MERCIFUL

Helping in Ways That Really Help – and Give Hope

MERCIFUL

THE OPPORTUNITY AND CHALLENGE OF DISCIPLING THE POOR OUT OF POVERTY

To Tracy:
You have been a great
support to me in the ministry
of Mercy in our denominations
Thank you for your love
and patience.

Randy Nabors

"Remember the Poor!"

Randy Nabors

ISBN: 1508434522
ISBN 13: 9781508434528
Library of Congress Control Number: 2015902416
CreateSpace Independent Publishing Platform
North Charleston, South Carolina

Dedication

I dedicate this book to the honor of my mother, Gloria, a single-parent mom who raised us in the projects of Newark, New Jersey.
She taught me to love God, one another, and to be kind.
She waits in heaven with Jesus for the resurrection from the dead.
And she would be so proud to know I wrote a book.

What Will It Take?

Through waves of sound and sight
Before us lays their plight:
It is the cry of the poor.
Are we listening, do we hear?
Is the picture becoming clear?
How far must it travel?
How sharp does it have to be?

From where does their cry come?
Will the poor's articulation
Resolve in recognition?
When will we know it
For what it is --
Discerning between noise or need,
To receive its truth,
And own its claim?
Their cry hovers in the air;
Is their breathless
Shallow rasp convincing of despair?
The poor are crying,
Poverty has a voice,
If you can feel
When you see its clothes,
When you meet its face,
When you touch its pain.

Can a man's running
Outdistance that sound?
If a poor man falls in a forest
Of wealth,
Will a rich man hear it?
One man lives louder
So it can't be heard;
Another wears dark glasses;
So that what he may distinctly see
We never actually know.
Another wears gloves of distance
So the poor won't be touched,
Or feverish flesh be felt.
Many wear hardness for hearts,
Substitute apathy for souls.
We posit some supposition,
A caveat inquisition,
For your sensory realization;
Does it take
A walk past Lazarus,
Or a separation from Abraham's bosom
For you to see another's sores
That the dogs lick,
And not dismiss
As daily ennui?

Those that won't be touched now
Will surely feel the heat then
And wish
Those whom they command here
Would assuage them there.

Sensory impressions of the poor
Which compassion elicits
Comes not through the eyes and ears
But through the heart!

What price must we pay
To engage our empathy?
Is it days of hunger,
Lean stomach or belly distended,
Rags, disassembled shoes,
Shopping carts with plastic sheeting
For our home and bed?

Does it require disease
Which could be cured
Except for the fee
We can't afford?

Will it take a loss of work,
Freedom, or home;
Foreclosed eviction,
Impoundment, prison?
The wrench of circumstantial loss
To gain our attention?

They cry now and you aren't disturbed;
You'll cry then, but you won't be heard.

Contents

organizations, and provide some principles and dynamics of which churches need to be aware in order to do mercy effectively.

Some of this material grew out of seminars the author has taught over the years to help congregations develop strategies, policies, and programs to give structure to their deacons and mercy committees, and to mobilize their people in ways that will help them make an impact on poverty and the lives of the poor. This may be the most practical, "hands-on" section of the book.

These last eight chapters close the book with some encouragement and challenge. We believe communities can be changed if churches are being what they ought to be in the midst of their neighborhoods. In this section we specifically talk about how to react to panhandling, the challenge to be generous, and close with a list of resources, both by way of bibliography and a listing of individuals and organizations that might be able to help you in the ministry of mercy.

Acknowledgements

I want to acknowledge and thank all of those who have helped me learn and do mercy ministry, those who assisted in gathering material for this book, and those who have enabled me to produce it. Thanks so much to Sam and Julie McCollum Van Voorhis for making it possible. Thanks to my editor, Robert Tamasy. Bob, thanks for your great insights, your kind way of pointing out how I could say or do things better, and your hard work on this project. Thanks to New City Fellowship for giving me an office and to the staff who have showed me much kindness.

Thanks to the various individuals and friends with whom I shared the manuscript and gave me encouragement, even to admit they did in fact read it, and for those who said it was worthwhile. I want to thank Gene Johnson, our full-time Deacon at New City Fellowship, whose phone number I have given out to hundreds of deacons around the country so they would have someone to call when they had a problem they couldn't solve. Gene has been my friend and colleague, and we have worked through bunches of individual cases as the years have gone by, Pastor to Deacon and Deacon to Pastor, to try and help people.

Thanks to those whom I mention in the book. I hope I have not in any way offended you, but your stories have helped to make my story, and especially the story of our church. My family has been very patient with me through this effort, and I love you all. And yes, Joan, I did mention you in the book.

Thanks to those who have taught me: pastors, professors, and leaders such as Pastor Grover C. Willcox, and the Rev. Tom Skinner, Dr. John Perkins, Dr. Harvie Conn, Dr. Roger Greenway, and Dr. Carl Ellis. Thanks to other colleagues from whom I have learned much, such as Manny Ortiz, Barry Henning, Mike Higgins, Jim Pickett, Kevin Smith, Paul Green, Stephen Davis, Thurman Williams, Mo Leveritt, Amy Sherman, Rick and Yvonne Sawyer, Andy Mendonsa, Dick Mason, Wayne Gordon and all the folks at CCDA. Thanks to other, some younger, men who have stretched me and from whom I am still learning, including Mark Gornik, Steven Smallman, Phil Edwards, Imbumi Makuku and Nathan Ivey. Some of these men are in the New City Network and are so encouraging

Thanks to Mission to North America of the Presbyterian Church in America, for whom I work, especially to Fred Marsh who has encouraged me and opened doors for me in the work of training others in the ministry of mercy for many years. I specifically mention some of my mentors in the body of the book, but in case their names are missed, they would include Rudolph and Collyn Schmidt, Sam Chester, Jr., David E. Mitchell and William S. Barker.

I want to acknowledge and thank some folks in Chattanooga who have worked long and hard to help poor people. Specifically, I remember the late Roy Noel, who worked off and on for the city and tried to get young people hired and encouraged me greatly in my early years in Chattanooga. I honor Callie Sue Chapman and her son, Alton Chapman, who put in so many years at Inner City Ministries. We have had some great urban pastors in Chattanooga who have also done great work in their own ministries, especially to help the poor, and I pray God's blessing on all of them.

I know it is unusual to tell a story in the Acknowledgement section, but I will include this: My grandfather, Harry Morgan (my mother's father), left a powerful impression on me. He was one of the blessings of my childhood. In the last years of their lives, my grandparents lived in a high-rise apartment for senior citizens across the street from my housing project. My grandmother had running sores on her legs for as long as I remember. Every day, twice a day, my grandfather would get down on his knees and wash her legs, and then dress them with bandages. I don't know why the sores wouldn't heal, but believe my grandfather had to do this for many years up until the time he had a stroke and died.

I wish I had realized then what I was seeing. I wish I could have told my grandfather what a powerful example and testimony he was of love and faithfulness and mercy. In both my mother and her father, I learned what loyalty in showing mercy was, through my sister's illness and my grandmother's. My grandfather died before I understood or could tell him what a great man I think he was, but when I became a man I realized what he had given me. I don't think I'll ever be half the man that he, or some others that I have acknowledged here, are or were. They have all certainly made me a better man than I would have become on my own.

Preface

Let me share a truth I've learned firsthand: Poverty is insulting.

So let me insult it back: Poverty sucks. Sometimes over the course of your life certain things happen that make you feel insulted. Sometimes it takes a while to realize you have been insulted, or that circumstances you live in are insulting. But they are insulting just the same. Poverty is one of those "things," and its insults hurt deeply.

One Christmas my mother told me my aunt and uncle had decided to give us Christmas presents. I was usually more than happy to get additional presents, especially since this particular aunt and uncle had money and the presents were sure to be worth having. However, this time my mom said, "They are going to leave the gifts at your Aunt Evie's house, so they don't have to come down to our neighborhood. They don't like to come this far down in Newark." I knew what this meant. It wasn't the distance but our neighborhood they were trying to avoid.

I suppose if I'd been more mature I could have been more understanding of their perspective, but at that moment I realized they looked at us as "the poor relatives." I told my mom to tell them if they couldn't come to where we lived, I didn't want their gifts. I never saw them except on their terms, and didn't like the way their decision not to visit us personally made me feel. I guess that reaction cost me any continuing relationship with them.

So yes, poverty is insulting. It insults you with the reminder today you don't have enough to eat, your clothes are inadequate, and your teeth won't be cleaned, filled, pulled, or fixed as needed. Poverty mocks you with the disappointing realization there are places you can't go, events you can't experience, and things you can't have.

Poverty humiliates you with vermin on your clothing, and forces you to make excuses as to why you can't participate in special activities at school, if indeed you're "wealthy" enough to be able to go to school at all. Poverty taunts you with the reality that this is where you live and these are the people you live among. This is the neighborhood where you can be beaten down, raped and robbed by your neighbors, and ignored by the police. What can be even more insulting is to be beaten by the police themselves for being on the wrong corner at the wrong moment.

Poverty afflicts you with the realization that corruption sometimes steals even the little bit that you have. Electricity can go out for anyone, during storms or due to weather. But our electricity went out every year because the housing projects in Newark were wired inadequately, and I'm convinced that was due to contracts padded by Mafia-controlled contractors. Poverty mocks you with the burden of obtaining credit, where salesmen "help" you to pay things off on time, but the time sure seems to drag on while the interest piles up – until you realize you could have purchased this item multiple times with the amount it eventually cost you.

Poverty can build community, but usually doesn't – at least not in many American urban environments. The hustlers, the addicts, the criminals prey on those closest and most available to them. Anxiety from not being able to pay your bills is bad enough, let alone being worried about walking home at night, or being caught in the hallway by someone who wants to take what little you do have.

Many poor people are good neighbors and willing to help each other. Some of the most generous people I have ever met were dirt poor. But the anonymity of living in the city can take all the good feeling of being "in this together" and make you feel like it's every man for himself. Sometimes the concept of community comes only later in life, when you sit around with others from the same neighborhood and can talk and laugh about all the things you mutually suffered – the funny, the sad, the stupid, the violent and the good, all together.

So as I said, poverty is insulting. And I believe the best way to insult it back is to help people to overcome it, to realize it doesn't have to be a lifetime sentence.

– *Randy Nabors*

Foreword #1

HOW DOES A FATHERLESS BOY who grows up in a housing project in Newark become a highly effective church leader who launches a growing network of urban, multicultural churches? It's quite the story, but the story hasn't ended. Indeed, this book represents just the latest chapter in the ongoing story of God's working in and through Randy Nabors.

At the heart of this incredible story is Jesus Christ, who is embodied in the local church as it ministers in word and deed to the poor. It is this type of church that rescued Randy and launched him into one of the most innovative American pastors in the past 50 years. It is this type of church that Randy wants your church to be. And that is the reason he wrote this book.

Drawing upon his personal experiences from growing up in poverty and from a lifetime of ministering amongst the poor, Randy shares a wealth of wisdom in order to equip your church for powerful kingdom service. As always, Randy's message is grounded in sound theology, honed through practical experience, and articulated with the directness of a street fighter.

And that is what Randy has had to be: a fighter. Planting a congregation committed to pursuing racial reconciliation and helping the poor gets lots of accolades these days, but that wasn't always the case. It took enormous courage for Randy, who is Caucasian, and his wife, Joan, who is African-American, to move into the inner city of Chattanooga, Tennessee during a period of substantial racial tension and civil unrest. Both personally and professionally they have had to fight against racial prejudice, economic injustice, church traditionalism, and institutionalized pride, often being wounded by "friendly fire" for simply trying to live out the gospel. It hasn't been easy, and they bear many battle scars.

This book is one of the many fruits of their struggles, documenting the lessons they have gleaned from years of ministering to the physical, emotional, and spiritual needs of the poor. One of the most important of these lessons is that when the local church provides material assistance in the context of an overall evangelism and discipleship process, it powerfully communicates the whole Gospel to the whole person, which can lead to lasting change. Indeed, this is the approach that helped Randy's own family to escape poverty.

This lesson is worth emphasizing because, as Randy notes, some people have interpreted the book that I have co-authored, *When Helping Hurts*, to be saying that material assistance – e.g., buying food or paying utility bills – should never be given to poor people. On the contrary! Material assistance is part of all three types of poverty alleviation: *relief, rehabilitation,* and *development,* but the *manner* in which material assistance is offered differs across these three types. In *relief,* material assistance is handed out to people who are unable to take actions to improve their situation, as in the story of the Good Samaritan; in contrast, in r*ehabilitation* and *development* the material assistance is provided in a way that complements the person's own efforts to improve their situation.

Of course, it's not always easy to determine whether a person needs relief, rehabilitation, or development. There is no magic formula, and it often takes a lot of wisdom to determine the best course of action in any situation. And that's where this book comes in. Randy lays out both broad principles and practical tips to help your church navigate through murky waters as you seek to restore poor people to what they were created to be: image bearers who are able to glorify God through sustaining work.

On a personal note, for the past 18 years my family and I have had the joy of attending New City Fellowship, the church that Randy founded and shepherded for 40 years. Under Randy's faithful preaching and ministry, we have seen the gospel transform black and white, rich and poor, young and old, educated and illiterate. And we have seen the Gospel slowly but surely transform our own family, shaving off our many rough edges and conforming us more and more into the very likeness of Jesus Christ. Randy and Joan, for all of this we are deeply grateful.

Thus, it is a profound honor to be able to recommend to you this wonderful resource, which represents another chapter in the incredible Randy Nabors story. May God use this book to equip your church to declare and demonstrate the greatest story of all: *Jesus Christ is ushering in a New City, where there will be no more crying, no more pain, no more racism...and no more poverty.* Come quickly, Lord Jesus!

Brian Fikkert
Founder and President of the Chalmers Center at Covenant College
Lookout Mountain, Georgia

Foreword #2

I have known Randy and Joan Nabors since about 1975, when I met them at a conference on Race & Reconciliation. Randy and Joan, and it is hard for me not to think of them together, have shown up again and again at conferences to hear me speak, or where we have both been teaching.

They have invited me many times to preach at the church Randy helped to plant in Chattanooga, Tennessee. I have always known them to be committed to justice, racial reconciliation, and ministry to the poor. Even Vera Mae likes them, and we have shared laughter and passion for ministry together. We have loved their people, been in their homes, and felt their love.

One time Randy and I were having breakfast at a Waffle House. We were talking about how so many middle-class kids seemed to be running away from their wealth, getting involved with our ministries to the poor, while both Randy and I were running away from poverty. We are thankful for those who have been moved by Jesus to love those whom Jesus loves, no matter where they come from.

To have someone who has been there, suffered in some manner the way we have suffered, been frustrated with the oppression of their environment, and turned around and come back to it for Jesus' sake is what we worked so hard to see in Mississippi. This book tells Randy's life story, and it is an important one for people to be listening to.

Randy comes from urban poverty, and it is good to see how God would not let him run away, like God would not let me run away from Mississippi when I was living out in California. I have built lots of parachurch organizations, and when they work well they can do really good work. However, I know God wants us to build his church, and it is wonderful to see what God has done at New City Fellowship.

Randy has a deep love for the church, planted in him by his church in Newark, New Jersey, who embraced him and loved him from the start. His love is not just for the church as an idea, but for the elders and the deacons and the people who support the life of the church. I wish we had more leaders who love the church like Randy does, and churches with a mission like New City Fellowship. I pray that God will make you live like the title of this book, *MERCIFUL!*

Dr. John Perkins
Jackson, Mississippi

Introduction

I GREW UP IN NEWARK, New Jersey, a place some people call "Brick City." I grew up in the bricks – the projects – and all the buildings I lived in have since been blown up and demolished. That being said, this is not a book about escaping poverty, but of going back to meet it – to confront it – in the power of God, with the wisdom He provides in His book, the Bible.

My desire to help others in doing mercy ministry (and to do it well) is born out of my own experience as a recipient of mercy. The family in which I grew up was blessed by a local church that loved and loved on our family in many ways. The deacons of Calvary Gospel Church in Newark, and the deacons of the church in which I ministered and pastored for 40 years, New City Fellowship in Chattanooga, Tennessee, have taught me many things about mercy ministry, things I'm happy to share with others.

My love and respect for the office of the deacon comes from one of my earliest memories of a budding relationship with the church where most of the members of my family came to faith. I vividly recall my mother crying one day at the kitchen table in our apartment. We were out of food and I imagine the cares of being a single mom, having a sense of failing her own parents, and now being unable to provide for her own kids must have overwhelmed her. As I remember it, right at that moment there was a knock on our door. We opened the door to find people standing there, bags of groceries clutched in their arms.

They were deacons from the church we had begun to attend. Later they would have a phone installed in our house because my mother was pregnant and they wanted to be able to come and get her when she needed help. From that time I've always thought of deacons as heroes, people who show up in the nick of time, people who rescue you when you don't know what to do.

I'm thankful and proud of the deacons who served with me at New City Fellowship. I've seen them go into scary and outrageous situations, and watched them sit with the desperate, the hungry, the sick, and the dying. I've known them to go under houses to fix broken pipes in the dead and cold of winter, wash the feet and cut the nails of a man with diseased feet, pay for coffins and graves, and repeat the story of carrying groceries and giving food to many other single moms.

As a pastor, I was thankful to them for being on call and leaving me to focus on the ministry of the Word while they went to help someone. I was thankful for their evangelism and leading people to Jesus as they prayed with the needy, the hurting, and the poor. And I was thankful and proud of their wisdom for saying "no" to the crooks and deceivers; and even after they were sometimes conned, for being willing to take a risk again.

I was glad they did the hard work of confronting the lazy, the wasteful, the foolish, yet still loving them. I am thankful for a church that gave ex-cons and recovering addicts another chance. I feel they gave meaning to the name "Christian" and gained respect for the name of Christ's Church.

In this book you will see my working definition of mercy:

> ***Mercy is compassion toward those who are in need, resulting in action to alleviate that need through acts of charity leading toward self-sustainment.***

This definition has a focus on care to the poor and helping people who are in need, with an emphasis on compassion and its works, rather than the mercy revealed in the forgiveness of sins. The forgiveness of our sins is certainly something we all need, but that's not the primary purpose of this book.

I like to tell people that mercy as it pertains to the poor consists of two parts: *charity* (or relief, and I will use those terms interchangeably in this book) and *development*. It's important to keep both in mind, as one can become the enemy of the other if they are not kept in the proper balance. Charity (merciful relief) is the response of love to immediate human needs. Development is mercy extended to the poor in ways that empower them to help themselves, not only so they can become independent, but also to be merciful to others.

Too much charity for too long makes people dependent and cripples them, while too little charity – when really needed and given too late – leaves people in desperate situations and causes them to suffer. Charity and development given without the Gospel or an articulation of the love of Christ is not a holistic or completed mercy, but simply a materialistic one.

In the context of poor communities, mercy without discipleship can be short-lived, only helping a person for one more day through one more problem, while condemning them to face the same trouble again. Therefore, mercy – if it is to be done well – requires a relationship that builds and fosters accountability.

Not all acts of charity will require a process of accountability, and neither does all charity require steps of development, since anyone could be in need of charity due to some momentary trouble or tragedy. Some people will only need help with one problem, and possibly only one time. Some of those that we help may have the resources, relationships and skills to take care of themselves once they are pulled "out of the ditch," so to speak.

Although mercy ministry can at times be dramatic, and can genuinely make you feel good about yourself once you have helped someone, it may also be confusing, at times difficult to do well, sometimes complicated, and even frustrating to the point of anger and despair.

There are romantic, idealistic, and heroic aspects to coming to someone's rescue. Yet the most consistent reality is this: Mercy ministry done right is hard work, at times fraught with self-doubt, often misunderstood and misinterpreted as to motives, and sometimes fails to achieve a positive outcome. Having acknowledged all this, we still want to motivate and enlist people in a ministry we firmly believe is absolutely close to the heart of Jesus.

We find many Christians and non-Christians alike believe it is a good thing to show mercy to the poor. Unfortunately, a lot of mercy is not done well and may actually socially cripple the very people it's meant to help. Some people who have addressed this reality, and spoken or written with the best motives have unfortunately seen their comments interpreted by some people in a negative way, so that a cynical attitude has developed toward ministries that provide relief as an immediate response to need.

Sadly, some of these folks have tended to dismiss relief as not only a hindrance to change but almost as an evil in itself. This is unfortunate for several reasons: One, it tends to belittle or diminish the reality of the suffering of the poor. Second, it's sometimes used as an excuse for doing nothing. And third, I believe one cannot honestly read the Gospels and not see Jesus putting emphasis on our immediate response to someone's need. Getting the act and process of mercy right is important not just for the poor, but also for our own obedience to Christ.

In this book we want to serve as advocates for mercy in all its parts. We especially want to advocate for the role of the local church in applying mercy in communities of poverty and human need. We want to advertise and celebrate that when mercy – through its component parts of relief and development – is performed through the local church, with wisdom and energy, then wonderful things can happen to change the lives of the poor and bless those who minister mercy.

This material was originally developed in response to studies at Westminster Theological Seminary in Urban Missions. It was actually a Power Point presentation, later developed with notes, and now into a book. I have used it to train deacons and congregations about how to do effective mercy. The poems are mine and use a different medium to approach the subject of poverty. I would never claim it is good poetry, for those of you who have high standards.

We have divided the book into six parts: Humble Beginnings; Perplexities of Poverty; The Magnitude of Mercy; The Church; Building a Working Framework; and What's Our End Game? As the reader, you may want to skip over the biographical background (in the Beginnings section), although this is where I speak from firsthand experience about the power of identity in the lives of poor people.

You might choose to move quickly to deal with the theories of poverty or mercy that are provided in parts two and three, or may want to move quickly to some practical ideas in parts four and five. Feel free to read the book in whatever way it best helps you and applies to your ministry.

Though my reflections on poverty may make passing mention of many aspects of this pressing societal and personal problem, this book isn't an attempt to create an academic, sociological or economic analysis of poverty. It's not about the politics of poverty. I can't claim it is a theological work about mercy. It's simply an attempt to use my own story and experience, personally and professionally, as a way of helping others.

I am certainly subject to error (and any matters of content that might be in error are solely my own responsibility), so I ask the reader's forgiveness in advance for any overstatement or misstatement in my analysis and understanding. I hope you will take the time to correct me, either directly by communicating with me or indirectly through your own reflection and application of ideas expressed in this book. I hope in doing so you will be merciful.

Part One:

Humble Beginnings

CHAPTER 1

I Know Where I Come From

"Brothers, think about what you were when you were called...."

(1 CORINTHIANS 1:2, NIV)

A FAMILY FALLS APART AND finds the mother raising her children in the housing projects of Newark, New Jersey. The one boy in the family learns fairly early that being ready to fight when you go outside is just a part of life. He begins to run with a gang of boys who spend their time stealing from local stores and learning about and observing stuff in the back hallways he is way too young to see.

His mother tries to make ends meet with her welfare check, but finds more month than money. The projects are better than the streets, better than being homeless, but they have their own kind of culture and hardship. Some families have someone with a job; many do not. Some families have fathers in the home; most do not. Some families will be there for only a short time, while others will raise all their kids on this one block.

One boy wakes up in his projects apartment and gets dressed for school. He forgets to check his shoes. This day he gets to his first period class and fortunately sits in the back of the classroom. He begins to feel something uncomfortable in his shoe, so he takes it off. Immediately five cockroaches jump out and scatter in five different directions. Mortified, he jumps up and does an amazing tap dance killing the bugs before anyone else in the class can see.

That kid...was me. In the movie "Rocky," the main character, Rocky Balboa, is asked why he is a boxer. His response is, "Because I can't sing or dance." If you come from the ghetto, the slums, or live in poverty you know what he means. Everyone is looking for a ticket out – a ticket to money and food, away from violence, a ticket to be somebody. When I saw "Rocky," I got it right away, because I knew where I came from: the (housing) projects of Newark, New Jersey. If you have any street smarts or sense of urban history, that's enough said.

I realize some people may wonder what my qualifications, credentials, or background might be to speak on the issues of mercy and justice. I don't come at the subject as an academic, but as a practitioner, so I hope the reader will be forbearing concerning any lack of scientific analysis of poverty, poor people, and the efforts to bring them out of poverty.

Admittedly there's much to learn, and I keep learning from many people who are engaged in significant work and ministry around the world related to this work of mercy. Obviously anyone is free to share his or her opinions about mercy and mercy ministry, who (and why some) might be deserving of help, and what congregations ought to be doing about it.

However, I'm often less than impressed by people that make pronouncements about the poor who have never experienced it. These are people who dismiss hunger, fear of violence, distress over how to buy medicine and clothes, and the possibility of losing what shelter you have by explaining them away as inconveniences, but not life-shattering.

Hopefully every minister of the Gospel is equipped to give a Biblical explanation of God's call for us to be merciful and how the early Church practiced it. Obviously some ministers have more credibility than others, whether from researching the issue or through firsthand experience.

I am a minister of the Gospel of Jesus Christ, and if I'm to preach the "whole counsel of God," then I certainly want to preach and expound on what Jesus defined as, *"the weightier matters of the Law: justice and mercy" (Matthew 21:21).*

My interest in the subject is built on what I believe Scripture teaches about it – and also because I grew up poor and my family received mercy from the church. I was discipled by a congregation that ministered to the poor, and learned much in that church, and also in the city of Newark, New Jersey where I grew up.

In God's providence I've had the opportunity to be a pastor in the inner city and in that context to challenge my congregation to be a church of mercy. Drawing from that rich and rewarding experience, I've been asked to help lead my denomination (the Presbyterian Church in America) in training deacons and church members in strategies, policies, and techniques about how to effectively perform mercy. Essentially, this has been my life's work, so I humbly offer to you some of what I have learned.

Mistakes and Bad Decisions

Providing me with a background in poverty wasn't the plan of my parents, who met near the end of World War II. My mother, Gloria, was coming out of a divorce from her first husband, who was an alcoholic and had left her with one daughter. My mother grew up in a very conservative home, but had been swept away by a sailor during a time of war, left her home in New Jersey for the West Coast, became a Navy wife, and within just a few years found herself in a place she thought she would never be: Divorced.

She was still fairly young then and met another sailor, my father, Allen Webster Nabors, at a dance. She didn't realize how much younger he was than herself, but in a fairly short time they were married. He brought her and his new stepdaughter to his family home in Memphis, Tennessee to become part of the Nabors family.

I don't know a lot about my dad, but from what I've learned from him, my mother, and family members, he could be very independent and rebellious. My mother didn't know it when she married him, but he'd first been married at the age of fifteen. That relationship didn't last very long and as soon as he was able, he joined the Navy and left home. I don't know if my father ever finished high school.

My father came from a Southern family that was religious (Nazarene), believed in marriage, hard work, and had survived the Great Depression by scraping out a living from dirt farming in Mississippi, and then carpentry work for the WPA. These were Southern folk whose lineage is noted on the membership rolls of Mississippi rifle regiments that fought in the Civil War.

My mother's parents were a product of a World War I marriage between a soldier from Alabama with a Methodist background and a New Jersey woman of German extraction and Lutheran influence. My mother's father, Henry Morgan, had been in the Army prior to the Great War and served as a medic in the trenches of France. Having met my future grandmother while on leave in New Jersey, Henry decided to settle up North. He made his living as a practical nurse, and the Morgans also believed in marriage, hard work, and loyalty.

My father and mother had one daughter together before I came along. When I was born I became my mother's third child, having two older sisters. Within a few years a third sister was born. It was this family, our mother and the four of us kids, my father decided to abandon. He put us on a train for New Jersey, assuring my mom he would come along later. Instead, he pursued another woman he would live with for the next twenty-five years or so. I would not see him again until I was 17, briefly as I was passing through Little Rock, Arkansas during my Christmas break from college.

I would realize later that divorce is one of the great causes of poverty in our country. The failure to create and maintain family-friendly moral and social laws was one of the great disasters of American civil society in the 20th century.

Devastation of Divorce

There are undoubtedly many philosophical and cultural reasons why state governments decided to change divorce laws, make the termination of marriage "no fault," and allow men primarily to abandon their family responsibilities while at the same time creating a financial infrastructure to support women and children who were not, at least legally, with their husbands and/or the fathers of their children.

Regardless of the reasons, including a sympathy vote for women to get out of abusive marriages and a determined effort to remove the stigma for sex outside of marriage, it resulted in widespread social disaster and a multiplication of the poor.

A legal divorce might actually have helped my mother, Gloria Eileen (Morgan) Nabors, in obtaining needed child support, but my father didn't give her the satisfaction of a divorce. This caused great legal difficulty for my mother in being able to acquire any help from my father. She was an abandoned wife, but not legally divorced, so we grew up without receiving any financial support from our dad.

My mother's problems were not simply a lack of financial resources. They had also become emotional and moral. We were living with my grandparents who were moral, working-class kind of people. They despised my dad for what he had done and graciously took in my mom with us kids, but I'm sure became appalled by the behavior of their only daughter. My mother was at the same time both smart and naïve. Still a fairly young and normal woman, she became lonely, and this made her subject to all kinds of temptations to seek love and relationships with men she easily outclassed.

Within a few years we had moved from our grandparents' home and into city housing projects in the city of Newark. My mother was working, but due to her interactions with men she became pregnant.

Even though I wasn't very aware of the friction at the time, I imagine the conflict between my mom and her parents must have been intense on both sides. Evidently the pressure they brought to bear pushed my mother into giving up what turned out to be my only brother for adoption. I've never met him, and know my mother lived with regret over her decision. But it didn't change her emotional need or her behavior, as she became pregnant again not long afterward.

I remember some of my mom's boyfriends, and vaguely recollect some of my experiences with them. I distinctly recall one of them slapping me in the face for trying to stand up for my mom when it was obvious he was upsetting her. At the time my mother was "illegitimately" pregnant yet again. She was no longer working, and we went on "welfare," now living in the projects of Newark. I don't know for certain, but suspect her relationship with her own parents must have been extremely strained by this point. Her self-image must have been close to rock bottom.

Receiving Mercy When Needed Most

Even if one doesn't know how to define mercy, we often can recognize it when we see it. Although sometimes we can understand it for what it is only through the rear window as our lives drive past it. I know our family was found and embraced by mercy at this low point of my mother's life. Even though I didn't realize it at the time, later years would reveal to me it was right then that our lives began to take a decidedly different, positive turn.

My oldest sister, Judy Lee, still had some connection with her birth father. He came to our home at least once to visit her. Suddenly we were told Judy Lee was going to leave us and go back to California to live with her dad. I suppose this was her best chance to get out of Newark, escape the poverty of the projects, and take her to the place of promise that California represented in those days. This parting caused great trauma in our family.

As it turned out, my mother would lose connection with her firstborn child and not see her again for years. Joyce, my next oldest sister, was very shaken by what she took to be abandonment by her sister. I can't adequately know her emotional sense of loss, and certainly didn't know much then about the grief and pain my mother and sister experienced.

Having grown up and learned much about people and families since then, I can't fathom the depth of the emotional wilderness in my mother's heart at that time. I don't have my mother's words to describe it, because never in my presence did she complain or blame others for her suffering.

Try to visualize this: By this time my mother had given away a baby son to adoption, released her oldest daughter to her birth father, and soon would have another baby daughter who would also be born out of wedlock. My mother didn't know what the city of Newark was to become, but knew it was already hard. She didn't realize how life on the streets already was affecting me, and didn't know how things would ever be fixed or repaired. My mother was living at the margins, without a job and relying only on the meager subsistence the government offered at that time.

Despite her hardships and unwise decisions, my mother was a woman with some sense of pride. She believed she was smart and talented, and treasured the memories of growing up and being loved by her family. Nevertheless, she had suffered repeated abandonment by men she had tried to love, was bereft of some children she loved, burdened with other children she was having to raise by herself (in what would become one of the worst cities in America). At perhaps her lowest point in life, as she was feeling her potential and her dreams crushed and beginning to slip away, God sent her a friend.

CHAPTER 2

I Didn't Have Wedding Clothes

"He chose the lowly things of this world and the despised
things – and the things that are not – to
nullify the things that are
so that no one may boast before him."

(1 Corinthians 1:28-29, NIV)

Another single-parent mother who also lived in our housing project invited my mom out to a midweek service at a little house church. My mother accepted and went to visit Calvary Gospel Church one night when an evangelist named Kennedy Smartt was preaching. He had been invited by the local pastor, the Rev. Grover Willcox, to lead a short evangelistic series. The Rev. Smartt believed that if you did an evangelistic outreach, the wise thing to do was to go and visit any new people who had come to the services the very next day. The day after my mother had attended the services, pastors Smartt and Willcox came to our apartment in the projects and led our family to Christ.

We had attended church occasionally with my grandfather, so I was a little familiar with it. I'd even been thrown out of a Sunday worship service once by the pastor's wife of my grandfather's church, and I can't blame her, knowing how unruly I was then (maybe I still am). This new church was different from what I'd experienced, however. It was like we had become part of a family, and soon our lives were caught up in it. I was going to be in Sunday school every Sunday, my mom sent me to Vacation Bible School, and the greatest thing of all, people at the church took me to summer camp.

As I reflect on this, I'm reminded of a parable that Jesus told about a wedding banquet:

"Then he (the King) said to his servants, 'The wedding banquet is ready, but those I invited did not deserve to come. Go to the street corners and invite to the banquet anyone you find. So the servants went out into the streets, and gathered all the people they could find, both good and bad, and the wedding hall was filled with guests. But when the King came in to see the guests, he noticed a man there who was not wearing wedding clothes. 'Friend,' he asked, 'how did you get in here without wedding clothes?'" (Matthew 22:8-12, NIV).

I was a kid on the streets, a guy from the street corner, and growing to be one of the bad ones at that. I got invited by the King to come to the wedding banquet, but I didn't have wedding clothes. But the day Jesus found me, He dressed me in His own righteousness and that's how I got to the wedding. He saved me.

Out of Food, Out of Hope

My mother was in her pregnancy, and one day the church had a phone installed so she could call for help when it was time for her to give birth. These church people picked us up and brought us home from events. Probably the greatest impression on me occurred one day when I realized my mother was weeping, seated at the kitchen table. We'd run out of food and there was nothing to eat. I'm not sure how close these two events were together – the church providing us with a phone and my mom crying at the table, unable to figure out where to get food. But I remember hearing a knock at our door. My sisters and I ran to open the door, and there were the deacons of Calvary Gospel Church, holding bags of groceries for us.

Many years later, I believe this is what churches do. It's what the people of God do for one another. I've stood in my pulpit and told my own congregation, "There is never a reason why anyone in our church should ever go hungry. If you are a member here, or attend here, all you have to do is let us know, or for us to find out that you don't have food, and we will feed you."

One of the things I appreciate about Brian Fikkert and Steve Corbett's book about assisting people in need, *When Helping Hurts,* is their acknowledgement of the psychological and emotional effects of poverty. Poverty creates a sense of shame, as I understand all too well. I began to develop a growing sense of this shame myself as I grew up.

At first I had no realization of poverty. I was just a kid, usually begging my mom for more, and when that didn't work I started learning to steal from her, from stores, or anywhere opportunity presented itself. As time went on I began to realize more clearly we didn't have much. I was embarrassed by the clothes I wore, ones that often didn't fit and would literally split apart, sometimes in public.

The housing projects were famous for roaches, the kind that crawl and seem to hide in every crevice. The story I told earlier is an example of the sense of shame and humiliation the experience of growing up in that environment gave to me. The roaches would climb up the pipes from one apartment to the one above or below on the next floor. When one family purchased and used enough roach spray, the vertical neighbors (above and below) would receive a fresh invasion of bugs. One of the bonding moments I had with my future mother-in-law was a day I showed up at her door, just in time to be handed a can of roach spray for initiating a war upon the bugs in her house.

Shame and Frustration

Many have endured lives much worse than mine. I'm not trying to compete for anyone's sympathy; I'm just saying I know what it's like to feel ashamed by my poverty. I know what it's like to feel frustrated and helpless in the face of having no money, no food, and no way to change my circumstances. I know what it's like having to wear clothes and shoes that are cheap, that rip apart at the most embarrassing, most inopportune moments. I know what it's like to want to do things and go places, but you can't because there just isn't any money. I know what it's like to at least have a television set, one that shows commercials where people have cars, washing machines, and refrigerators full of food, grimly reminding us that "we" don't have those things.

I also know what it's like to come to believe, to have faith, to know that God has become my Father – my Heavenly Father – and to be absolutely sure (when I am not wavering in my faith) that He would take care of me. I don't want to give the impression that living by faith is something I learned once and never had to relearn. Even though God's mercy has come through for me time and time again, it seems the lesson of faith is one I must learn...again and again.

If you're reading this and grew up poor, then I know you can relate, maybe even laugh about some of those times now. Once after preaching at a suburban church, a nice white lady walked up and told me, "Listening to you tell those stories I gasped, leaned over and I told my husband, 'I forgot where I came from.'" What a great but bittersweet moment for her. Never forget where you came from.

Some people have willingly experienced temporary poverty by using their power of choice to go to school. Poverty that comes from a choice you make – such as to go to advanced schooling, locate among poor people, or take a job that pays very little so you can accomplish some goal – is different from growing up in it, being forced to live in it. Nevertheless, even "temporary poverty" can still be frustrating.

I will tell you more about my wife, Joan, in later chapters. Suffice it to say at this point, she and I grew up in the same housing project in Newark. We had chosen to take the risk of being poor again by going to school. I remember a time, while in seminary, Joan and I were having a hard time making it financially. I didn't have a job yet, and she'd been looking for employment without success during the first two months we'd been in St Louis, Missouri.

Prior Experience Doesn't Make It Easier

She and I had found a place to live, but the rent was coming due and we still had no income. We'd been living off of the little bit of money we had saved to make the move to seminary and that money was just about gone. We prayed and prayed, but there was still no job and no money showed up. Since Joan had grown up in the same housing projects that I had, she understood what it was like being broke. And as was the case for me, she didn't like it much. Previous experience didn't make it any easier.

As we drove home from campus one day, my eye staring on the declining gas gauge, I began to wonder out loud what God was doing. I told Joan maybe we'd made a mistake, that maybe I needed to quit school and find a job. She was quiet for a moment and then responded with words I've never forgotten: "If God won't answer our prayers, we'll just have to trust Him anyway."

I looked over at this woman I had married and wondered where she, the non-seminary student, had learned such a thing. Soon after that we received help from the deacons of a local church who had learned we were in need, and not long after that Joan found a job and I took part-time employment as a security guard. We at least had options due to our education, making this what I call "poverty-by-choice" in order to go to school, but we still needed faith. Such moments of poverty for students who are poor by vocational choice are emotionally trying, but not psychologically devastating. That's because having a choice means you have power to change your circumstances.

DON'T TELL ME THE POOR ARE 'BETTER OFF'

I know for a fact that poverty is terrible and ruinous. This knowledge comes from experience and study, but I also know it's true because the Bible says so. *"The wealth of the rich is their fortified city, but poverty is the ruin of the poor" (Proverbs 10:15, NIV).* No matter how anyone might like to romanticize it, or claim the poor are better off because they don't have to worry the way wealthy people do, all I can say is, "Get a grip!"

There's no doubt in my mind how harmful poverty is to people. It not only hurts to be hungry, it's demeaning and demoralizing to not have enough money to feed your kids or pay your rent. It's humiliating to try to explain to your spouse or your kids why you can't keep the water running and the lights on. It's a sad way of life to feel as if roaches, mice and rats have more freedom than you do. And it makes me angry to know some kids are forever mentally behind because they inhaled and ingested lead from the paint in their dilapidated houses.

It's maddening to know how poverty affects the education many children receive in public schools. Many of those children live in communities where poverty is a way of life and the dynamics of those communities affect the quality of the job teachers are able to do. It's distressing to know some kids move almost every month during a school year because their mom keeps getting kicked out of one place after another.

Poverty impacts its victims from many different directions all at the same time. It's not just too little food, or too little cash, or a bad house, or a bad school, or a violent neighborhood, or no employment. In many cases it's all of these and more, often happening simultaneously.

Poverty affects the way people are treated by the police and the courts, either with not enough attention or way too much of it. There's the lack of adequate medical care, lack of decent diet, and lack of care and services available for families that are dysfunctional. In many of these homes young children are left vulnerable to being sexually abused and exploited, sometimes simply because no one else is paying them any attention due to the chaos in the life of their family.

Sadly, in some quarters these powerless, voiceless poor become used as fuel for political commentary that regards them as a national burden. Some commentators act as if there exists a permanent class of people so despicable that all they do is live off the government, like human parasites. There may be some like this, of course. However, for politically opinionated people to be so obnoxious and callous as to dismiss the millions legally receiving some assistance from the government – describing them as desiring and being satisfied with such a life – amounts to not just ignorance, but to a pernicious and cynical exploitation of the poor by politicizing them through creating a political myth.

Hope That Overwhelms Hopelessness

For the Christian there's another side to this problem, however. A gloriously positive side. In the midst of hopelessness, fear and weakness, there's a Savior whose name is Jesus. He is able to take the victims and transform them into being members of God's royal family. Unless you've experienced it yourself, it's difficult to explain how great and wonderful a difference it makes for someone trapped in poverty to enter into a personal relationship with the living God.

At one moment they have no significant name, no family, no connections, and no resources. They are despised, rejected, and pigeonholed, labeled as insignificant and disposable. Then for the first time they encounter the good news – the reality that for the poor, and even the wicked, there is a God who can intervene.

Jesus enters their life. They become intimate with the Son of God. They (the poor person no one cared about who has now come to faith) can actually speak to this Jesus constantly in prayer, calling out to Him for their daily bread, trusting Him to make it through the day and through the night, go from this place to another, get medicine, or simply find a ride when it's needed. Suddenly the very definition of being marginalized (what the powerless poor truly are) is changed to being right in the center of the game.

If one knows the Creator of the universe and the One who runs it, and is in a daily speaking relationship with Him, then one can't truly feel powerless. It's actually rather heady, even exhilarating, to know that I have access to God the Father – even though nothing is in my pocket – while on the other hand some rich man is stuck at the eye of the needle, like a camel that won't fit, and can't get God's attention because he doesn't know what it is to have faith.

As our family began to participate in the life of Calvary Gospel Church, we progressed through various stages of distrust, suspicion, and damaged pride in receiving their help. These feelings were remedied by the church quickly recruiting us into ministry. Even though the church gave us mercy over many years in various ways, we also were becoming contributing members, owners and participants in ministry, learning how to offer assistance to others.

By the time I was in high school, I was helping bring groceries to other families, doing evangelism on the streets, and learning how to work and help my family whenever opportunities to take on small jobs became available.

My new life in the church not only helped me learn how to work and earn money of my own, which I usually spent to finance some type of participation in the youth group, but also showed me how to pray to God and ask for things to happen.

Once while in high school I told the pastor I wanted to go to the Urbana Missionary Convention in Illinois. I'm sure he looked at me with some exasperation, and at first may have thought I was asking him to come up with a solution, but he did the absolute best thing he could have done. He told me if that was what I thought God wanted me to do, then I should start praying about it. Within a few weeks he called to tell me someone had paid my way, and someone else would give me a ride there and back. Wow, I was beginning to learn – God does answer prayer!

CHAPTER 3

Identity: Who's Your Daddy?

"And God raised us up with Christ and seated us with him in the heavenly realms in Christ Jesus."

(Ephesians 2:6, NIV)

I vividly remember two important encouragements to my faith when I was in high school. One day Pastor Willcox spoke to several of the leaders in the youth group. He opened up his Bible to 1 Corinthians 1:26-31, but before reading it he reminded us of who we were and where we came from. He pointed out most of us had no fathers in our homes, some came from the projects, and some were on welfare. He told us no one expected much of anything from us since we were from Newark, which by that time was turning into one very hard place to live. We all knew what he was saying about us, and to tell you the truth we even gloried in the toughness of it. Yet, he was right – our prospects didn't look very good. Then Pastor Willcox read:

"Brothers, think of what you were when you were called. Not many of you were wise by human standards; not many were influential; not many were of noble birth. But God chose the foolish things of the world to shame the wise; God chose the weak things of the world to shame the strong. He chose the lowly things of this world and the despised things-and the things

that are not – to nullify the things that are so that no one may boast before him. It is because of him that you are in Christ Jesus, who has become for us wisdom from God – that is, our righteousness, holiness and redemption. Therefore, as it is written; 'Let him who boasts boast in the Lord'" (1 Corinthians 1:26-31, NIV).

I took these words to heart and began to realize there was a sovereign hand behind my life and God could use even my family's poverty for His glory – and that meant He could use me.

Another wonderful boost to my young but growing hope in Christ was what I heard from Tom Skinner. The Rev. Tom Skinner was an evangelist who had grown up in Harlem, a borough of New York City. If you wanted respect from someone in Newark, all you had to do was tell them you grew up in Harlem. I didn't know then how much influence Tom would have on my life and the creation of the congregation I would eventually lead as pastor, but at that stage of my life his message filled me with hope.

Tom came and did a crusade in our city, and as he preached I was able to grasp a new sense of identifying with what God had done for me. One of his stock messages was to go into a riff about how when someone comes to Christ they are "seated with Christ in heavenly places." When one is a Christian, he said, they are a son of God, a member of God's royal family. Therefore the Christian doesn't have to break his neck to be in anybody's country club. We can walk through our neighborhoods feeling 10 feet tall because we take second place to nobody. I began to believe and do just that.

I was getting in touch with what I now call "ironic grace." It's the praise and liberation expressed in the prayers of Hannah and of Mary. One of the phrases in Hannah's prayer I've taken as a theme for my life. It's found in 1 Samuel 2:1-10, especially verses 7-8:

"The Lord sends poverty and wealth; he humbles and he exalts. He raises the poor from the dust and lifts the needy from the ash heap; he seats them with princes and has them inherit a throne of honor."

I think the Hebrew word translated here as "ash heap" is actually even stronger, so it almost could be paraphrased, "from the outhouse to the White House."

This turning the tables on human expectations is reflected again in what is often called the "Magnificat" in Luke 1:46-55. This is where Mary pours out her heart in praise to God for what He has done for her, taking a poor young woman from a despised town and who was unknown to everyone, and making her the mother of our Lord. If I were preaching right now, I'd say something like, "Hallelujah! Somebody needs to start shouting right here!"

Physical and Mental Consequences of Poverty

There were complications from poverty in our lives. One was our lack of dental care at that time, and it wasn't until I was in my forties that I could get my teeth fixed. The bigger problem was the mental health of my older sister, Joyce. She had a problem, but with no father in the home to help control her behavior, and due to inadequate income, we couldn't get her the care she needed. What made this even harder was no one seemed to know exactly what kind of help that should be.

Hers was a progressive disease that exhibited itself by incredibly fast mood swings, rage, violence, and then withdrawal. Later she would lose her balance, the ability to swallow and to talk, and would spend the last years of her life in a nursing home being fed through a tube in her stomach.

Understandably, this caused great damage to the unity of our family. My mother had to spend an inordinate amount of time dealing with Joyce's problems. This created resentment among her siblings (myself included), and Joyce's sometimes violent attacks during her times of rage caused us to become embittered toward her.

When I was younger, Joyce being three years older than me meant she was able to physically hurt me as well as my younger sisters. She would attack with little warning, slashing my face with her nails, once chasing after me with a knife. I remember us sitting around the kitchen table when suddenly Joyce, in a rage, took a mop and smashed the face of another of my sisters against the kitchen wall.

It was hard not to hate her. Some people thought she was just being a disobedient and rebellious child, but somehow, in some way her brain had been damaged. Although my mother took her to counselors and doctors to the extent she could, there was no diagnosis. When the physical symptoms finally became clear, I think we were all relieved to know there was actually a physiological reason for all of our ruined family gatherings and holidays, the physical attacks, and the venomous verbal abuse.

Tragedy Without Options

Families living with a relative who has mental or emotional problems live with a heavy burden, even if they have money and are able to pursue treatment. The greater tragedy is there are many poor families who have no options – at least until the police are involved – and even then it becomes a succession of 911 calls until suicide, murder, or prison give them a tragic way out.

Our society has progressively consigned our mentally ill to the prisons or to the streets, producing battalions of homeless individuals who can't seem to live with anyone but that must fight to survive by whatever wits they have left. Our leaders have explained we just can't afford to institutionalize them anymore, saying community care is better. What is often left unsaid is that they often refuse to finance community care that might enable the impoverished mentally ill to be treated and given much-needed attention.

As I grew in my understanding of the Christian faith, along with a clearer awareness of my circumstances, I realized the Bible did have things to say about my life, my family's economic condition, the social situation in the city in which I grew up, and in fact, virtually every socio-economic situation.

I resented the fact I didn't have a father in my life. I didn't realize how much of a hole existed in my heart, my emotions and my psychology because of this. Who did I belong to, and who would go to bat for me? Who could protect me, who could mentor me, and who would love me? These weren't questions I consciously asked very often, but these nagging questions were anchored deeply in my heart. One of the verses that spoke to me early in my Christian life was John 1:12. It changed my perspective on whose child I was, and assured me I had one very powerful Father. This truth greatly impacted my life:

"Yet to all who received him, to those who believed in his name, he gave the right to become children of God – children born not of natural descent, nor of human decision or a husband's will, but born of God" (NIV).

Identity in the Midst of Racial Conflict

I lived in a racially polarized city, one that during my teen-age years was becoming increasingly violent. Sides were being drawn as the civil rights movement began to have its impact on Northern cities. Until the 1960s, I believe many Americans thought the problems of racism were confined to the Southern region of our country.

As African-Americans and non-white immigrants began to fill Northern cities, racial attitudes became exposed. The competition for jobs, housing and political power all began to create tension. Poverty in cities like Newark, as well as Gary, Indiana, Washington, D.C., and Detroit, Michigan, was real and could no longer be hidden or isolated to rural areas. It was up front and visible, in insultingly sharp contrast with the wealth of America paraded before us on television. This disparity created a sense of bitterness among those who felt disenfranchised.

As I moved from high school to college, I began to realize various individuals, groups, political parties and nations had differing and sometimes conflicting views on what caused poverty, and what if anything could be done about it.

The Black Muslims were very active in Newark and were preaching a work ethic, self-determination, and manhood, all from a distinctly ethnocentric position with a covering of pseudo-Islamic rhetoric. The Black Panthers were teaching an essentially revolutionary, Marxist model of liberation from oppression, of racial empowerment, of opposing systematic injustice with violence "by any means necessary." Communism beckoned as an answer for the oppressed masses, a way of collectivizing everything so it could be "evenly" distributed.

As a young Christian, I struggled with these messages and had to admit the appeal these movements had, especially for black young men, because it was fairly easy to see the racism of our country's history. By this time I'd begun reading a lot of black history and would read a lot more. I couldn't deny the reality of oppression, recognizing it not as an accident or byproduct of the assertiveness of one group and the slowness of another, but rather as systematic and intentional.

This ranged from the invasion and confiscation of Native American lands and resources; to the stealing of people from Africa and forcing them to give their labor in return for the barest means of sustenance; to the manipulation of the needs of poor people to force them into a lifetime of indentured servitude drawn from the sharecropper system – as in the lament of the mining industry, "I owe my soul to the company store." Once you began to notice it, there seemed to be injustice everywhere you looked.

Was anybody speaking to these issues? By the late '60s in America, Christianity appeared to be a segmented religion of theological Liberals opposed by various shades of Conservatives. I didn't yet understand the historical depth of this phenomenon, but did know some of us believed the Bible to be the Word of God, true in *every* part and applicable to *all* of life. Some of us believed people really had souls that needed saving, that people were facing judgment and unless they believed in Jesus they would be lost. I was very much a product of a so-called Fundamentalist approach to Christianity at this point.

Two Conflicting Views of the 'Gospel'?

At the same time I was getting angry at both racism and poverty, and frustrated that the people who seemed to be speaking about these things didn't appear to be preaching the "Gospel" as I had come to know it. How come we couldn't put these things together?

I had a bad taste in my mouth for the welfare system, based on personal experience. My family had been a beneficiary of the government's largess. I lived in federally financed city housing projects with a subsidized rent based on our income. This meant my family had an opportunity to have potable water, heat in the winter, a roof that didn't leak, and a foundation that wasn't collapsing under us. My family received a check every month that allowed us to buy food and certain other things, but not much more.

The social workers that came every once in a while to see if my mother had a man living in the house, along with the government surplus food distributed to us every great once in a while, made us feel special – but not in any good sense. I'm grateful for the generosity of the American people that allowed my family to survive during those years, but became determined to never live off of it again if I could help it. I've personally never met anyone living luxuriously off of welfare, but do know there are some who have settled for it when they shouldn't.

As I have already mentioned, while in high school I was introduced to the preaching and ministry of the late Rev. Tom Skinner from Harlem in New York City. This was the first time I had heard anybody begin to connect the Word of God with social issues. It was a great encouragement to me, opening a door to understanding that God did care about people like me, that His concern wasn't just to get souls to heaven but to reveal His glory in the practice of mercy and justice by His very own people.

My pastor, Grover Willcox, was using the Scriptures to point out what I have referred to as "ironic grace," where God uses the poor, the left out, the overlooked, to overthrow what the people of the world would ordinarily look to as wisdom and power. I was beginning to develop a theology that spoke to the world as I was coming to see it, no longer a theology that ignored it or attempted to overlook it as unimportant.

When poverty is "happening" to you, being hungry and worse, it takes on a sense of personal importance: Freezing to death is *personal,* being illiterate and ignorant is *personal.* Not being able to buy medicine when you or your babies have a chronic or life-threatening disease is *personal.* Being beaten or imprisoned unjustly by the police, forbidden to work or live in certain places because of the color of your skin or your ethnicity, are all personally important when it's happening to you or your family.

Poverty is not theoretical to those who suffer. I was beginning to understand it is also important to God. This was really not new truth or information; it was just becoming new to me. It had always been there in God's Word, that God heard the groaning of His people. If He heard the groaning back then, it meant He could hear it now.

One day the pastor gets a call from a businessman he knows from another church. The businessman says he knows a wealthy individual who has mentioned he would like to help a kid from the inner city go to college. The pastor considers who among his young people is getting ready to go to college but doesn't have any scholarships.

The pastor calls one particular young man and tells him to be ready to get picked up to go and meet with this wealthy benefactor. The inner city young man and the wealthy man, the owner of a music company who has invented a significant electric musical instrument, are introduced. At the end of the meeting the elderly gentleman tells the young man, "I will pay your way wherever you want to go." The businessman keeps his word and covers the young man's college costs for all four years.

That young man was me, and this great gift was made possible because that pastor – my pastor – felt a call to the city, to the poor, and was able to use his contacts to leverage a kid from the projects and a broken home into a college education so he would have no debt at graduation. I became – and am today – a recipient of mercy.

CHAPTER 4

"Let Freedom Ring from Lookout Mountain, Tennessee..."
(Dr. Martin Luther King, Jr.)

"The Sovereign Lord is my strength; he makes my feet like the feet of a deer, he enables me to go on the heights."

(HABAKKUK 3:19, NIV)

I HAVE TO CONFESS TO my immaturity and arrogance as a young man. To be honest, I admit to still being sometimes confident to the point of arrogance, often because I'm simply heedless to the possible circumstances. My hope is I've gained some maturity so as not to be too obnoxious. I left Newark for California because a wealthy man offered to pay my way to college – "anywhere you want to go." So I got out a catalogue of Christian colleges and turned right to the California section. That was about as far away from Newark as I could get.

When I left for California, I don't think I realized how much I was imprinted with an urban mindset and a commitment to the black community. I was in love with a young woman named Joan McRae, who had grown up during the same time as me and in the same housing project, the Otto E. Kretchmer Homes. We both went to Dayton Street School and Arts High School, although she was one year ahead of me. Joan is African-American, so falling in love with her meant I had to begin thinking about race, reconciliation, and justice.

Newark had experienced a terrible riot in 1967 and again exploded after the killing of Dr. Martin Luther King, Jr. In the late 1960's, Newark was a place just boiling with issues of race and injustice. We had studied issues of race and poverty in my senior humanities class in high school, and talked about issues of race and poverty in our church youth group. For those of us in Newark these issues were real; they weren't abstract for us since we had to deal with them firsthand every day.

Transplanted into Suburbia

By September 1968, I was in Southern California on a Christian college campus with only a few black students. I was in the heart of predominantly white suburbia. I enjoyed many things about being at Biola College (now Biola University), yet felt homesick and out of place.

Things perked up for me when Keith Phillips came out to the campus to recruit students for ministry with (as it was named at that time) World Impact/Urban Impact. Keith had been working in the inner city and partnered with the Student Missionary Union to bring college students to the projects in Watts and East Los Angeles.

In my home church I had been trained in how to do street meetings, children's open air meetings, youth group evangelistic services and rescue mission Gospel services. I was a fundamentalist Christian and an evangelist. I was thrilled to be able to get off the campus and do ministry in the inner city. The Imperial Courts were different in appearance from the projects of Newark, but many of the issues were the same. Poverty, fatherlessness, and violence all were there. I was thrilled to be back (albeit only to visit) in the projects again.

As I participated in the children's Bible clubs I began to realize my philosophy of ministry was different from some of the other students. I'd never done ministry as a passing service to inner city kids; they were always seen as individuals and people we were seeking to bring into the church and into our lives.

Many of those students meant well, but too often they were patronizing and paternalistic to the children. I hungered for more urban ministry and soon became involved in a black church in Compton whose pastor had a son at Biola. I began to help with their youth group.

As the school year went on, I realized the friends I had from Newark, most of whom were black and had gone to Covenant College on Lookout Mountain in Georgia, were people I desperately missed. Joan (who would become my wife) was one of those people, and after making a few visits on the way home for holidays, I became convinced I needed to transfer. Biola was undoubtedly happy to see me go as I was becoming somewhat rebellious, challenging the rules.

Closing One Door, Opening Another

In the Lord's providence, Joan had been recruited to Covenant College (a Presbyterian college on Lookout Mountain) in the summer after she graduated from high school. One might call it lucky, a coincidence, a cosmic convergence, a serendipitous event – or as we Calvinists see it, a predetermined act of God's will – that a recruiter for Covenant College "happened" to be in upstate New York at Camp Peniel that summer day. It was during a week in July that Joan had come up to the camp to see me because I was working there for the summer.

Pastor Willcox had tried so hard to get Joan to apply to a Christian college, but she dodged him at every turn. He had people come to her house to help her fill out applications and she'd fill them out, but would not mail them. It had been the history in her family that kids would finish high school and then get a job, so she saw no reason to be different.

Our pastor felt he could best seal the discipleship of inner city young people by getting them to a Christian college. He was a Wheaton College graduate and never regretted the effect it had had on him. He just couldn't seem to get Joan to buy into it.

When Pastor Willcox realized there was a college recruiter at the camp and Joan was there, too, he jumped into action. I can tell you Pastor Willcox had an agenda for almost everyone in his church, especially among the youth, and felt it was his job to guide them where he thought they should be going. So he instructed Joan to go to the special presentation at the chapel building to hear about Covenant. Instead, Joan decided to go swimming – which she cannot and doesn't do – but that day she went down to the swimming area at the "channel" so she could escape the college recruiter.

Our pastor looked over the group in the chapel and realized Joan was not there. Asking around, he found out where she had gone. He then took the recruiter practically by the hand and walked him down to the swimming area. After finding Joan he sat her down on a large boulder, put the recruiter next to her, and asked him to help her fill out the application. He then asked the recruiter to take the application with him so Joan would have no opportunity to sabotage the process. One month later, Joan flew from Newark, New Jersey to Lookout Mountain, Georgia

Looking back, I consider this one of the best things that ever happened to Joan, me, Covenant College, New City Fellowship, and the Presbyterian Church in America. I am, of course, a bit biased, but I do think the simple fact of her attending and graduating from Covenant has made a tremendous impact on the lives of so many people. She was the second black student at Covenant, and the first black female to attend and graduate.

This pretty, musically talented, believing, and faithful young woman would encourage many people in the ministry of racial reconciliation, inner city church planting, and Gospel witness. There is no doubt in my mind (and probably no doubt in the minds of anyone else who know us) that marrying Joan has made me a better man, and together given us a ministry we could never have found on our own.

Joan had come into my life at first simply as a girl I "noticed" in my school and neighborhood. I certainly liked what I saw, but had no idea how to meet and get to know her. One day my best friend told me his sister had invited Joan out to our youth group at church. I was excited to hear that, and as we stood waiting for our ride to youth group on the sidewalk of the projects, Joan came walking around the corner. As soon as I saw her I had the impression that this was the girl I would marry. A few months later she came to believe in Jesus. And by the next year, I think the deal was pretty much sewed up.

Third Street Sunday School

During Joan's freshman year it turned out a Mr. Rudolph Schmidt was conducting a Sunday school class at the Reformed Presbyterian Church of Lookout Mountain. This class was studying a book by my friend, Tom Skinner, called, *Black and Free.* Mr. Schmidt was the dean of admissions at Covenant, and after reading this book, he (with his wife, Collyn) along with the doctors Barker (brothers Will and Nick Barker), Steve and Mary Kaufman, Arlene Wetzel and several students, decided to go downtown and start a Sunday school in the inner city.

By this time in my life I was beginning to realize the lesson that God had begun to teach me back in the projects. When I was a freshman in high school, before I met Joan, I was fervently praying for friends (and in my heart I meant white, Christian, girl-type friends). About two years later, one night at a Bible study in my house, I realized God had given me the friends for whom I had been praying. They all turned out to be African-American and from my same neighborhood. Joan was one of the teenagers in that room. The affluent, white Christian community I had seen in California, a context I knew little about, held less and less appeal for me. It seemed so out of touch with reality, at least the hard, bitter reality I saw in the inner city.

Upon arrival at Covenant College for my sophomore year, I was immediately recruited by Joan to come down to the city of Chattanooga on Sundays to help with the "Third Street Sunday School." If one is attempting to plant a church, this may be the slowest way to do it. In those early days I don't know if anyone imagined this was really the beginning of a church plant.

If one wants to plant a church in the inner city and hopes to have the children they are reaching be the nucleus of the new church, there are certain realities one needs to face. In order to have leadership, or even active volunteers, they will have to wait for those kids to grow up. Maybe their parents will get saved and be brought into the church, but either way no one has any money. The kids certainly don't. Even if everyone tithed in such a church, the meager income wouldn't be enough to afford a pastor.

In any event, the Reformed Presbyterian Church of Lookout Mountain (a congregation in the Reformed Presbyterian Church, Evangelical Synod) commissioned this group of faculty, staff, and students to go downtown and conduct a Sunday school. The team was led by Rudy Schmidt, a man who would become one of my dearest friends and a faithful mentor to me for as long as he lived.

Dutifully, every Sunday morning the team would go knock on doors and see what children they could get to come to the Sunday school apartment. A simple program of singing and Bible classes was presented, and over the first year it began to grow. As the semester went by, I began to desire to do more than just serve on Sundays. I asked Mr. Schmidt for permission to start a youth ministry, and he asked me to write up a proposal. Although I never got to the proposal, I did get to the work.

CHAPTER 5

Embracing an Inner City Calling

"Then I heard the voice of the Lord saying, 'Whom shall I send? And who will go for us?' And I said, 'Here am I. Send me!'"

(ISAIAH 6:8, NIV)

I AM NOT SURE HOW it started, but I began to ask people if they would go off Lookout Mountain with me and try to do some evangelism. One fairly consistent partner was Dr. Nicholas Barker, a brilliant scholar of English who was absolutely not a basketball player. (I wasn't much of one, either.) He and I would try to find places to play basketball in the city and meet young men, and hopefully have opportunities to witness to them.

We went to Howard High School, Ninth Street, and the McCallie Homes in Alton Park. One time my friend Jim Coad, a fellow student and future missionary to Mexico, and I took the Incline Railway down the famous mountain south of Chattanooga and walked to the McCallie Homes projects from the station at the bottom. I remember this distinctly for several reasons. That day we met some guys who would become part of a youth Bible study and with whom I would continue to have a relationship for several years. On the way back up Lookout Mountain on the Incline, we caught a ride back to the college with the noted theologian/

philosopher/evangelist Dr. Francis Schaeffer, dressed in his usual lederhosen. We represented two different worlds, to be sure.

I began to pour myself into both the Sunday school and the youth work. The previous summer, between my year at Biola and my sophomore year at Covenant, I spent working for the Newark Evangelistic Committee in the inner city back home. They paid me twenty dollars a week, but I was given freedom to do all kinds of outreach and ministry. It was a great summer of ministry in the Central Ward of Newark.

As the summer after my sophomore year approached, I wondered what to do. I received an offer to go work in the inner city of Detroit, but realized my immediate future was tied up with the work in Chattanooga. Mr. Schmidt worked it out so that the Reformed Presbyterian church on the mountain would hire me for the summer, and I'd live in the Sunday school apartment.

Raising the Level of Consciousness

Several of my high school classmates had come to Covenant, even before I did, and we all had a consciousness of what was happening racially in the country, as well as how that contrasted with the white church community to which we were being introduced. One of the young women from Newark, Patty Reilly, was attending a wealthy church on Lookout Mountain. She began to tell some of their leaders and members what I was doing downtown, that I was beginning to gather young people into Bible studies, and actively pursuing street ministry.

In God's mercy, one of the elders from Lookout Mountain Presbyterian Church, Mr. Dave Mitchell, took an interest in me. He told me to come see him when I returned from a short trip home to visit my mom. When I went to see him at his fire protection company, he gave me my first car, and recruited Sam Chester, Jr. to pay the car insurance. These men, along with Rudy Schmidt, became my spiritual godfathers and supporters of the early work. They bailed me out of financial trouble over and over again, and encouraged me when I felt overwhelmed and lonely.

I moved into the apartment on Third Street and began to build a pattern of playing basketball in the recreation centers, walking around the streets, and hanging out with inner city kids and their families. After a week or two living in the Sunday school apartment, I got a call from Rodney Alexander.

Rod and I had roomed together during our sophomore year at Covenant. He and I had gone to high school together in Newark, and he'd been a leader in our church youth group. Rod was an exceptionally gifted athlete, smart, and a gifted preacher and leader. He said he felt God wanted him to come down and work with me in Chattanooga. I told him, "If you come, I'll share all I have with you." He came and as promised we shared the car, I slept on the box spring, he got the mattress, and we split the salary.

Rod is black, so he and I became a noticeable twosome on the streets and the recreation centers. That summer found us in all kinds of little adventures in pool halls, in the middle of potential gunfights, and playing basketball at recreation centers and on parking lots until the wee hours of the morning.

A Harvest Just Waiting

The Lord was with us and by the end of the summer of 1970 we had gathered dozens of teenagers. We took them up to Cedine Bible Camp in Spring City, Tennessee; we took them swimming wherever we could find a pool, and we tried to proclaim the Gospel to them. It was as if the harvest was just waiting to be reaped, and kids were waiting to be loved. We made lots of mistakes, and had little if any adult supervision, but God used us in spite of ourselves.

Out of that summer grew a two-pronged ministry for me. I was invested in the Sunday school, and also became part of the preaching team (Dr. William S. Barker and myself) after a worship service had been added. I need to say one of God's great gifts to me in my life has been the wonderful mentors I've had. Dr. Barker was one of them. I don't know if I've ever met a more soft-spoken, humble, affirming, generous, and brilliant man.

We began to form a coalition of churches and businessmen to support what would become our first parachurch ministry, Inner City Missions, Inc. For the next three years I would be heavily involved in both ministries and found this was my essential calling: to live and work for the Gospel of Jesus Christ in the city and among the poor.

By January of 1971, Joan and I were married and lived in an apartment next to the one that hosted the Sunday school on Third Street. After growing up in the projects, going to college had been a step up for both of us in terms of living conditions. Now we were right back in the ghetto. The dear lady who owned the apartments had inherited them from her deceased husband, and it would be hard not to have called him a "slum lord."

We had no heat in our apartment that winter until Sam Chester found out about it and then paid to have a plumbing company install a gas heater. We might have been okay, but the heater in our car went out, and then things got a little rough. We lived off the money from wedding gifts for a few months until Joan graduated and got a job, and I started getting paid again for doing ministry in the summer. I still apologize to Joan (Honey, I'm sorry!) for putting her through all that by marrying me before I was financially stable. Of course, who knows when that would have been?

Adjusting to Married Life

I had to adjust to being married. I could no longer hang out in pool halls until the wee hours of the morning as Rod and I had done that previous summer. One day, I can't remember the reason, Joan's mom sent her five dollars in a card. It was all the money we had. Sure enough, while Joan was at school someone knocked on our door and said his family was freezing, his sister had pneumonia, and they needed five dollars for a bag of coal. It was hard to explain to Joan where the five dollars went. It's also hard to explain how we are still married today, but by the grace of God she has stuck with me in spite of the many dumb things I have done.

By the summer of 1972 we had organized the parachurch into a 501©3 non-profit, the little church was growing, and we had moved the worship service into the Southside YMCA, also known as "the Industrial Y," but to the people on the block, it was simply "the pink Y."

A growing number of college students began to attend the small church and wanted to participate in ministry during the summer. This gave us a lot more "boots on the ground," and I was moving from being someone who did street ministry to one that was supervising and directing a whole group of people that wanted to do ministry in the city. Joan and I decided to delay leaving for seminary and stayed to preach regularly at the mission church for one more year.

We were conscious that not many evangelical churches were involved in inner city evangelism or church planting. We began to reach out to others we knew who were also pursuing ministry cross-culturally and to the poor. We helped to organize and hold a conference we called a "National Conference on the Inner City," in 1972 and 1973.

A highlight of one of those conferences was when Dr. William Bentley of the National Black Evangelical Association (NBEA) had a debate with Dr. Francis Schaffer on the question of, "When was America Christian?" since Dr. Schaffer had spoken so often of the "post-Christian era." Dr. Bentley was pretty scathing about how "Christian" America could possibly have been, given the realities of slavery and racism. Dr. Schaffer later made some corrections to his description of American Christianity in an article in *Christianity Today* magazine.

Our Next Spiritual Adventure

When Joan and I left Chattanooga in the summer of 1973 for Covenant Seminary in St. Louis, Missouri, we did not know if we would ever return. We turned over the mission church and Inner City Missions to those leaders we left behind, and Rudy Schmidt especially became the guiding force in helping things to continue.

During our time in seminary, Joan and I participated in ministry at Grace and Peace Fellowship (RPCES) and during my second year I took a job as a youth minister at Sutter Ave. Presbyterian Church (UPC), pastored by the Rev. William McKonkey. My job was to lead and develop a youth group in University City and Wellston, where Joan and I lived in a church apartment.

Wellston was as hard an inner city environment as anywhere else I have lived or served. We also became part of a regular ministry to the state women's prison in Tipton, Missouri. Through all of this, we were still immersed in ministry to inner city folks and those in poverty, and in all the drama that characterizes broken families, violence, prison, and challenges of discipleship across racial and cultural barriers.

As Joan and I examine our own lives today, we know our past scarred us in many ways. As a fundamentalist, I was almost entrenched in my ignorance about the effect that my dysfunctional family, abandonment by my father, our poverty, and other psychological influences had on my personality and behavior.

My understanding of theology taught me I was saved and forgiven, so I didn't allow myself to think very much about how those things affected me, both emotionally and behaviorally. My legalism propped up a good front for me on the outside as I appeared to be a zealous worker for Jesus, and to a large extent I was.

Joan had her own share of emotional baggage, and many of our struggles were hidden from others. We knew we were having problems; we could see all kinds of sins taking hold of us, but didn't have many folks we could talk to about this. Those were days when there just weren't many (hardly any) Christian counselors available, and it was almost shameful to admit if you needed to go see one of them. I think it's important to acknowledge these things since someone might get the mistaken idea that we were somehow heroic Christians in doing the kind of ministry we did.

Doing What Few Others Were Doing

At the same time, we were overconfident, presumptuous, even arrogant, because we knew few people who were doing what we were doing, or even understood how to do it. Lots of white people seemed afraid of black people, and black people didn't trust white people. Sometimes I will admit I was too dumb to be afraid – and there were plenty of times I should have been afraid.

The real danger, though, wasn't from thieves, muggings, or getting shot or stabbed. The real danger was pursuing ministry without getting in touch with our own brokenness, our own internal mess, our own inability to resist temptations of various kinds. If God had not been merciful and faithful, I'm afraid our sins would have led us to blatant hypocrisy and eventual spiritual shipwreck.

It's God's plan to use broken people to achieve His will. (I'm wondering if any readers are saying "amen" at this point?) My life has been a growing realization of His love for sinners, of love for me, His ability to forgive, cleanse and make righteous, to deliver from besetting sins, to heal the past, and to "restore the years the locust has eaten." Dr. William Barker once pointed out to me that I usually start my public prayers with, "Lord, please forgive us of our sins." I was simply revealing that my sins were conscious realities to me. I hadn't realized most people don't do that.

Work among the poor, serving in the inner city, having a zeal for justice, along with a conviction of the need for ministries of mercy, can make one very self-righteous. Maybe God's saving grace to us was to make us so aware of our own wickedness, our own weakness and failures that we began to realize we had (and still have) no right to judge others.

I write this as a sinner saved by grace, calling on other sinners to do something great for God – not to *earn* His pleasure, but only *by* His pleasure – and become amazed at the joy of being a participant *in* His pleasure through His wonderful grace. When I read that phrase in Scripture about a bruised reed and a smoldering wick (Matthew 12:15-21), I know how it applies to us.

Recipients of Great Mercy

So, by the skin of our teeth we remained in the ministry, over the years learned the joy of our sonship in Jesus Christ, and were given the grace of repentance in overcoming addictions, exposing secrets and darkness in our hearts. Again I tell you this so you would not think we are in any way special. If anything, I am sure others are probably more qualified to do ministry, show mercy, and reach the lost. So if God can use us, He obviously can use anybody.

During our time in seminary we had the opportunity to meet Dr. John Perkins at the Race & Reconciliation Conference held in Atlanta in 1975. For the first time I found a mentor who had some practical economic vision for helping poor people in the name of Jesus. Dr. Perkins was a man who had a rare combination: a fundamentalist's view of the necessity of evangelism and the salvation of the lost, a civil rights leader's commitment to racial justice, and a revolutionary's passion for social change for the poor. Besides that, he was loving man, and had an acerbic wit.

By the time of my graduation, I had helped Covenant Seminary hold an Urban Institute, with Dr. Harvie Conn of Westminster Theological Seminary and Dr. Perkins coming to teach. The preaching, teaching and writings of these men deeply affected me. My hope was that this kind of Urban Ministry Institute would continue at the seminary, but unfortunately it didn't.

I was a little conflicted about my future. I'd taken a commission in the U.S. Army in preparation for being a chaplain. I wasn't sure where else I would have a call to the ministry, so I was ordained as an Evangelist for the Chaplaincy. The elders from New City Fellowship, as the mission church in Chattanooga was now called, came to see me in my last semester of seminary. Ed Kellogg and Rudy Schmidt asked me to come back, organize them as a church, and retake my position as the Director of Inner City Missions. I would have to be bi-vocational in order to make a living. I told them if the Army didn't take me on active duty I would come – and so the Army duly lost my application. Coincidence? Being a believer in a God who works all things after the counsel of His will, I think not.

In the Lord's providence, being tri-vocational as an Army Reservist was the only way we could have made it in those days, and times were still hard. So we came home to Chattanooga and led New City to become a Particular Church (though it would take years for us to be self-supporting) in November of 1976. It was a congregation that would grow in its self-awareness of its calling to minister cross-culturally to the black community, to be inclusive and welcoming to the poor, and promote the radicalization of the middle class into ministries of justice and mercy.

Questions for Reflection and Discussion

1. What passages of Scripture in this first section speak to the issues of a person's identity in Christ?

2. How does poverty affect someone's identity and his or her feelings of worth or value in the world?
3. What other passages of Scripture that you might know speak to the issue of value and self-worth for a person who is a believer, or simply that God loves us?
4. Where does the Bible speak to such social issues as poverty, injustice, and oppression?

Part Two:

Perplexities of Poverty

CHAPTER 6

Is Poverty God's Fault?

"The Lord sends poverty and wealth; he humbles and he exalts."

(1 SAMUEL 2:7)

IT IS MY HOPE THAT by sharing my personal narrative in Part One, you have a sense of my own journey through the world of poverty, as well as my passion for helping the poor and disenfranchised. At this point it might be helpful to address some foundational concepts to establish a basis for common understanding.

Let me begin this section by acknowledging that not all poverty is the same or arises from the same cause. People are poor for a great many different reasons, which means our solutions to poverty should not be simplistic.

We are beset with all kind of debates about the causes of poverty. These debates become important as they result in action or inaction in our response to the poor. The decisions leaders make, as well as individuals, in what benevolence they will or will not fund or where they will make contributions often are derived from their perspectives on why people are poor. If the fault of poverty lies with the poor themselves, this may steer our choices, and certainly our attitudes.

If the fault of poverty lies at the feet of those who have defrauded or exploited them, our feelings may be more compassionate toward the poor (and angry at the oppressor) and even begin a cry for justice. If we feel the poor are poor through no fault of their own, but rather because of ruinous circumstances or acts of nature, we may feel kindly inclined to give them some relief – help either in dealing with or escaping from their circumstances.

The causes of poverty are scientifically analyzed, measured by economists and sociologists, and recommendations presented as to how to curtail or even end it. But the underlying causes are not new, nor are they a great mystery. Unfortunately, even in the face of facts and evidence, our political predispositions tend to make us categorize people, label them, even dismiss them. This sometimes causes us to miss what is obvious about poverty – and people – in general.

In our discussion of poverty let's start with God. Sometimes those in very difficult and disastrous circumstances blame God, and I use "sometimes" advisedly, because this is not a universal reaction. I have heard more armchair philosophers blame suffering on God than I have heard it from people who are suffering.

The poor and the needy quite often find themselves looking to God even as they suffer. The Marxist may find this to be part of the problem, as if religion were a drug to ease the pain of suffering, and one that keeps people from taking the materialistic steps to change their situation.

The reality is that faith is an engine for the poor, and historically has helped them survive in their poverty, as well as deal with the suffering created by unjust governments. Thankfully the human heart is not universally bathed in bitterness. Amazingly, sometimes trouble just creates more faith.

The Poor You Will Always Have With You

Starting with the assumption that there is a God, what role does He have in allowing poverty, or perhaps even planning it in the lives of people or nations? Does God even care about the poor?

People will sometimes quote Jesus as saying, *"the poor you will have with you always"* (Matthew 26:11). Some people will cite this passage without any knowledge of where the original quote comes from. They just as often misunderstand the intent of Jesus in his reference. Jesus was using a statement God made in the Old Testament from the book of Deuteronomy, chapter 15.

In the Pentateuch (the five books of Moses), we are told of God choosing the children of Abraham, the nation of Israel, as a special nation through whom he would eventually bless all the nations of the earth through His "seed," namely the Messiah, whom we know as Jesus.

As proof of His favor to Israel, God delivered the Jews from Egypt where they had formerly been slaves and made them His covenant people. God told Moses about the covenant He wanted the children of Israel to keep once they came into the promised land of Canaan. Simply put, God wanted obedience and He promised that if Israel obeyed him, then there would be no poor in the land.

The promise of "no poor people" (Deuteronomy 15:4) is astounding. The land itself would respond to the Jews by growing abundant crops without drought, blight, or anything that often adversely affects agriculture. The beasts would cooperate, the bugs would cooperate, and the weather would cooperate – all if Israel obeyed. If Israel truly loved God with everything they had, and loved their neighbors as themselves, then there would be universal sufficiency and abundance.

But just in case someone became poor, God demanded the children of Israel should respond in compassion and mercy to those in such situations (Deuteronomy 15:7-8), and when they did that the blessing of prosperity would continue for them as a nation. To this end, God set up a plan of economic justice and economic recapitalization for times when people might become poor.

God established a sabbatical system, a Sabbath year, and the year of Jubilee with a plan for debts to be forgiven, for sharing with those who became poor. This is where He told them there would always be poor people in the land, so they should remain openhanded (Deuteronomy 15:11). This was not a statement of resignation, but a challenge and opportunity for the people of God to do good.

When Jesus makes reference to this Old Testament passage, He is not condemning people to stay poor, but only comparing the reality of continual poverty with the transitory nature of His time upon the earth. As with all suffering, poverty is a result of the judgment that fell on the world when the human race sinned against God. Presbyterians refer to the situation that mankind fell into as "an estate of sin and misery." This misery is general to all of us, like death. Just as it does not come to all of us at the same time or the same way, suffering does not to come to us all in the same magnitude.

Judgment Brought Upon Themselves

One of the reasons Israel suffered judgment from God was because they did not treat the poor with compassion, nor did they faithfully execute the system of economic justice and recapitalization as He had commanded.

Included in this plan was the forgiveness of debts after seven years; the freeing of indentured slaves; the rest given to workers, servants, and animals on the seventh day of each week; the resting of the land every seventh year; and the returning of lands of inheritance to families at the 50th year, which was called Jubilee. Recapitalization for the poor was to take place each Jubilee (50th) year as people were able to receive back their family's property. Families could use their land to rebuild their lives.

The sad fact is that Israel never celebrated the Sabbath year, and as a result of their missing seventy of them for 490 years, God took back each of those years: He sent them into exile to Babylon for seventy years (2 Chronicles 36:20-21). The Old

Testament system of economic justice and equity builds on the understanding that the land belongs to God, that it is a gift and blessing from Him to His people. Wealth was God's blessing, not an inherent right, and certainly was not something people should attain by taking it from others. It was, and still is, something that can be achieved by blessing, diligence, and righteousness (both personal and social).

Along with God's system of economic justice was the responsibility of individuals to help those who needed help. The foremost categories of those He commanded His people to help were widows, orphans, and aliens, because these were the very people whose cause God declared He would defend.

"For the Lord your God is God of gods and Lord of lords, the great God, mighty and awesome, who shows no partiality and accepts no bribes. He defends the cause of the fatherless and the widow, and loves the alien, giving him food and clothing. And you are to love those who are aliens, for you yourselves were aliens in Egypt" (Deuteronomy 10:17).

With the command to help these categories of folks was the principle of "gleaning" and allowing the poor to help themselves. The best picture of this in the Bible is the story of Ruth, who was a widow with her mother-in-law, Naomi, and they gleaned in the fields of Boaz.

Boaz was a near relative of these two widows and it made sense that they would choose his fields from which to glean. Under God's law the poor were allowed to come behind the reapers during the harvest. Owners of fields were to not reap the corners of their fields, nor shake their fruit trees twice, so the poor would have something left behind to glean for themselves.

So we see that some people were poor because they became widows, or had become orphans, or had been forced from their homeland and had become aliens in a strange land. In each of these cases, we can see poverty was not their fault but happened because of circumstances that befell them. Did God make that happen?

Complicated Causes and Effects

The Bible reveals the issue of cause and effect is complicated. It does teach God has eternal decrees, making decisions about destiny and futures of individuals, families, nations and thus the world. Many of these kinds of workings of God's will are unknown to us, except that the Bible does say, *"The Lord makes poor and makes rich"* (1 Samuel 2:7).

So we are told behind all of our circumstances is His unseen hand at work to bring about His will. This idea can create resentment toward God and the teachings of the Bible. In my case, however, it gave a sense of relief. In other words, this truth told me my family's poverty had a purpose, and for me it provided a great comfort. So you might understand clearly, I am saying God sovereignly planned for my family to be poor – and in retrospect I am thankful for it. Admittedly, I am more thankful for it now than I was at the time!

The secret, unseen hand of God in determining our futures is not so much our daily worry. Whether one agrees or not with the theology or philosophy of this idea (destiny, predestination, etc.), it will not change the reality as to whether God is behind things or not. Isn't that so?

God's revealed will (as seen in the Bible) in declaring our responsibility about how to conduct our affairs and the warnings of the result of that obedience – or disobedience – should be our concern. The Bible's view is that, ultimately, all poverty and suffering has come to the world because of the sin of humanity. The poor are always with us because of our sins.

God uses poverty not just to punish us, but also to afflict us so that we might turn back to Him. We understand death and all suffering as His judgment upon humanity for our collective sin and sinfulness. However, at the same time we see them as a result of the continued malice, evil, neglect and wickedness on the part of individuals, families, and nations. Therefore they are our responsibility.

It is this part of sin, suffering and poverty that is our business because it is something we can act upon and seek to relieve.

Questions for Reflection and Discussion

1. What role do you think God's intention, His plan, plays in people being poor?
2. What purpose could poverty possibly serve in God accomplishing His will? You might want to discuss the story of Joseph in Genesis.
3. What place do the choices that people, families, or nations make have to do with their poverty?
4. What was the sabbatical plan of God, and how did that affect issues such as justice, debt relief, and poverty?

CHAPTER 7

Then Whose Fault Is It?

"Do not love sleep or you will grow poor...."

(PROVERBS 20:13)

THE BIBLE MAKES CLEAR THAT there are several causes of poverty. Sometimes poverty is not the direct result of anyone's lifestyle, but the result of circumstances over which a person has no control. In other cases the poverty of others can be directly related to their behavior and poor choices. This means that not all poverty is the same; it doesn't all flow from the same source.

For that reason our response to poverty has to be as different as the causes, especially if someone's behavior will keep them in poverty no matter what we do to help them. In addition, as Christians the poverty and suffering we see others going through is not the only thing that should concern us about them.

For us as believers, our love of neighbor means we must care about their relationship to Christ – their need for a Savior. This care for the souls of our neighbors is built on our hope and faith in the reality of God's ability to forgive and change people. This is directly related to how we treat the poor. We are not allowed a simple dismissal of anyone who is poor due to their own misbehavior.

The Christian church cannot and must not simply condemn those who have failed in their choices. So what should a Christian do when he perceives someone's poverty as being brought about by that person's own laziness or dissipation? Does the Christian despise all the poor, explain all poverty by this example, and refuse to help this particular person? A generalized explanation for poverty from a few examples is not logical. In the face of a poor person's sin, do we still believe the Gospel is able to change people? Is our compassion compromised by our own self-righteousness?

Mercy Totally Undeserved

What right do any of us have in being self-righteous at all, considering our own sins? As the Church preaches the Gospel of Grace with its attendant call to repentance and faith, we must also welcome back the prodigal. This means extending mercy (even physical mercy) to those who don't deserve it. In Jesus' story of the Prodigal Son, doesn't the father extend physical mercy to his son, as well as the forgiveness of the heart?

Mercy from God is not given to those who deserve it. In fact, it's just the opposite. Mercy is given to those who by definition do not deserve it, i.e., sinners. Like me and you. For some reason when it comes to economics, we tend to dispense with this side of grace and simply start categorizing people as "deserving poor versus undeserving poor."

The children of Israel were commanded to show mercy and love to their neighbors who had need because God had shown them mercy through their deliverance from Egypt. All of us who are followers of Christ should know that none of us deserve mercy *("while we were yet sinners Christ died for us,"* Romans 5:8). So in response our hands are forced to be open; we must not be hardhearted. At the same time, wisdom will show that neither should we be thick-headed and unaware of the best ways to show mercy so that it is truly helpful.

Without a doubt there are some people who are poor because they are lazy, and some because they are wasteful and stupid in their choices. Some people become poor because of their greed and selfishness; they live beyond their means until everything falls down around them. Some people force their children into poverty by their immorality, their addictions, and refusal to accept their own responsibility.

It is not helpful to the poor for us to excuse their poverty by depriving them of the dignity of being responsible for their choices. However, there is poverty that is brought about from injustice, just as there are natural disasters in which people lose all they have worked to achieve. So we must not regard all poverty as arising from the same source, nor are the results coming from it all the same.

The Available Poor

The poor are often victims of crime because they are the most available victims to other poor people who have chosen to use criminal means to satisfy their wants and desires. My own mother was mugged five times before she was finally able to move out of the projects. Many times our church has helped people who, after cashing their welfare or Social Security checks, had the money taken by strong-armed robbery, purse-snatching, or theft (often by a neighbor or relative).

How frustrating it is for those who have hardly anything and count on the little bit of money coming in from a government check, and then to have that stolen. Rich people get better police protection, build gated communities, and hire security guards to protect their wealth, but the poor live in great danger every day of seeing their food and rent money taken from them. This experience from our church will show you what I mean:

One of the teenagers in our youth group called one day: "My grandmother has been sitting in the dark for two weeks. Her food has gone bad because the electricity has been shut off." "Why?" we wanted to know. "Because my Auntie who lives with her steals her Social Security check and drinks it up." We found out where she lived and went to visit.

This elderly widow was 85 years of age when we met her. Paying her light bill was the easy part, but getting family members to intervene with the alcoholic daughter was harder. Getting that daughter to rehab, and protecting this elderly mother, would be part of a long, challenging relationship. She became our church's oldest member, dying at 103 years of age as a devoted member, having first come to Christ in a cotton field in Alabama.

She scandalized the elders of our church when they gave her a membership interview. When asked why she thought she was qualified to go to heaven, she responded (and I quote), "Why, you don't think niggers can go to heaven? When I was young I was picking cotton in Alabama. I fell asleep in the middle of the day and I had a dream. I saw Jesus and he said, 'I'm gonna take out your heart of stone and give you a heart of flesh, I'm going to take out of you a heart of damnation and give you a heart of salvation,' and that's the day I got saved!" The Presbyterian elders said, "Amen," and gave her the right hand of fellowship.

Breakdown of Values

Poverty in and of it itself does not cause crime. Amazingly, most poor people choose to obey the law and would rather suffer than lose their own self-respect. However, the breakdown of a strong value system instilled by good home training (now often absent, and that largely due to there being no father in the home to provide impulse control) leaves many children in poor communities at risk to the temptations of violence and fast money. When addictions to alcohol and drugs are pursued to deaden the boredom, loneliness and pain of poverty, crime spreads pretty quickly.

I have seen the violence in poor communities many times and have often thought of the passage in Proverbs 1:8-19:

"My son, if sinners entice you, do not give in to them. If they say, 'Come along with us; let's lie in wait for someone's blood, let's waylay some harmless soul; let's swallow them alive, like the grave, and whole, like those who go down to the pit; we will get all sorts of valuable things and fill our houses with plunder; throw in your lot with us, and we will share a common purse' – my son, do not go along with them…."

Question: Does this remind you of gang activity?

In this passage we see "a father's instruction." Most kids in the inner city aren't getting the instruction in this passage because there isn't any father to give it. We see in this passage a warning against the "enticement" to young men for violence, and that is what happens when a peer value system is built by and among a generation of other fatherless young men.

As hard as it is to concede, gangs and violence are attractive. They are, in fact, "infectious" and in a very real sense a public health problem, especially to those of the public (often the available poor in the neighborhood) who are the ones robbed, mugged, beaten, and shot. Peer value formation among fatherless males creates climates of violence, and that climate creates one more obstacle for people trying to climb out of poverty.

Understanding what has made people poor and what continues to keep them poor is essential if we want to change the reality on the ground. The Bible views poverty as a curse, a ruin for the poor. *"The wealth of the rich is their fortified city, but poverty is the ruin of the poor" (Proverbs 10:15, NIV).* We will find this verse several times in this book.

Poverty is not something we should simply accept or tolerate, since all that does is perpetuate people in their suffering. We don't treat the sick as if their suffering was normal; we seek to heal them. We know every sick person that is healed by doctors will someday die, but we don't give up on them because of that. Not only is a person's suffering something we want to alleviate, but we also know the poverty of one generation can – and often does – leverage the next generation into deeper poverty.

Some poverty is momentary, an anomaly in the life of a person who is suddenly unemployed or who has been beset with devastating circumstances. If a person has the resiliency, value system, family background, right connections and access to resources, then they are usually able to recover and come back into self-sufficiency. However, generational poverty destroys most of those things. As Proverbs says, *"Wealth attracts many friends, but even the closest friend of the poor person deserts them" (Proverbs 19:4).*

Relentless, Continuing Patterns

Poverty often begins with the destruction of the family and in turn initiates a continuing pattern. Many young adults in the inner city don't even consider marriage. Far too many become pregnant outside of marriage. For those who do get married, as in all of American society, there is far too much divorce. For those growing up in poor neighborhoods or living in generational poverty there is the pattern of aborted education and functional illiteracy, with the consequent inability of finding a job and thus, lack of ability to earn a living wage.

We seem to be creating in America a permanent "underclass" of folks who seem caught in a system of cyclical poverty. The question is where do we break that cycle, and how? There are certainly historic patterns of racism in America that explain many of our housing patterns, our employment patterns, and our declining public schools: Real estate and banking red-lining of neighborhoods, city planning for where to put black people, engineering patterns of enclosing them in areas bounded by interstates and highways, developing school districts to edge them out of the best schools. These are not just impressions of how things look; they are documented decisions by politicians and municipal governments.

Patterns of segregated housing and schools became accompanied with patterns of single parent families, which affected the quality of education in inner city schools. As some achieving black folks were able to move out of such neighborhoods, they took with them much of the positive human resource necessary for the modeling of achievement. The patterns of inadequate home training, misbehaving children, inadequate school education, misbehaving teens, generating early pregnancy and single parent homes, young adults with functional illiteracy, inability to go to college or to find solid career type jobs, susceptibility to gangs, drugs, and criminal activity (and thus higher rates of incarceration) deprive many black communities of the human capital by which to build a future, namely marriageable and employable males.

Generational poverty tends to destroy an achiever value system (I confess I borrowed this idea from the Rev. Dr. Carl Ellis, an African-American scholar, who is also part of New City Fellowship), and finally results in the loss of aspiration. Generational poverty creates a vicious cycle where cause and effect seem predestined to continue endlessly. Unfortunately, too many anti-poverty programs have not helped the generationally poor recover those non-monetary resources. Instead, they simply sustain them in a survival mode, stuck in the quicksand of economic scarcity while living in a land of plenty, lacking a substantial "values" ladder that would enable them to climb out of their plight.

Bad choices. If a person's poverty is due to their own bad choices (laziness, dissipation through addictions, bad financial management, etc.) it will affect our strategy in trying to help them. Unfortunately, people who make bad moral and economic choices often drag and keep their children in poverty. Thus it complicates any strategy we might employ for helping them.

Social injustice. If the poverty of an individual, or community, is due to unjust economic systems or circumstances for which they are not responsible, this presents other challenges. *"A poor man's field may produce abundant food, but injustice sweeps it away" (Proverbs*

13:23, NIV). Sometimes poor people are working hard, doing all they can, but injustice steals away all their best efforts.

Deliverance from a corrupt government or unjust laws can often bring about economic change. In some nations this might mean a political upheaval and may require a liberating army to bring in a new administration. Usually those changes are not so readily available. If the cultural value system of people is from generational poverty, then simply giving them more money is not going to create long-term change. It takes a good value system to know how to earn, use wisely and keep the money one needs.

Many advocates for the poor focus on the reality of injustice as the central basis for the existence of poverty. Their strategy is to expose injustice, resist it, be an advocate for change, and hopefully mobilize the poor in a fight for their rights and their own communities. My own thinking is that if there were more justice we would need less mercy to bring about restoration and hope, but even if and when the system is just, individuals can still have a terrible value system that keeps them in poverty.

Combating Injustice

God hates injustice, and I believe individuals, institutions, businesses, and government have a responsibility before God to practice justice and to fight, resist, and stop injustice wherever they know it to exist.

Although this book is about mercy and specifically advocates that the church should practice it, as well as giving suggestions for how to make the administration of mercy effective, we cannot neglect a call to justice where we see injustice bringing people into poverty or continuing to lock them in it.

Discerning where there is injustice, and how to alleviate it, can sometimes be difficult. People often have vested economic interests, presented as legitimate exercises of free enterprise, which actually exploit the poor or discriminate against them. We advocate economic freedom, but not to justify the exploitation of the poor. *"Do not exploit the poor because they are poor and do not crush the needy in court, for the Lord will take up their case and will plunder those who plunder them" (Proverbs 22:22-23, NIV).*

Do we pay a fair wage – not simply the market rate, but what it takes for people to survive and thrive? Do we charge ruinous interest and excuse it because we loan to the poor (who at times certainly do need capital) and no one else will? Do we realize we haven't hired any minorities in our privately owned company and always seem to have a reasonable economic or self-justifying reason why that hasn't happened? If you are a business owner, has there been a pattern of ethnic prejudice in your hiring history? I give these as possible examples of exploiting or discriminating against the poor.

There were certainly cries for defending the rights of storeowners to discriminate against black people during the days of segregation. Didn't their personal property rights take precedence over the rights of the public to frequent their establishment? That issue was in one of the central lawsuits against the Civil Rights Act of 1964.

Though that cry for the freedom to discriminate might have been confusing, although it might have sounded as if storeowners and businesses were losing their freedom, the reality was that satisfying their desires would result in the perpetuation of injustice, based not on any behavior but on ethnic or racial origin.

Lack of Freedom in 'Free' Marketplace

Legal segregation locked many black people out of what is known as a free marketplace. They were not allowed to buy, sell, or compete in various kinds of markets in this country. Discriminating against people because of the color of their skin when it came to open and fair housing or equal opportunity for education and employment caused many black people to suffer economically.

Dismantling that discrimination has undoubtedly allowed many black people to climb the ladder of economic success. There is no denying the difference in the amount of collective wealth of the black community today compared to what it was during the days of segregation. Unfortunately, there remain a much greater percentage of black people still in poverty relative to the overall black population in this country, though the total of poor white folks far outnumbers them.

In those places where injustice is allowed to flourish, the work of churches or any institution to bring people out of poverty is hindered. As I have mentioned previously, such places would include a self-justifying loan industry, which exploits the poor because they are poor. This exploitative industry purposefully targets poor people and even gives an excuse or justification for it. Only people with bad credit need such places, and the revolving door of loans with ever-increasing interest rates does not deliver people from poverty but instead, chains them to it.

The criminal justice system, with its abundance of laws, the propensity for police to focus on African-American males, and courts that favor the wealthy through their ability to at least have competent counsel, produces rates of incarceration that are often racially biased and unbalanced. Such skewed law enforcement practices have had terrible effects on the ability of the black male population to thrive and provide economically for their own families.

Assigning Blame Where It Belongs

These are not attempts at finding scapegoats or offering excuses for bad individual decisions. But neither should we make scapegoats of the poor to excuse systemic injustice. Advocating justice, voting and campaigning for candidates that champion justice, organizing to protest, and researching and exposing issues – all are things Christians ought to do in a free country where this is part of our civic right and responsibility. When any of us achieve a position where we can make just changes in policy, or make decisions that dismantle unjust systems, we should take that responsibility as sacred.

Even the amount we pay employees for their work, and the time we give them off for rest or worship, are part of practicing justice. Creating industry that learns how to use low-skilled workers, keeping factories accessible to marginalized communities, and investing in work, jobs and employment strategies for people desperately in need of legitimate income – all are parts of doing justice.

Just as we can make mistakes in how we do mercy, we are subject to making mistakes in how we seek justice. We can be self-righteous; we can become "cause-oriented" and not keep Jesus Christ first in how we respect authority, persons, or even love the wicked. In this struggle to help the poor, we have to be aware of the various causes and complications of poverty. We also have to be aware that none of us can be involved in everything. There are times when we must find the place where we can be the most effective in helping to effect change in the lives of the poor for their good.

Questions for Reflection and Discussion

1. What do the following verses teach about being lazy, or a "sluggard"? See Proverbs 18:9, 19:15,24, 20:4,13, 24:30-34, and 26:13-17.
2. What do these verses teach about being wasteful? See Proverbs 21:17,20.
3. Is it sinful to be poor? See Proverbs 15:16-17, 16:19, 19:1.
4. Whether it is their fault or not, how are the poor often treated? See Proverbs 14:20, 18:23, 19:4 and 7.
5. Where does wealth come from? See Proverbs 13:4,11,18, 16:26, 19:14.

CHAPTER 8

The Need for Good Government

"How long will you defend the unjust and show partiality to the wicked? Defend the cause of the weak and fatherless; maintain the rights of the poor and oppressed. Rescue the weak and needy; deliver them from the hand of the wicked."

(PSALM 82: 2-4, NIV)

I DON'T WANT ANYONE TO think I am speaking against good government strategies, but must emphasize the importance of the phrase, "good government." Whether you are a large government or a small government ideologue, I think we can all agree that, large or small, the quality of programs can be remarkably disparate. Obviously there are some who think any government program is bound to be a failure, and others who think without government no real change is possible. I reject both of those ideas since neither stand up to Biblical scrutiny or a reality test.

There are some Christians who rail against government programs to help the poor, as if government had cheated the church out of doing ministry. While there are certainly grounds to indict some government programs for sustaining people in poverty, and in the process enabling them (or worse yet, "disabling" them) to remain in poverty, Western governments have rarely prevented churches from doing ministry among the poor. I do believe, however, government has at times made it harder for poor people to emerge from poverty and engage in their own progress, encouraging them instead to acquiesce to a survivable but inadequate standard of living.

Government has sometimes deprived poor people of the hard, realistic choices that would have made the Church's mission of mercy easier. Obviously if the church teaches there is moral responsibility and moral choice, and that there are and should be economic consequences for those choices, but government then removes the accompanying consequences so people can remain in destructive lifestyles, then poverty continues while subsidized by our taxes.

Government also extends people into poverty not only by shortsighted welfare or economic programs, but also by choosing to retreat from dealing with social ills created by things such as bad divorce laws, public begging, the failure to care for the mentally ill, and abandonment of the policing of unscrupulous lenders (everything from balloon payment mortgages, check-into-cash, and title loan practices), and what has been an unjust medical and health care complex. These issues of justice have real effects in pushing people into poverty and holding them there.

The 'Clumsy Giant'

My criticism of government is not that it has pursued a theological and ideological warfare against the ministry of the church to the poor. Rather, in addition to sometimes really bad social welfare policy, government structures have often performed like a clumsy giant. Because of unfeeling bureaucracy, they have sometimes crushed the impoverished people they claimed to be helping.

I firmly believe God ordained government. I also believe the Scriptures speak clearly to the "king" and thus to all kinds of government (regardless of the particular system) that it must provide justice for the poor. Being an American, I know there are those against taxes of any kind, and plenty of us who complain they are too high or inequitable. There is such a thing as a "tax burden," and a just society needs to determine through the political process how much of that burden should and can be carried for the poor.

Some would venture to say all government programs for the relief of the poor are bound to be ineffective simply because they are big. This neglects the reality that in a country as large as the United States, whole segments of our population have suffered at various times until a national or systemic strategy was introduced to help them.

Someone's ideology might lead them to say the government should not have done these things, but nonetheless, many elderly people are no longer threatened with starving who otherwise would have been without the aid of a pension. Many people are no longer homeless because there is subsidized housing, and many are no longer without some kind of emergency or chronic medical assistance because the government allocates funds for these things.

Thankfully there is an abundance of historical stories, incidents, and patterns of individual Christians and local churches performing effective ministries of benevolence, but it has been the programs and policies of government that have affected the largest number of poor in our country, keeping many from sinking further into their misery, or at the very least protecting opportunities for them to help themselves.

Economic advancements produced by free enterprise, along with some targeted government programs, have given our nation an amazing standard of living. Government cannot provide for all the poor if they outnumber the people who work, if jobs are not there for those who are willing and capable of taking them, or if there is not reward for the labor of people giving them incentive to do the work. Democratic capitalism, bounded by moral conscience in the culture of our society, has given our nation incredible blessing – sometimes in the face of greed and oppression – even to the point of fighting the Civil War.

Necessary for Justice and Well-Being

The reader might not like Social Security, Medicare, Section Eight, and other such assistance programs, yet the poverty that existed prior to these programs was massive compared to what it is today. America has used land grants, homesteading, the G.I. Bill, and subsidies for all kinds of industries to increase wealth and opportunity. Our country is much richer, and wealth is more broadly distributed, due to this largesse. People who insist government can't create wealth evidently haven't been paying attention to history. As I advocate the use of the local church to minister to the poor, I recognize the need to acknowledge government's place for insuring justice and providing for the social welfare of our people.

To some degree, all taxation is redistribution of wealth, but that does not make it evil. According to the Scriptures, taxes are to be paid by Christians (Romans 13:7). Our responsibility as citizens who elect our government is to decide at what level and for what purpose they should be demanded.

Some historical redistribution in America was not Biblical, but most of us still enjoy the benefits of it. This redistribution was indeed theft, such as taking land from Native Americans and taking labor from Africans. I mention this so that as we develop and defend whatever our ideology about government might be, we can try to remain honest and not be mythical about the wealth of our nation.

There are some who hold to ideological views that insist charity, mercy and all other forms of relief for the poor should never be the concern of government. Rather, they contend, it should only and always be performed by the private or religious sector. However, in reading the Bible, especially the Pentateuch, I see the Lord demanding that the people of the nation allow the poor to glean (in essence, to re-harvest fields that have been once gone over); that God's people (the nation at that time) forgive debts; that slaves are allowed to go free; and that the poor are recapitalized by returning to them their landed inheritance after a certain amount of years. As I understand it, that was how Israel was governed at that time. Individuals may have resented it or disobeyed it, but it was the Law. God punished Israel harshly for their failure to redistribute their material blessings during the Sabbath and Jubilee years. Thus government did require some form of redistribution, and there was a penalty for the failure to obey that law. The law of Jesus, which requires love, is far more radical.

If you use the Bible to justify economic arguments, how then can we apply those principles to public policy today? How do we apply them in a capitalistic system? How should we apply them to the kind of constructed economy of the United States, which is not simply capitalistic but historically has developed a social welfare infrastructure as well?

Positives from Capitalism

I am one of those that think history proves democratic capitalism has done a great deal of good for poor people, and not simply oppressed them. We are not a nation where everyone is suffering due to socialist experiments in which everyone is impoverished in an attempt to bring about equality. Nor are we a society where there is no incentive for people to take personal initiative, as in some socialist dictatorships. Even China has figured this out. There is no comparing the economic conditions enjoyed by the masses of Chinese people today compared to what that nation suffered just three or four decades ago. And that, I believe, is due to their willingness to pursue capitalism.

There is no denying that economic systems and governments without moral constraint or just regulation have often been rapacious to the environment, and oppressed the poor. I include both capitalistic and state-controlled economies in this indictment. It is essential for a culture to develop moral capacity, self-reflection, and moral boundaries for what it will allow as individuals and state-run economies eager to make fortunes sometimes take without restraint. This is why just and good government is necessary – to promote and provide justice for the weakest in its midst. It is also why it's so necessary to strive for a Gospel and Biblical impact upon every culture. Without positive moral impact in a culture it is difficult for democracies, let alone state-controlled economies, to restrain greed and exploitation.

I believe governments have a responsibility to help and protect the poor because it seems evident to me the Bible clearly teaches governments have that duty (Psalm 72, Isaiah 1:21-23, Proverbs 23:10-11). I invite those who demand the private and religious sector shoulder all the needs of the poor to go ahead and lead the way for us by example. We certainly haven't been waiting on the government to take care of the poor in our church and community. However, I would suggest we refrain from spinning fantasies that our government programs have never helped people, insisting they have only hurt them. That is simply not true.

Let me be blunt: If the reader is one that believes the government shouldn't be helping the poor, and mercy ministry belongs solely to the church instead, then I hope your life and church are where your mouth seems to be. If your church isn't doing effective ministry to the poor in ways that can bring people out of poverty, and you are not personally doing your part in that effort, you should probably stop whining about the government taking the place of the church – because you are leaving the poor with no options.

Our country needs lots of reform in how we do things, as well as in how we pay for whatever we choose to do. The nation and its people also need a much greater awareness of how the poor are actually affected. We certainly don't need to keep repeating mistakes of the past based on ideological commitments.

If you feel your calling is to change government policy through politics, or to fight against injustice in regard to government neglect or abuse, then I encourage you to pursue the effort with honesty, faith, diligence and courage. Our purpose in this book, however, is not to articulate what we think are proper governmental solutions, but rather to call for God's people to do for the poor what He has commanded us Christians to do – as individuals, as families, and especially as congregations.

One sobering lesson we can learn from both history and the Bible has to do with God's judgment upon the people of Sodom:

As surely as I live, declares the Sovereign Lord, your sister Sodom and her daughters never did what you and your daughters have done. Now this was the sin of your sister Sodom: She and her daughters were arrogant, overfed and unconcerned; they did not help the poor and needy. They were haughty and did detestable things before me. Therefore I did away with them as you have seen" (Ezekiel 16:48-50).

Questions for Reflection and Discussion

1. What do the following passages teach about the role of government and the poor – Proverbs 28:3, 29:4,14, and Romans 13:1-7?
2. What do these verses teach us about righteous people and their relationship to justice – Proverbs 28:5 and 29:7?
3. What are these passages teaching us about justice and dealing with the poor – Psalm 72, Proverbs 28:8, and James 5:1-6?

CHAPTER 9

The Culture of Poverty

"Of what use is money in the hand of a fool,
since he has no desire to get wisdom?"

(PROVERBS 17:16)

PEOPLE WITH MIDDLE-CLASS BACKGROUNDS SOMETIMES remark on the bad spending choices of welfare mothers and other poor people. They might wonder why poor people don't seem to learn to pass up the enticements of comfort food at the Quick Stop and invest in healthier choices instead. Why is it the poor don't start saving for tomorrow? How come they don't know better than to become indebted to "rent-to-own" stores, or buy things through ruinous financing schemes of lenders?

Many of these questions begin with the assumption that poor people have both the same values and same knowledge as the middle class. However, this ignores the reality that the poor live with a mentality of survival aimed at just getting through another day.

Obviously one approach for helping people that are in a hole financially is to get them to stop digging it deeper. We should have no illusions about this being easy to do, however, especially if the person doing the digging thinks he or she has a reason to do so.

I am not saying their reasons are good ones, but it would be naïve to think people do what is against their own best interests without there being some basis for it – at least to their way of thinking.

This leads to a need for understanding the "culture of poverty," which is a quagmire of thinking and behaviors that keep people poor and give them a distorted way of interpreting reality. Not all of that culture is wrong or evil, but it is a way of seeing and doing life that is distinctly different from how people in the middle or upper classes typically would see or do it.

Differences in Poverty

Among the exciting movements in fighting poverty is the concept of micro-finance. This idea of capitalizing very poor people with small amounts of money, which they have saved themselves, so their own ideas and effort can bring about even minute or fractional economic changes in their lives, has been a great blessing to many places and people in the world.

One of the problems of introducing micro-finance programs into the inner cities of America, however, is that poverty in the developing world is different, at least in my experience. Many people in the Two-Thirds World have a wonderful work ethic, strong family ties, and often a supportive sense of ethnic or geographic community. Generational poverty in the U.S., on the other hand, has tended to erode and even destroy those foundations.

In addition, the scale of the financial system that surrounds American poverty is very different from the developing world where a little bit of savings (i.e., investment capital) can often begin to leverage a person or family into different sources of income. I am not speaking against savings plans or savings clubs at all. It is just that the scale is different, and the values necessary for pursuing and utilizing the discipline of it are often absent in American poverty.

There is another significant factor in Two-Thirds World poverty: The options in those regions are far fewer and stark, so poor individuals and families are quick to realize if you don't take advantage of every opportunity, the result could well be death for you or your kids.

Creating savings clubs, church savings and loans, and establishing Federal credit unions with programs such as IDAs (Individual Development Accounts) are all helpful strategies. However, some internal structural work and preparation has to be done in the way individuals think before they can realistically regard these as viable options for themselves. This is one reason I strongly advocate for churches to be doing evangelism and spiritual discipleship, as well as providing complimentary and simultaneous discipleship into Biblical values and economics.

Listening to how some development folks talk about helping poor people makes me suspect they believe the poor in America could all become successful entrepreneurs if they just had some investment capital. How I wish that were true. But we have to understand too often a strong value system that reflects the profile of a wise man described in the book of Proverbs has been destroyed systematically among many families over the generations. It has turned many people into fools when it comes to the use and handling of money.

Dr. Ruby Payne, a Texas educator, has done great work in describing the distinctions of poverty culture versus that of the middle or upper class in this country. She has written several books, but *Understanding the Framework of Poverty* is an especially good one to read. (You can find details in the Resource Section in the back of this book.)

Disadvantages Not Easily Overcome

I am indebted to a recent book by Graham Scharf, *Apprenticeship Of Being Human.* It shows the average child raised in a poor home is at a distinct disadvantage from a child born and nurtured in a middle-class home.

Besides the obvious problems of not having enough money to handle their basic needs, children born in families that have been caught up in generational poverty start further behind even before they qualify to go to Head Start or some other pre-school program. It is alarming to realize how disparate pre-school programs are in terms of quality and their educational impact on pre-school children. Some that are little more than money-making schemes to "baby-sit," so parents can work, are not helping children get ready for the school system.

In their first three years of life poor children, in far too many cases, are not being spoken to in the same way as middle-class children. They are generally not receiving the experience of being read to by their mothers, let alone their fathers – if there is one still in the home. Their vocabulary is only half that of middle-class children by the time they are three years of age. They hardly have any books compared to the deluge of children's books that most middle and upper-class children enjoy.

Mr. Scharf shows poverty affects the growth and structure of a child's brain due to the insufficiency of linguistic interaction. This means poor children enter pre-school and the early grades of elementary school already behind in the literacy and education race they must win if they are to become capable of earning their own way in this society.

Having been raised by a single parent mom, I know firsthand how difficult it is for a poor mother, with no supporting husband/father, to spend the time needed to adequately nurture her children. It is not a question as to whether poor mothers love their children or care about their success. Let us assume that for the most part they really do. Time and resources are not there, however, for them to give each child what they will need to succeed in school.

I want to share an email message I received from our full-time Deacon, Gene Johnson, exactly as he describes some of the challenges he faces in helping single parent moms:

"Yesterday I met with six different 'families' here at the office who needed assistance. Four were single mothers or grandmothers from East Chattanooga who are not a part of New City; one was a neighbor and member of New City raising grandchildren; and the other was a married, middle-class church family with three kids. All were African-American. There are 17 children under the age of 12 in these families. All are in public schools except for the three at a Christian school whose parents are struggling financially to keep them there.

The dysfunction in the remaining five families is so strong I sometimes wonder if there is any hope for these children. The parents that are working have no skills that allow for more than a minimum wage job. Others receive a meager disability check. Their ages ranged from 27-55 years of age.

(Referring to a recent article in the Chattanooga newspaper, he proceeded.)

The articles title could have read, 'Inequality is the OLD normal,' because things haven't changed, even though the black middle class has grown in Chattanooga quite a bit. I was saddened by the fact that the 'church' was not mentioned at all in the state of black Chattanooga. In fact, many black churches have fled to the suburbs or have become commuter churches themselves. In many cases the church has not just abandoned the city, but has abandoned the Gospel as well.

Yesterday, as D.T. and I met with these families as we do every week, once again we saw that the real need in people's lives is the Gospel, the 'good news for the poor.' Sure, we try to help pay a bill or provide food or job training, but money comes and goes. They need to know the truth of the Word of God, that someone hears them, cares about them, and prays for them. That's what only the Church can give them."

A mother caught up in poverty, possibly being the third or fourth of her lineage to have become a single parent as a teenager, might (and I stress the word *might)* understand education is not only important but also vital for her children to escape that cycle of impoverishment. At the same time, she might feel it is impossible to do anything to change the situation.

American poverty, much of which is built on generations of functional illiteracy, dependency on government largess, and the eroding of the extended family network for support, has helped to produce too many inner city moms who view a child as something for themselves. The child is the emotional source, not just (or even) the object of love. The child becomes an emotional crutch, and sometimes an economic instrument to provide a living. The child is not the family's future, but the mother's present.

Compounding the Problem

Children who find it difficult to learn in school eventually find it hard to continue to pay attention. As a consequence, their behavior becomes a problem. If the majority of the children in a teacher's class have this same problem, one can imagine a good part of the day is spent on behavior management, and not on teaching. Our society is spending enormous sums of money on education in the hope the schools somehow will make up for those first three formative years, but sadly it is rarely happening.

In inner city ghettos, trailer parks, Appalachian mountain communities, Native American reservations and suburban apartment complexes, there are huge numbers of single parents trying to raise their children. For all intents and purposes, they are functional widows with functional orphans who are learning – often through no fault of their own – to be dysfunctional in our society.

Fatherlessness is both a cause and effect of poverty, and makes it seem like the cycle is never-ending. All the statistics reveal it to be a constant marker for all kinds of maladies in our country. The problems in our public schools, the violence in inner city neighborhoods, and the vast number of young men going to prison, all are related to being raised without a committed and loving dad in the home.

These communities are often not where good churches (I will be defining what I mean by "good churches" more closely as we go along) are being planted, and in some ways for the same reason as grocery store chains aren't built in them. It is economically unfeasible to start a business in a community that cannot support it, and the same reasoning is often applied to churches.

But let me ask: Do poor communities need good churches? Do they need full-service grocery stores? I think they need both, but unfortunately we have allowed the reality of the need for profit and economic sustainability to affect where we place both of those institutions. It might make economic sense not to do so, but ultimately it doesn't make any societal sense.

All of the social, medical, and criminal costs to our cities, states, and national governments are impacted by poverty and fatherlessness. It makes sense for government leaders to care about these issues and attempt to do something about them, even if is just for our nation's economic self-interest. Over the long term, the financial burden of incarceration, public health needs, emergency medicine, remedial education and other services costs society much more than if we did something to prevent the problems in the first place.

Think 'Missionaries to the Neighborhoods'

Christians have a Biblical and spiritual reason for reaching out to these communities. Ironically, our record as Christians reveals it might have been better for these poor communities to have been in a foreign country, since then we would send missionaries to them. Missionaries have a record of doing community development work, and churches support overseas what they often seem to have no willingness, imagination, faith or tenacity for doing in their own home country.

Without proper nourishment, which a full-service grocery store can provide, the poor are forced to eat an unbalanced diet. The poor often live in "urban deserts" where there are no affordable grocery stores to provide fresh fruit and vegetables. Most often the communities are served only by gasoline/convenience or stop-and-go type stores that sell lots of junk food, along with sodas loaded with sugar and salt.

Public health maps demonstrate that in communities with little or no access to full-service grocery stores that offer fresh and healthy produce, residents are prone to having much higher rates of diabetes, obesity, and early death.

I am sometimes confronted with questions about whether poverty in the U.S. is real or not, compared with what is experienced in Africa, Haiti, Asia or anywhere else in the Two-Thirds World. I have read from Christian writers that the poverty of America is nothing like it used to be (with the implication that people in America today are no longer really poor), that if anyone really wanted to make it in this country, they could.

Occasionally someone confronts us with what the Federal government spends on poor people. We listen with amazement to someone who does the math and calculates an amount postulating that if we just divided all the money spent by government on the poor by the number of the poor in the U.S., and simply gave it to them directly, they then would have an income even higher than the median income in America.

I describe this as "funny" math because it dismisses the system of conveyance of relief as unnecessary, as if in a country this large cash could just be given out without employing someone to distribute it. It often compares apples to oranges in categories of people (often not taking the plight of children into consideration), and I believe it leads to some unfounded conclusions. It is as if they want to prove several things at once. They seem to say there really are no poor people in America, that we give them enough to get by. Then they want to say the poverty rate hasn't changed so all these programs haven't worked. I wonder what America would be like for those who do receive help if we actually gave nothing?

I agree the government wastes an awful lot of money, but if the system is broken, then let's fix it and not let our anger at government inefficiency make us despise poor people for needing legitimate help. I absolutely despise corruption, waste, and spending tax money on things that actually bind people into dependency. However, I really don't like it when these pundits suggest everyone receiving government help is a deadbeat, a source of Democrat votes, and simply a drain on the country. This sets up a class divide where the working and wealthy are portrayed as righteous, and the rest of the people are enemies of America.

Sometimes the questions are based on sincere ignorance. I confess it is too easy for me to dismiss all of this curiosity as coming from a political agenda, not as an honest appraisal of the suffering of the poor. I am no stranger to Two-Thirds World poverty. I have been a missionary to Africa and visited many countries where I have seen people living in horrible conditions, as this story will tell you:

One Sunday a man came to the church I was pastoring in Nairobi, Kenya. He told me he had spent time in prison, but now was going back into the prisons to do ministry. He also told me he had a ministry to "parking boys" or street children in downtown Nairobi. He invited me to join him in some of his activities, and we did some prison ministry together. Later he said if I could go with him one morning I could preach at the farmer's market, and then I could meet some of the children with whom he worked.

So one morning at about 5:30 we arrived at the farmer's market entrance. We stood on the sidewalk in front of a huge mountain of trash and garbage right by the market gate. He told me to start preaching and he would translate. As men and women carried their bags of vegetables into the market, they stopped to hear the sermon. My friend put his hat in front of me, and after I preached he asked for an offering. The people put in their shillings. I was a little embarrassed and told him I didn't need the money. He told me, "This isn't for you."

My friend went over to the garbage pile and stuck his foot in it and began to shake it. Suddenly it seemed like the whole pile of it was shaking, and then one by one, children began to sit up and come out of the garbage in which they had been sleeping to keep warm. Then he took us all into a little kiosk where he used the money to buy the children mandazis (deep-fried sweet donuts) and chai (tea cooked in milk and heavily sugared). Given such unusual circumstances, that became one of the most gratifying breakfasts I have ever had.

Seeing Misery Firsthand

Once you have seen the misery of poverty, it's hard not to keep seeing it. I have tried to help start a home for street children in Nairobi who either had lost their parents or whose parents could not provide for them. I have delivered food assistance in times of famine and drought in rural Africa. I have walked in the alleys of Kibera and Muthari Valley slums in that great city. I have visited the sick in hospitals where three people must share a bed.

I have worked with prisoners in Africa in several countries who would get no food unless their families carried it to the prison. I have seen children who would walk five miles in a morning to dig in a dry riverbed to retrieve potable water, and then carry it home in a jerry can on a donkey. I know they had to do this almost every day. This is real poverty. Yet many of those same folks, as I have said, often displayed aspirations and were not broken in spirit. To this day, I am amazed and in awe of their resilience.

Yet, there is real poverty in the U.S. as well, and it is often accompanied with other problems that destroy aspirations.

I had tried to make friends with a man named John who walked around on crutches in the neighborhood of our church. He was elderly and lived homeless on the street. His nickname on the street was "Eat'em up," because he ate out of the dumpsters.

As I came to know him, I was able to convince him to let me move him into a Christian community. Once there he sometimes became belligerent because they asked him not to smoke in the house. Finally his mental problems would not let him stay in a place where he had shelter and plenty of food. I last saw him as he stood in the pouring rain. I told him the Social Security office had called and said they had several checks waiting on him. I told him that if he would wait, I would go get my car and take him there so he could collect them. When I got back he was gone. I drove around looking for him, but never saw him again. That winter he was found frozen to death on an empty lot.

Sometimes the demons in people's minds keep them locked in misery and cause them to die in it.

Some children I have carried to Sunday school and youth group didn't know if there would be food in their homes when they got back, or if their mother will still be living in the same apartment when they came "home" from school.

And I know some of the people in my church can't find jobs because there are none where they live or they lack access to due to inadequate public transportation. And if they do work at minimum wage, they can barely make it through the month if they pay their rent. Their income and living arrangements are often so fragile, it takes just one emergency and everything falls apart for some of these families.

Living on the Brink

Hurricane Katrina provided a vivid example of the precarious nature of American urban poverty. It revealed many of the urban poor live in a tenuous balance of survival, and if anything happens to the urban system that sustains them, their lives are not just inconvenienced – they are immediately thrust into mortal danger. Frankly, many poor people in America don't realize how precarious their lives are. Ironically, part of the reason for this is a comprehensive and amazing infrastructure of government and social services that usually seem ubiquitous. Many of the urban poor depend completely on these services being available.

Consider if you lived in a government apartment and when there was a flood, you were told you had to evacuate the city, but you didn't own a car. Suppose you had no money to get a bus out of town, or to get a hotel, and had no extended family that could take you in. There would be government shelters, but suppose they became flooded, or overwhelmed as well. Suppose the stores were all closed, so now there was no food, and of course you had no money with which to buy it anyway. What do you do if you are a young mother with several small children in that situation?

When I hear people declaring we have no real poor people here in America, and at the same time complain about how much we spend on helping the poor, imagine how much poverty there would be if we weren't spending what we do? Again, I am not justifying the amount or the waste of ineffective programs. I am just asking you to consider what it would feel like to see whole families starving and dying in the streets because there was no longer any assistance available.

Is Their Poverty Real?

If a child in America goes to bed hungry, or homeless, or unable to get medicine for a chronic illness, or has his toes bitten by rats, then I must ask the question: Is his or her poverty real, even if he or she lives in America? Is it real, no matter what choices his parent has made? Where do they turn if we dismiss them as "not really poor" compared to other people in the world? Do we really believe this, or is it just convenient for us to make such a declaration, freeing us from any sense of guilt, responsibility or obligation?

My desire is not to dismiss or minimize the wonderful opportunities present for economic advancement in America. Nor is it to remove the responsibility of people to make their own way whenever possible. Rather, my goal is to help leverage the ministry of the Church of Jesus Christ so that the poor, one by one, can take advantage of these resources.

Great multitudes of the working poor are just that – poor people who are working. Their wages are criminally too low. The wages they make can't get their families through the month, but they have nothing to be ashamed of in their honest efforts to put food on the table. When we generalize about poverty and condemn even those who are doing all that their education or skill levels will allow them to do in the present economy, we are in fact slandering some very good people.

For anyone who dismisses the poor of America as people who simply won't try, who deserve their suffering, and if you should believe they need to change the way they think and live, my first question is not, "Will you help them?" My question is, presuming you are a Christian, "Why won't you take the Gospel to them?"

This is what was said about Jesus:

"He went to Nazareth, where he had been brought up, and on the Sabbath day he went into the synagogue, as was his custom. And he stood up to read. The scroll of the prophet Isaiah was handed to him. Unrolling it, he found the place where it is written: 'The Spirit of the Lord is on me, because he has anointed me to preach good news to the poor. He has sent me to proclaim freedom for the prisoners and recovery of sight for the blind, to release the oppressed, to proclaim the year of the Lord's favor.'

"Then he rolled up the scroll, gave it back to the attendant and sat down. The eyes of everyone in the synagogue were fastened on him. And he began by saying to them, 'Today this scripture is fulfilled in your hearing'" (Luke 4:16-21, NIV).

If the commission of Jesus, the purpose of His anointing by the Spirit, is to preach the Gospel to the poor, then shouldn't it be ours as well? If we sincerely think poverty is a result of a moral condition, and we have within our means the ability to change that moral condition by presenting the Gospel to people and discipling them in the Word of God, then why aren't we doing that instead of complaining about the poor?

Questions for Reflection and Discussion

1. Discuss the various levels of opportunity for economic success in the U.S.A. What might keep people from having equal opportunity, or being able to take advantage of it?
2. What are the variations we find in place for people in the U.S. economically, socially, family-wise, and health-wise?
3. Can you list some obstacles for economic achievement in our country? Which ones did you overcome personally? Is your example normative, in your opinion?
4. What possible difference can the Church make in helping people deal with the discrepancies in their backgrounds that affect their opportunities for success and well-being?
5. How does the Gospel, once it is believed, call people, in spite of their backgrounds, to improve their situation?

CHAPTER 10

Strategies For Dealing With Poverty

"For you know the grace of our Lord Jesus Christ, that though he was rich, yet for our sakes he became poor, so that you through his poverty might become rich."

(2 CORINTHIANS 8:9, NIV)

FOR THE POOR, AND THOSE who would like to help them, there are various strategies for surviving or being delivered from their situation. Some people have the skill to ***exploit*** the poverty of their surroundings. Sometimes this is done through crime – stealing from or exploiting the vulnerable around them. But there are also positive strategies of exploitation. Here's an example:

One African-American man I knew told me he owned a candy store in Piney Woods. He was the "candy man" for that neighborhood. I admired his energy and business sense. The surprise came when he told me he was using the profits to buy cinder blocks so he could build a church on the empty lot on which his little candy shack stood. Sure enough, within a few years he had built his church. I guess candy money mounts up after a while.

Another strategy is ***escape,*** and I referred to this earlier by quoting the movie character Rocky Balboa. Sometimes getting a family or a child out of a bad neighborhood is the only thing left that can save their lives. We have sometimes used this strategy, but at other times have realized it was not going to be possible. We have learned the hard way that some mothers will refuse to let their children go to a boarding school or a safer place because that child fills an emotional need for them. Even as they watch their child be swept away by gangs or drugs, they adamantly refuse to let their child escape.

Some children have been blessed with exodus-type programs and scholarships or grants to get to good schools or institutions where they can really thrive. My wife, Joan, and I – as I have already said – are examples of that. It would be naïve, however, to think it is not tough on them and for their families to see them being placed in cultures that sometimes can seem very foreign. Sometimes the experience of being an alien in a strange land produces negative results.

Many inner city kids dream of making this exodus through sports, particularly the NBA or NFL. The stories of those kids (very few in number) who do make it against the odds are moving and inspiring, especially for those that aren't ruined by the fast and massive amounts of money. Even those for whom sports was just a vehicle for getting through college, even if they never reach the professional level, can serve as glimpses of hope for others.

Taking an Engagement Approach

There is another strategy and that is one of ***engagement***. We don't want to simply snatch families and kids out of bad neighborhoods and send them all to middle-class suburban land. Our great challenge is to bring Jesus into the "hood" and have people of churches planted there develop a sense of ownership in their own community. The challenge is to have poor people who come to Christ in *that place* love the people of *that place,* and seek to change *that place* through the power of God.

One time in Tulsa we were meeting with some middle-class African-American families who were talking about moving back into an inner city neighborhood. One of the men said, "I've seen people shot. I've seen a girl raped. I don't know if I want my children to have to go through that." He had grown up in that kind of neighborhood, but now his faith was calling him to go back instead of running away. He was counting the cost, and he had no illusions that the cost would be cheap.

How do we do it? One time I spoke to a group of church folks about this kind of ministry to the poor. The pastor had asked me to dialogue with them. After the meeting I noticed he looked a little disappointed. I asked him what he thought. He replied that he was surprised by how the meeting went because he had expected I would have presented a curriculum for discipling the poor out of poverty.

Although there are certainly some helpful curricula and training programs for helping the poor – for educating them in financial literacy or budgeting, or learning how to save and work for tomorrow – our call to disciple the poor out of poverty is not and should not be based on a curriculum.

Discipleship is not a curriculum. It is a relationship, it is a lifestyle, it is a life experienced in community within a local church. That makes it harder, longer and difficult to quantify. One can't simply say we have trained this many folks in this period of time and as a result, now there is no longer any poverty in this city. Oh, that it could be so easy!

We are advocating the Jesus method of incarnation, of not just becoming flesh, which Jesus did for us so he could partake of death for our sake, but of identifying Himself with us in our poverty. I am not suggesting that we all must become poor to help poor people, but if we don't live among them, if we don't know them as friends and neighbors, if we don't plant churches among them, it will be very difficult to build those relationships that will help liberate them.

Planting a church among the poor and living your life with them in the pursuit of Christ – modeling, coaching, explaining, forgiving, restoring, encouraging and learning from them – are all part of the process. Some of us who planted the seeds will not see the fruit; it will bloom after we leave or die. But we know – we are promised in the Scriptures – if there is to be an increase, God will give it.

We will be articulating a strategy of church planting and ministry in the coming chapters that will hopefully give the reader ideas on how to effectively engage poor communities for the sake of the Gospel, and for the sake of the people who live in them.

Questions for Reflection and Discussion

1. What are three strategies for the poor suggested in this chapter?
2. If you wanted to plant an effective, fruitful church among the poor, what steps would you take to get to know them, to become involved with them?
3. What do you think should be the curriculum for discipling the poor out of poverty?

Part Three:

The Magnitude Of Mercy

CHAPTER 11

Mercy Covers a Whole Lot of Brokenness

"Blessed are the merciful, for they will be shown mercy."

(Matthew 5:7, NIV)

Definition:

Mercy is compassion toward those who are in need resulting in action to alleviate that need, through acts of charity leading toward self-sustainment.

God's mercy is broader than acts of charity or development for the materially poor because it is also a matter of forgiveness and healing, the mending of relationships, and reconciliation. Mercy covers and repairs a whole lot of things that are broken. As we explore some of that here, we will be using the definition of mercy above so we can have a common understanding of what it means to be working with the materially poor.

In this book we want to discuss not only the idea of mercy but also some of the wisest ways to give it. It is in the failure to show or give mercy at all where we have our greatest challenge as people, as Christians, and as churches. Our second greatest problem is in doing it badly, so that instead of helping people we sustain them in a poor condition or make it worse.

Many of us have good intentions, but so many times those intentions are left unrealized, are thwarted by our inept and ineffective methods, or aborted by complications we meet in the attempt. Our desire is to help the reader gain wisdom in getting it done and doing it right, along with some practical observations and suggestions. We will draw these from the Scriptures, as well as from what we think is some common sense based on experience.

Churches seem to approach mercy in distinctly different ways. Some congregations, as organizations, avoid the issue and leave it to the members themselves to figure out what they should do about the needs of people. Some churches only see this as an issue when it concerns a church member, and even then they may be resistant to helping very much.

Differing Levels of Concern, Interest

Sadly I think we would all have to admit there are some individuals and churches that come across as hardhearted and don't seem to care very much about others. These churches may even have a "spiritual" reason for not showing mercy, thinking it hinders or redirects their primary mission of Biblical preaching, teaching, and evangelism.

How can someone preach the Bible, however, and miss the demand from God to love people and show mercy? It may be beyond us to understand that, but there are some churches that preach about a merciful God while refusing to show mercy to the poor. Sadly, there are churches that preach the gospel of grace yet fail to demonstrate grace.

Eventually there will be a reckoning for individuals and congregations that think and live in this way, so we leave that to God. Our hope, however, is that even in writing this book we might awaken the consciences of some, encouraging them to love their neighbors as themselves – especially the poor.

There are congregations that do preach and encourage mercy to be done intentionally by their members, but have failed to have any active vision for doing mercy as a congregation. Some churches have deacons or mercy teams within the congregation for responding to the needs of church members, while others don't. We must acknowledge that regardless of the intention and organization, there is a vast difference in the quality and skill by which things are done. We all need to "up our game" so to speak, so we can become more effective in doing what God has called us to do.

Thankfully (and obviously this reveals my opinion about what is more effective and Biblically obedient), there are churches that see mercy not only as something that becomes a ministry for individual members, but also as a ministry that should be done by the church itself (as an organizational entity) through its projects and programs. Still other churches see the need to take mercy further by helping to create economic development in a community, possibly spinning off separate non-profit or parachurch organizations to accomplish it.

Multi-Faceted Approaches

Some congregations have created ministry, business and institutional entities to take their mission into various areas of need. These might include economic community development organizations, school or literacy programs, clinics or hospitals, tutoring and after-school care, preschools, rehabilitation and drug treatment centers, halfway houses for released or probationary prisoners, thrift stores, vocational training and business start-ups, credit unions, and homes for women who have been abused or are leaving the sex trade. The list of the various forms of ministry attempted and active is vast.

Some congregations focus primarily on the needs of their own members, while other churches use approaches like those mentioned above as a strategy for outreach. Sadly, some churches create ministries without giving much thought as to how those ministries will relate to the originating congregation. For instance, taking on programs that don't motivate their own members or bring the poor into discipling relationships. Still others pursue these types of ministry through a coalition with other area churches.

We do not advocate every church trying to do everything. It should be common sense to begin with whatever gifts and opportunities the Lord puts before you. We suggest you start small, and attempt to do that small thing well before you take on more.

It is not necessary to reinvent the wheel, as they say, by duplicating services and ministries already available, as long as they are compatible with the ministry of the congregation and those services can be made available to the poor you are trying to help. It takes some research to know what is accessible around you and what a church can utilize in order to complement its mission and not compromise it.

The Gospel of Jesus Christ and the Church of Jesus Christ are uniquely suited for responding to a vast amount of brokenness in different forms. Most of that response is best realized in the forming of healing and nurturing relationships. This does not mean the Church, or one local church, has to respond to every need and seek to heal every problem in its neighborhood. There are limitations: Each church has a limited set of people, with a limited array of gifts, skills and resources. Each church has a limited set of training and expertise, and most likely a limited budget.

What is not limited, however, is our God, and what we should stretch is our faith. Prayerful wisdom and prudence will help church leaders know where to start, humility will help us to learn, and compassion will help us to see and feel more and more of the needs of the people.

The promise revealed in the doxology/benediction of Ephesians 3:20-21 is real and available to God's people:

"Now to him who is able to do immeasurably more than all we ask or imagine, according to his power that is at work within us, to him be glory in the church and in Chris Jesus throughout all generations, for ever and ever! Amen" (NIV).

Questions for Reflection and Discussion

1. What limitations might your church have in dealing with the poor in your community?
2. What would be your congregation's greatest asset?
3. As you read the previous chapter, what advice or wisdom do you think should be considered before beginning a program or ministry?
4. Some churches struggle with mobilizing their people into any kind of outreach, especially in any organized sense. What kind of programs do you think the members of your church might become excited about or be willing to participate in?

CHAPTER 12

God and Mercy

"He raises the poor from the dust and lifts the needy from the ash heap; he seats them with princes and has them inherit a throne of honor."

(1 SAMUEL 2:8)

BEFORE WE WRITE MORE ABOUT how churches should *DO* mercy, we need to reflect first on *WHY* we do mercy. This, of course, all starts with God. So let's spend a little time talking about that before proceeding in our discussion of the practical, everyday outworking of mercy for those in need of it.

In attempting to describe God, we usually speak in terms of His "attributes." We don't use that term as if God was divided into parts, but as a way of taking what the Bible says about God and explaining His being and nature. Understanding His attributes helps us to answer questions such as, "what is God like, what does He do, and how does He conduct Himself?" We think the Bible does reveal these things about God. We admit we don't know everything about God, and even the things we know we don't always fully understand.

Yet, we believe the Bible reveals God to be knowable. Not only can we know certain things about Him, but we also can know Him in relationship – a personal relationship to ourselves. This for the believer is both awesome and wonderful.

One of the things the Bible reveals about God is that He is good. One truth about God's attributes is He *always* is all the things He happens to be. In other words, God is good – and He is *always* good. He is unchangeable in His goodness. He never wakes up and decides to be bad. He never has a bad hair day, never needs another cup of coffee, and is never irritable because He hasn't had enough sleep. He is not like us at all in this regard, because He is a spirit and doesn't have a body that would be subject to hormones, hunger, adrenaline, or chemical imbalances of any kind. This is perfect protection for the world and especially for God's children – those who have believed in him.

Mercy Flowing from God's Goodness

One of the things that flow from the goodness of God is His mercy. The Bible tells us, "His mercy endures forever" (Psalm 136). The word "mercy" in Hebrew can be translated several ways, but it basically connects our English concepts of both love and mercy into one expression, and sometimes we refer to it as "loving kindness." God's love and mercy are aspects of what makes Him good. He is always a God of love – and always a God of mercy.

There are, of course, struggles with this in our faith due in part to the reality of the works of providence, which sometimes make it appear God is mad at the whole world, or mad at one particular place or person. I am referring to the troubles we face in a broken and messed-up world. It makes us ask questions such as, "Where does suffering come from? Why is there pain, why is there poverty, why is there hunger?"

Bible believers accept the reality that the sin of mankind brought misery into the world. Everybody, even those who don't believe the Bible, somehow have to deal with the fact there is trouble in the world, evil, and death. I suppose some people may attempt to deny the reality of evil or suffering from some religious or philosophical basis, but their denial doesn't affect the reality because they too will still die someday.

Skeptics often pose the question, "If there is evil, pain and suffering, then how can God be good?" This is a valid question that many find difficult to understand, let alone answer. Of course, most of us understand that even among humans, good people sometimes cause others pain – often for good purposes. Parents discipline their children, doctors give shots to heal illness, policemen shoot bad guys to stop crimes, soldiers kill to defend their nation. We don't usually deny that people can be good and still do these things, although what they do can certainly seems negative to the recipient of the action at that moment.

We do want to point out that we speak about God with the understanding He is not a creation of our minds, nor is the way He acts and treats the human race something over which we have any control. Just as with the rest of life, we have to play the cards we are dealt. Someone might think they have a superior morality to the God of the Bible, or they may assume suffering shouldn't be so. But it is so, no matter what you believe. We only know what we do about God because He reveals Himself in the Scriptures, so that is the source of our information about why there is judgment, suffering, and also redemption.

God is holy, and He is always holy. God is just, and He is always just. All of these attributes operate simultaneously for eternity. He never compromises, never grades on a curve. What we are saying is that part of God's justice is realized in our suffering because our first parents sinned, and then we did as well. Suffering from that judgment is not necessarily directly attributed to individual causes; it falls generally, seemingly arbitrarily at times, upon all people.

Because God is personal, and because He does discipline those He loves, we can also say suffering is sometimes attributable to our personal disobedience, or even to God's plan for our growth. However, here is the good news: In the Gospel we see that God's justice and holiness are satisfied due to His mercy.

Manifestation of Mercy, Love and Justice

God's mercy (prompted by His love) and His justice met 2,000 years ago at the cross of Jesus Christ. This is where the justice of God was satisfied in the sacrifice of Jesus, who died in our place for our sins. God's just anger against the rebellion of His created beings was forever consumed in the willing death of the Son of God. 2 Corinthians 5:21 puts it this way, *"He became sin for us who knew no sin that we might become the righteousness of God in him."*

Jesus took our sin and gave us His righteousness. His blood has washed away our sin. God loved the world so much, so intensely that He willingly did this, the giving of His Son, on our behalf. This was all of mercy; all of what we call grace. Every person who has believed in Christ is a recipient of this mercy. All true Christians become Christians because God forgives them.

One of the great English phrases in the Bible comes from Zechariah's praise to God in Luke, chapter 1, in which he thanks God for giving him a son who would be known to us as John the Baptist. John would set the stage for the Lord Jesus, who is the Christ, the Messiah:

Zechariah says, "And you, my child, will be called a prophet of the Most High: for you will go on before the Lord to prepare the way for him, to give his people the knowledge of salvation through the forgiveness of their sins, because of the tender mercy of our God, by which the rising sun will come to us from heaven to shine on those living in darkness and in the shadow of death, to guide our feet into the path of peace" (Luke 1:76-79, NIV).

The phrase, the "tender mercy of our God," is realized and experienced by everyone who finally comes to believe that Jesus is God and that He came in the flesh to save us and shower us with the forgiveness of God. The millions of people who have come to faith in Jesus tell many wonderful and varied but consistent stories of redemption, conversion and reconciliation – people who were down and out, sometimes at the point of death, victims of their own corruption, mired in confusion, overwhelmed by spiritual darkness. These testimonies all are examples of the tender mercy of God.

This forgiving and healing mercy leaves its recipients astonished, humbled, broken, amazed, and thankful. It is this mercy everyone needs, but as Jesus said, it is only the ones who come to realize they need a physician – the Great Physician – that get well. This is one reason the poor receive such news gladly.

In the Gospel is the message that God loves the poor, the marginalized, the oppressed, those who have been shut out, the forgotten and rejected. If we receive this message as little children and believe it, whether we are materially rich or poor, we become heirs of God and joint heirs with Christ.

Bound By Mercy

If each Christian is only a Christian due to God's mercy and forgiveness, it binds them forever to the necessity of mercy being a defining aspect of their life. We must forgive each other because He has forgiven us, and we must have mercy on others because He has had mercy on us. This is what we pray in the Lord's Prayer, where in public and corporate worship we ask God to forgive us our trespasses, our debts, our sins – as we forgive those of others (Matthew 6:9-15).

Does this spiritual mercy mean we are obligated to show physical mercy to others? In their Biblical expression, love and mercy are inextricably bound together. We cannot really love without showing mercy because God never loves without showing mercy. We must love our neighbors as ourselves.

"This is how we know what love is: Jesus Christ laid down his life for us. And we ought to lay down our lives for our brothers. If anyone has material possessions and sees his brother in need but has no pity on him, how can the love of God be in him: Dear children, let us not love with words or tongue but with actions and in truth" (1 John 3:16-18, NIV).

So, mercy is revealed and demonstrated in both forgiveness and in caring for those in need. We are concentrating in this book on the kind of mercy that those who are in physical, material distress desperately need. Our spiritual forgiveness, the spiritual experience of receiving mercy, absolutely obligates us into a lifestyle of showing physical mercy. So what is mercy, and how do we define it? We will look at this question next.

Questions for Reflection and Discussion

1. Why do you think there is suffering in the world?
2. If there are evidences of goodness and mercy in the world, why do these virtues exist?
3. How did God demonstrate His mercy toward the world – and to each of us?
4. Why do bad things happen to good people?

CHAPTER 13

Mercy Means We Have to Think About the Poor

"If anyone has material possessions and sees his brother in need but has no pity on him, how can the love of God be in him?"

(1 JOHN 3: 17, NIV)

DEFINITION: ***Mercy is compassion toward those who are in need resulting in action to alleviate that need, through acts of charity leading toward self-sustainment.***

THIS, AS WE STATED BEFORE, is our working definition of mercy. We will now attempt to discuss various aspects of mercy and how it can and should be applied. We realize there are apparent acts of mercy that don't necessarily come from any emotion or passion, or even concern, for the poor. Someone might give money to help the deacons and the poor for all the wrong reasons. On the other hand, there are those who feel great compassion and yet fail to give or do anything.

Still others, while feeling compassion and respond with the intention of showing mercy, produce unmerciful results. An example of this would be to show mercy only as charity and never allow an individual to grow toward self-sufficiency, ultimately leaving people crippled through dependency. Later we will have a discussion about the important differences between charity and development.

One of my favorite passages in the Bible about mercy is when the apostle Paul tells what happened when he went to Jerusalem to make sure he was not running his race "in vain." He says the apostles didn't change his message at all. *"...All they asked was that we should continue to remember the poor, the very thing I was eager to do" (Galatians 2:10, NIV).*

As you read about the concern of the apostles and elders, do you think that would have been on your mind when asked what to add to someone's working theology? I am sorry to say that for many theologically astute church leaders this never enters the conversation. It is not a priority for them. I am wondering if we can give Paul's response today? Is this the "thing" you are eager to do? I want that to be the "thing" on my mind, and try to pray every day, "Lord, help me to help the poor today."

The following are a series of questions I think would be appropriate for you to consider at this point in our discussion:

Questions Worthy of Consideration

- If you are a church planter, or pastor, or leader in your church, do the poor enter into your thinking and planning? Or are the pleading poor only an interruption and a nuisance?

- Are there poor people in the neighborhood of your church, or more specifically, are there any in your congregation?

- Do you think it might be safe to assume someone, someday, in your own congregation will need help?

It is hard to imagine any church without people needing help from time to time. I don't know if we can safely assume the people of the your church will want to be led in how to do mercy, although my experience has shown me many believers want to know how to do it – and to do it well.

One of the issues, of course, rests with our own inability to empathize with others in their need. Most of us don't like to live a life filled with worry or anxiety that bad things might suddenly happen to us. In fact, the Bible teaches us that the righteous man doesn't fear bad news (Psalm 112:7). However, it is wise to consider that disaster, illness, economic collapse of the company we work for, even violence could happen to any one of us without much warning.

Bad things don't always happen to someone else. Sometimes it is to us, our children or family, fellow church members or friends to whom trouble comes. No matter how much preparation we make, life has a way of surprising us, even though we often arrogantly live and ignorantly think bad things only happen to people that deserve it.

Remembering the poor and caring for them is a way of showing our understanding that we ourselves are not exempt from the possibility of suffering and hardship. Loving the poor is part of being humble before God in the world. Being prepared to respond to human need, along with helping our churches be prepared, gives us great perspective on our own dependency on God.

Questions for Reflection and Discussion

1. If you are a church planter, pastor, or leader in your church, give examples of how the poor enter into your planning.
2. How does you church typically handle it when the poor come to your church and plead for help?
3. Give some description of the amount and kinds of poor people in the area around your church. Are there any poor people in your congregation?
4. What kinds of needs would you anticipate that folks in your own church might have someday, even if they don't have them now?

CHAPTER 14

Some Things Mercy Is Not

"Do not pervert justice; do not show partiality to the poor or favoritism to the great, but judge your neighbor fairly."

(LEVITICUS 19:15, NIV)

MERCY SHOULD NOT BE:

- **Enablement of bad behavior.**
- **Creation of dependency.**
- **Paternalism and patronizing.**
- **Sweet words without action.**
- **For doing later, when help is needed now.**
- **Merely good intentions.**
- **The circumvention of truth and justice.**

IT IS HELPFUL, BY WAY of contrast, to understand some things that mercy is not, or what it should not be. We are not really showing mercy to people if we support their addictions, or excuse them. We are not showing mercy to people if they lose their dignity and personal initiative by having to depend on us. Our relationship with those in need of mercy might begin with people telling us they need our help, and at first they might be dependent on us for very basic things. But it must be our intention to move them, if we can, to the place where they are helping themselves. Mercy that is healthy seeks, even for the mentally challenged and physically disabled, to encourage them to do for themselves as much as possible.

We realize there are those who are so feeble, disabled and poor that they might always need some kind of help. Especially for them we must be very careful not to take a superior attitude and treat them in a condescending manner. We have to be very careful not to rob people of their dignity. It is not merciful to give someone shame on top of a few dollars or a meal to eat. At the same time, to wish someone well and not help them when they are in desperate need is not mercy.

"What good is it, my brothers, if a man claims to have faith but has no deeds? Can such faith save him? Suppose a brother or sister is without clothes and daily food. If one of you says to him, 'Go, I wish you well; keep warm and well fed,' but does nothing about his physical needs, what good is it? In the same way, faith by itself, if it is not accompanied by action, is dead" (James 2:14-17, NIV).

Proverbs also teaches we should not tell our neighbor to come back later when we already have what they need right there present with us.

"Do not withhold good from those who deserve it, when it is in your power to act. Do not say to your neighbor, 'Come back later; I'll give it tomorrow,' when you now have it with you" (Proverbs 3: 27-28, NIV).

For those who insist there be no immediate relief, I wonder how they interpret these Scriptures. It is right and good to build development strategies, but it is wrong to use that as an excuse to deny immediate and necessary help to our neighbors. In that case, the Good Samaritan might be still working to create a "Traveler's Aide Society" so everything could be done "decently and in order," while the poor man who was beaten dies of his wounds.

Many of us mean well. We really do intend to help, someday. Of course, in the meantime the hungry will remain hungry, the homeless will freeze to death, and those in debt will be evicted. You get the point.

The radical response that Scripture calls for sometimes puts us in a dilemma as we seek to break the habits of dependency, begging, and the avoidance of accountability that often complicate ministries of mercy among the poor. We don't want to stop hearing the cry of the poor and lose passion for rapid and effective response. We don't want our hearts to become calloused and have our attitudes become cynical while we build strategies to help the poor for the long term.

Mercy is not trying to keep someone from getting arrested if they break the law. Mercy is not lying to a landlord, or the IRS, or to anyone in order to deliver the poor from the consequences of any illegal choices they have made. Mercy helps people as it tells the truth, accepts consequences, and faces facts. We certainly can be advocates for people, but must not use our integrity and status to cover up for some folks that are not yet spiritual, not yet mature, and not yet trustworthy.

Questions for Reflection and Discussion

1. What side have you erred on – only or mostly giving immediate and fast relief, or only or mostly working toward long-term solutions?
2. What would be some symptoms that would indicate you have helped create dependency in people, or found yourself being co-dependent in their struggles?
3. What good have you been intending to get to, good that you never seem to get around to doing?

CHAPTER 15

Showing Mercy Across Ethnic and Class Divides

"But a Samaritan, as he traveled, came where the man was; and when he saw him, he took pity on him."

(Luke 11:33, NIV)

When I was a Chaplain in the Tennessee National Guard, one of our soldiers received the news that his trailer, in which his family lived, had burned down. This happened while our unit was away on our annual training. The soldier didn't know where he could house his family, since he didn't have many resources. I told him if he wanted our help, my church back in Chattanooga could step up and find an apartment for them, and give them some basic things to get started. He seemed happy to receive the help.

When we returned to Chattanooga I was glad to see my congregation had taken care of his family. However, it seemed this poor white family was not accustomed to receiving help from black folks, or a mixed group of people. Within a week or two – I suppose after the soldier got his pay – he and his family left the place in which we had helped them get situated. They drove in front of my house yelling all kinds of racial epithets and curses, and then peeled off in their car. I never saw the soldier again.

Receiving help is a tender thing. Most folks have a sense of pride that is offended when other people do for them, and sometimes they are suspicious as to why they are being helped, even if they really need it. I can remember my own family struggling to understand the gestures of charity the church was extending to us. We didn't like being asked a lot of questions, and even though their help was given out of love and kindness, we seemed ready to bite the hand that was feeding us.

Manipulation and Cynicism

When panhandlers and beggars ask for help with no sense of embarrassment or shame, it is usually because this is how they are making a living. They in fact don't want to be held accountable for what they are being given and begin to look at people as "marks" or suckers. In turn, people who often find themselves being asked for money become cynical and hardened to the hustlers on the street. We will discuss ways to think about and plan for professional panhandlers later in chapter 35.

All people come from a certain ethnic and social context, and this means they interpret the actions and words of others from that context. What you might mean in all sincerity as a gift and an effort to help may be taken as an attempt to control, demean or manipulate.

When middle-class folks give help to individuals or families, they might expect the recipients to respond as they assume people "should." Maybe they expect gratitude and some measure of humble thanks. If the people helped don't seem properly grateful, the givers can become resentful and decide such acts of charity are wasted.

I remember once being met by a man in the church parking lot asking me for help in finding a place to spend the night. I knew the Salvation Army had a shelter not too far away. In my attempt to help the man, I told him I could give him a ride down to the shelter and would pay the nine dollars so he could spend the night. On the way there, however, he became angry. He demanded to know why I couldn't get him a hotel room. Finally he made me stop the car and got out, furious with me that I hadn't helped him according to the standard to which he would like to grow accustomed.

It is easy for us to say, "Beggars can't be choosers." Yet even when times are hard, we each still have our innate sense of dignity. That is a gift from God and the dignity of other people needs to be treated with care by all who would do well and mean well in what they do. We must take care not to despise the poor. *"He who mocks the poor shows contempt for their Maker; whoever gloats over disaster will not go unpunished" (Proverbs 17:5, NIV).*

It is shortsighted of us to think somehow the chronically poor are going to have the same value system or same set of social skills that we do. It is naïve to think the poor are going to know the middle class rules of charity etiquette.

Some Humility Required

As Christians we are the ones who need to have humility in our giving. We must be constantly aware of the danger of being paternalistic and patronizing to people when they need help. When a stranger comes into your church office, if that should happen, and he or she is of a different race than you, there is the strong possibility they have some preconceived notion of what you might be like.

You also may have a preconceived idea or even a prejudice about what that person of a different color, ethnicity, or accent is like. You might normally be an abrupt, rude or demanding person, so you might not mean anything by it in terms of your racial feelings. However, the person hearing you is not likely to give you the benefit of the doubt.

My suggestion is that you listen to yourself talk. Ask yourself if your demand for information, or desire to quickly move this person on down the road, won't be taken as arrogant, racially negative, or condescending. Remember, this could have been you – and it might yet be you in a similar situation, but for the grace of God.

People say kindness doesn't cost you anything, but I believe it does. Sometimes I am too busy to be kind. Being kind to you might just slow me down. Being kind might mean my sense of importance is threatened, because allowing myself to be interrupted by you means you are as important as I am.

We do advocate having a system or process by which your church might help people, but please don't hide your lack of caring behind whatever process you create for helping the poor. Ultimately, this is a spiritual work, and you will need the power of the Holy Spirit to do it well.

Questions for Reflection and Discussion

1. Do you have any stories you can tell about times when it was hard for you to receive help from others?
2. What things have people done or said that made you think they were judging you (or pre-judging you) racially or socially?
3. How have you felt when someone was giving you help but made it obvious they thought they were better than you?
4. How do you want people to act and feel when you give them some financial or merciful help?

CHAPTER 16

For Mercy's Sake, Get Your Attitude Right

"...if it is showing mercy, let him do it cheerfully."

(ROMANS 12:8, NIV)

THE CHRISTIAN'S ATTITUDE ABOUT THE poor must be built on his relationship to Jesus. It doesn't matter if you don't like the poor or anything about them. It doesn't matter if you have never been around poor people and don't think this has to be your concern. If you are a Christian, your attitude about the poor has to be derived from your relationship with, and submission to, the Lord Jesus Christ.

This means for those of us who are Christian, the poor (those who are in need and those who are in our path) are inescapably tied to our faith and our life as believers.

"To keep up the exercise of brotherly love, God assures us, that all men are our brethren, because they are related to us by a common nature. Whenever I see a man, I must, of necessity, behold myself as in a mirror: for he is my bone and my flesh (Genesis 29:14)." –John Calvin, *Commentary on Matthew, Mark, Luke.* [Matthew 5:43-48, Luke 6:27-36]

The very commission of Jesus is related to God's anointing him for a certain task. What task was that? We are told what Jesus was commissioned to do in Luke 4, verses 16-19:

"He went to Nazareth, where he has been brought up, and on the Sabbath day he went into the synagogue, as was his custom. And he stood up to read. The scroll of the prophet Isaiah was handed to him. Unrolling it, he found the place what it is written:

"'The Spirit of the Lord is on me, because he has anointed me to preach good news to the poor. He has sent me to proclaim freedom for the prisoners and recovery of sight for the blind, to release the oppressed, to proclaim the year of the lord's favor'" (NIV).

I think it is a fair extrapolation of this text to deduce that if we follow Christ, we join him in His commission and in the task He was anointed to complete...*to preach the Gospel to the poor.*

Walking As Jesus Walked

We are the Body of Christ (1 Corinthians 12:27) on this planet and we are to walk even as Jesus walked. Jesus is God incarnate, in the flesh (John 1:14), so that we might behold Him. Now that He is in heaven on the right hand of the Father, we (the Church) are the representation of God on earth. We are called the "Body of Christ" on purpose, as we are the members of that body and He is the head. Dr. John Perkins preaches that almost everywhere he goes, and it is an understanding of the Church, and of the local church, that we all need to understand.

Let's look at what Jesus taught in Matthew 25 about how our reactions to the poor will be judged:

"When the Son of Man comes in his glory, and all the angels with him, he will sit on his throne in heavenly glory. All the nations will be gathered before him, and he will separate the people one from another as a shepherd separates the sheep from the goats. He will put the sheep on his right and the goats on his left.

"Then the King will say to those on his right, 'Come, you who are blessed by my Father; take your inheritance, the kingdom prepared for you since the creation of the world. For I was hungry and you gave me something to

drink, I was a stranger and you invited me in, I needed clothes and you clothed me, I was sick and you looked after me, I was in prison and you came to visit me.' Then the righteous will answer him 'Lord, when did we see you hungry and feed you, or thirsty and give you something to drink? When did we see you a stranger and invite you in, o needing clothes and clothe you? When did we see you sick or in prison and go to visit you?' The King will reply, 'I tell you the truth, whatever you did for one of the least of these brothers of mine, you did for me.'

"Then he will say to those on his left, 'Depart from me, you who are cursed, into the eternal fire prepared for the devil and his angels. For I was hungry and you gave me nothing to eat, I was thirsty and you gave me nothing to drink, I was a stranger and you did not invite me in, I needed clothes and you did not clothe me, I was sick and in prison and you did not look after me.' They also will answer, 'Lord, when did we see you hungry or thirsty or a stranger or needing clothes or sick or in prison, and did not help you?' He will reply, 'I tell you the truth, whatever you did not do for one of the last of these, you did not do for me.' Then they will go away to eternal punishment, but the righteous to eternal life" (Matthew 25:31-46, NIV).

Many Approaches for Helping

Many people have been emotionally affected by what they have learned about the poor and their suffering. To that end, some individuals have given their lives in sacrificial service, and some with wealth have created foundations by and through which to dispense aid. Some people have gotten involved in politics and tried to legislate initiatives to help the poor by creating institutions and agencies, from the neighborhood level to the United Nations, or by ending injustice. Some have even become revolutionaries and sought to create new governments and economic systems to end economic disparity and raise people from poverty.

Some of these individuals have become heroes and examples of greatness. And some of these initiatives, foundations and movements have had a positive effect and changed people's lives. On the other hand, others have created havoc, tyranny and slaughter in the name of trying to create some materialistic or philosophical good.

I confess to admiring anyone that is generous to the poor and seeks to serve them and change their condition for the better – if they do that with integrity, justice, and respect for life in all individuals. We cannot excuse murder, slaughter, and theft (although I once thought Robin Hood was a great role model) as a way of helping the needy. As a Christian, my tools for delivering poor people from poverty are limited by what the Scriptures teach, and that limitation is nothing but the boundaries of love.

For those who love God, the end can never justify the means; the means must be consistent with the end. They are in fact one and the same. If love is what we seek, we find it in loving. I am commanded by God to love people, even my enemies.

I have to use truth. I am bound by admitting my own sinfulness, my own need for God, and my commonality with all other people, so I cannot lord it over them even if I am doing a so-called good thing. In short, any heroic activity I pursue doesn't make me better than anyone else.

Well-Meaning, But Misguided?

So I can rejoice in all good works that are done in conformity with Biblical ethics and morality, ones that result in good to people. We realize some attempts for doing good to others have arisen from ulterior motives, for the personal gain and aggrandizement of charismatic leaders or organizations by way of exploiting those supposedly being helped. Some good works have gone awry through poor leadership, mismanagement, and sincere but ignorant vision of what to do or how to do it.

Unfortunately, there are ripple effects from the failures of well-meaning but misguided efforts, but especially from those with corrupt purposes. Donors, the public and the poor all have become disaffected, angry and resistant to other legitimate efforts and appeals once they have been disappointed by unscrupulous ministers or workers among the poor, or by those who have simply been inept. Church members and deacons become burned-out, calloused, and then indifferent as they sense nothing ever changes.

There seem to be many sound reasons for not helping the poor. It can be hard to trust the poor themselves, for some of them are con artists and thieves. It can be hard to trust charitable organizations when so much money is either wasted, through programs or projects that are not well-thought-out or led, or worse, skimmed off by white-collar hustlers.

One becomes discouraged when money raised to help the poor is spent disproportionally in maintaining inflated administrative salaries and corporate offices. It can be disheartening and frustrating to help the poor because the poor can be so intransigent in their dysfunctionality. (I challenge you to unpack that phrase.)

Whatever negative experiences we have had, or frustration our efforts have encountered in trying to show mercy, we need to refresh our determination to continue by reminding ourselves that we are all recipients of God's mercy. From the beauty of a sunrise or a sunset, to the blessing of a spring rain, to a landscape full of glorious color in autumn, or the blooming of dogwoods and azaleas in the spring, to our daily bread, God has blessed us. If you have eyes that can read this type, ears to hear music, or skin to feel a hug, then you are blessed. Mercy ministry requires and receives a constant renewal from the fountain of an attitude of gratitude.

Attitude affects just about everything. So often we find ourselves defeated in achieving our good intentions because when a need arises, our *attitude* is self-focused and self-centered. The attitude of Jesus is what we need, as we are encouraged to have in Philippians, chapter two:

"Your attitude should be the same as that of Christ Jesus: Who, being in very nature God, did not consider equality with God something to be grasped, but made himself nothing, taking the very nature of a servant, being made in human likeness. And being found in appearance as a man, he humbled himself and became obedient to death – even death on a cross!" (Philippians 2:5-8, NIV).

To use another Denzel Washington movie quote, "Attitude reflects leadership" (from the movie, "Remember the Titans").

Questions for Reflection and Discussion

1. Recount a personal story of a time when you knew God had mercy on you?
2. What, if anything, keeps you positive about showing mercy to others?
3. What has discouraged you about showing mercy to strangers?
4. What do you think could give you a better attitude about doing works of mercy?

CHAPTER 17

A Right View of Good Works

"And let us consider how we may spur one another on toward love and good deeds."

(HEBREWS 10:24, NIV)

AN ELDERLY MAN LIVING IN a boarding house across from where the church meets has diseased feet, and sometimes he can't even walk. One of our members is told about his problem – she is a nurse and goes to visit him. She washes his feet, massages his feet and toes, and clips his nails. Over the course of that year she voluntarily repeats this ministry several times. She does it in the name of Jesus, and each time she does it he gets to walk that week.

Evangelicals, it seems, have had a schizophrenic relationship with good works. We seem (in a lot of our preaching) to despise good works because we think that if we advocate them it reveals that our theology is a "theology of works." Such a theology of works is one that says, "if we do good things God will reward us, and if we do enough of those good things we gain eternal life." All good evangelicals know (or should) that we are saved by grace through faith, and by grace and faith alone. That was what the Reformation was all about.

To make the statement that Evangelicals despise good works seems like an overstatement, yet we find our preachers having difficulty knowing how to call their congregations to actually do those good works. If we speak so much against them as a false hope for salvation, it might not be any wonder Evangelicals aren't quite sure how to pursue them. When we do preach about doing good it seems like moralizing, so we fear floating back into another legalism. What we need are sermons that stress the power of grace and the joy of the Gospel as empowering us to finally do the good works that God has already prepared for us to do in our lives and through our churches.

Issues Surround Good Works

There are several issues that keep surfacing as I have gone around calling the Church to engage in those good works the Lord desires from us. One issue is the silence of the church about such good works; another is that when mentioned or taught, it seems more of an emphasis on personal morality without a corresponding call to acts of public justice. Another issue is the question some seem to have about whether good works are something only the individual believer is supposed to do, or if there is also a corporate responsibility to be laid on congregations as well? Consider the following:

Ephesians 2:8-10 says, *"For it is by grace you have been saved, through faith-and this is not from yourselves, it is the gift of God-not by works, so that no one can boast. For we are God's workmanship,* ***created in Christ Jesus to do good works, which God prepared in advance for us to do"*** *(NIV).*

This is a very clear statement, declaring that God has something for us to be doing. When it comes to salvation, our work is to believe in the One God has sent, namely Jesus. But after salvation has come into our lives, we begin to realize our purpose is to do what we have been created to do.

Yes, those who are good Presbyterians understand this purpose is to glorify God and to enjoy Him forever – but that glorifying is fulfilled in doing those good works that evidently God has already prepared, and which are waiting on us to get done. When it comes to acts of mercy, which our Lord has commanded us to show to those who are suffering, to our neighbors who are in trouble, to our brethren who have need of this world's goods, and to all men in general, it shouldn't be a mystery as to what God wants us to be doing.

The book of James certainly spells out that our salvation (the reality of our being saved) is revealed in our deeds. "In the same way, faith by itself, if it is not accompanied by action, is dead" (James 2:17).

Skewed Theology of Works

I am afraid, especially in America, we have built an Evangelical subculture that sees doing good as only those activities we perform within the local church, or in our evangelism to the unsaved. Some churches work their people so hard in church activities they seem to have no time for anything else, and then we use our inadequate theology to excuse our lack of love and mercy to those who are our neighbors and those who are in need. There isn't anything wrong with the theology of the New Testament. Rather it is the wrong emphasis we have given it that limits the effective witness that deeds of love and mercy can give us.

Jesus spelled out how He wanted the Church to act in the world when He preached His Sermon on the Mount:

"You are the salt of the earth. But if the salt loses its saltiness, how can it be made salty again? It is no longer good for anything, except to be thrown out and trampled by men. You are the light of the world. A city on a hill cannot be hidden. Neither do people light a lamp and put it under a bowl. Instead they put it on its stand, and it gives light to everyone in the house. In the same way, let your light shine before men, that they may see your good deeds and praise your Father in heaven" (Matthew 5:27-30, NIV).

When I attended Sunday school as a boy, I remember singing, "This little light of mine." I always understood that song as a call to live my Christian life so people would see my "light," which I took as my witness as a Christian. Most of the emphasis seemed to be for an individual piety that would reveal to others my personal holiness. I don't remember ever hearing anyone say this particular Scripture was a call to the Church as a community to do good works before the people of the world, which is what I believe it actually means. But we will talk more about this when we discuss the role of the church in mercy.

The apostle Peter adds to this when he says, *"Dear friends, I urge you, as aliens and strangers in the world, to abstain from sinful desires, which war against your soul. Live such good lives among the pagans that, though they accuse you of doing wrong, they may see your good deeds and glorify God on the day he visits us" (1 Peter 2:11-12, NIV).*

In this text Peter is calling us to a personal moral righteousness, but is also saying unbelievers look at our deeds, our works. It is what Jesus taught in the Matthew passage. How can unbelievers give glory to the Father? I don't think it is because they are impressed necessarily by what we say we believe. Nor is it by what we do in the church house.

Being Out Among Them

Often I challenge congregations, when I have the opportunity to be speaking at their locations, to look around and see if there are any non-Christians looking in the windows of the church. People don't really care what we do as we practice our religion in corporate worship, in the privacy of our church settings, except those few that might come to visit on a given Sunday.

I certainly think our worship is important, and essential. What I am also saying, however, is that our corporate worship, Sunday school classes, small groups, growth groups, etc. are not the arena for the people of the world to see our good works. It is out among them, where they live and work – and among the poor especially – where our faith will be revealed as to whether it is genuine or not.

Yes, as we live out our lives in our specific vocations, jobs and callings, we reveal to people what kind of people we are. I don't want to minimize the importance of the witness we can have through our vocations, whether it is the quest to do them with excellence or in taking the opportunity to give a verbal witness of our faith. Yet we don't always get to do that vocally in the name of Jesus, and we usually don't get to do it as a church.

Later in the Sermon on the Mount, Jesus warns against doing good deeds for our own personal aggrandizement:

"Be careful not to do your 'acts of righteousness' before men, to be seen by them. If you do, you will have no reward from your Father in heaven. So when you give to the needy, do not announce it with trumpets, as the hypocrites do in the synagogues and on the streets, to be honored by men. I tell you the truth, they have received their reward in full. But when you give to the needy, do not let your left hand know what your right hand is doing, so that your giving may be in secret. Then your Father, who sees what is done in secret, will reward you" (Matthew 6:1-4, NIV).

This might seem confusing. Does Jesus want us to help the poor or not? Does Jesus want us to go and perform good deeds? Yes, but when they are done personally, we should be careful not to seek glory for ourselves.

We should especially seek to do them as a church, as a congregation, and be glad when the world sees it so they can glorify God for what is done. The good we do corporately, even if we try to keep it quiet, is going to become known. Widows are going to tell their families, orphans are going to tell their friends, the hungry are going to tell those who have not yet eaten, the prisoners will tell their cellmates who we are. The oppressed, the beaten down, the ones treated unjustly are going to know who their heroes are, and we need to be those heroes. This was the reputation the Church of Jesus Christ had during the Roman Empire, and we turned that empire upside down. Church, hear me, you who are faithful followers of Jesus Christ: We need to get our reputation back!

The following passage gives part of the reason for why we go to church:

"Let us hold unswervingly to the hope we profess, for he who promised is faithful. And let us consider how we may spur one another on toward love and good deeds. Let us not give up meeting together, as some are in the habit of doing, but let us encourage one another – and all the more as you see the Day approaching" (Hebrews 10:23-25, NIV).

The So-Called 'Social Gospel'

We are not called to replace the true Gospel with something called the "Social Gospel." The Social Gospel idea, first introduced more than a century ago, was that people needed improving, that the savage needed to be civilized, that the poor needed to be delivered, and that the very act of helping them rise up was what the Gospel was all about. It basically was a dismissal of the supernatural in favor of a naturalistic attempt at helping mankind.

If one doesn't really believe the supernatural aspects of the Bible, we can see how they might take that route. We, on the other hand, believe true Christianity has always been a spiritual and faith-based religion built on the miraculous and historical revelation found in the Bible.

However, we also believe the true Gospel has always had social impact and societal results, as well as spiritual. To not care about people as whole human beings is not the true Gospel either. We believe in a supernatural God who still works in the world, who still calls people to be spiritually saved but also to be physically and earthbound obedient in doing justice, loving mercy, and walking humbly with their God, as God declares in Micah 6:8. John Calvin said,

"But it is his will, that we should imitate his fatherly goodness and liberality. This was perceived, not only by heathen philosophers, but by some wicked despisers of godliness, who have made this open confession, that in nothing do men resemble God more than in doing good. In short, Christ assures us, that this will be a mark of our adoption, if we are kind to the unthankful and evil. And yet you are not to understand, that our liberality makes us the children of God; but the same Spirit, who is the witness (Romans 8:16), earnest (Ephesians 1:14), and seal (Ephesians 4:30) of our free adoption, corrects the wicked affections of the flesh, which are opposed to charity. Christ therefore proves from the effect, that none are the children of God, but those who resemble him in gentleness and kindness." – John Calvin, *Commentary on Matthew, Mark, Luke* (Matthew 5:43-48, Luke 6:27-36).

Law of Charity

Wow, did you take that in: "*...none are the children of God, but those who resemble him in gentleness and kindness*"? One of the things I like about this section of Calvin's Commentary is this comment: "We ought simply to enquire, what is demanded by the law of charity; for if we rely on the heavenly power of the Spirit, we shall encounter successfully all that is opposed to it in our feelings" (ibid). I like this because he makes two really great points. One is that we need to rely on the "heavenly power of the Spirit," and the other is that sometimes we are opposed to being charitable in our "feelings."

My theology has given me the great joy of preaching the Gospel of grace: God's grace in sending His Son, God's grace in opening my eyes to believe in Him, and God's grace in empowering me to live the Christian life. So with charity, and with mercy, I need God's grace to do it at all, and certainly to do it well. Calvin speaks of the "law of charity" because he believed Jesus had commanded us to love our neighbors as ourselves, and Jesus wasn't just giving us advice.

Some might resist the idea of any mention of law, yet love is the law of Christ. Don't let your passion for the Gospel rob you of the ethical implications of being saved by it. It doesn't matter if it makes you feel guilty; maybe you are. We deal with guilt at the cross; we believe our sins are paid for and paid for completely at the place where Jesus died. However, the proof our lives have been redeemed is that we are not only moved emotionally by the moral law of Christ but also move toward obedience. The moral law of Christ calls us on to righteousness.

The Holy Spirit-empowered response to the call of Christ to love – even our enemies – is possible only by faith, and for us not to pursue obedience by faith is indeed sinful. If you love the Gospel, if you love hearing about grace, don't mock Christ by resisting His call to mercy and love as if it were a new kind of works (in the salvation sense). It is work, good work, empowered by grace, done in faith, and through the work of the Spirit.

Questions for Reflection and Discussion

1. What kind of good works could (or should) a congregation be doing as a body of believers?
2. What might be the theological dangers of doing good works, as well as not doing them?
3. What kinds of good works is your congregation engaged in at present?
4. What would be the contrast between a "spiritual" way to do good works and doing them "in the flesh"?

The Drink of Kindness

Another hot African day
Whose high sun beating low
Finds a white man sweating
Mops his brow and waiting
Upon a rural bus
In an obscure little market town
Somewhere 'tween Mwingi and Ngai.

The African woman lays out her mangos
On a market day,
Cloth spread upon the ground.
Anonymity in proximity
African and American sit.

She is curious that a white man
Is not only here
But waits upon a bus,
Whose kind roar by in Rovers,
Seldom with any need but speed
To pass her by.

Enthralled, she wonders
In a non-English way,
Is poverty
Emanating from a Mzungu,
Is she deceived?
Maybe God inculcates
Humility,
At least in this moment
In one whose
Very clothes
Could send her kids
To school

Or purchase bread for a month.

He is stranded
From too many flattened tires,
On his way back to recover
Another now repaired
In a town recently passed.

With her lithe arm
She reaches for one shiny moist
And succulent fruit
On whose skin
Sunlight prances in sparkling invitation.
She offers fruit to him, and in
Thirsty dismay he says,
"Hapana pesa,
I have no cash money,
Save for the bus."

Undeterred, no hesitation,
Withdraws not her hand,
Smiles – and offers again.

When there is no water
On a hot Kenyan day,
There is the drink of kindness
And it is a gift
Long remembered.
Without words,
From a stranger,
A kindness from poverty to wealth
That had no money.
-- Randy Nabors, February 2010

Part Four:

The Church

CHAPTER 18

God's Institution Is God's Instrument

"His intent was that now, through the church, the manifold wisdom of God should be made known…."

(EPHESIANS 3:10, NIV)

THE BEST THING WE CAN DO FOR THE POOR IS TO PLANT THE RIGHT KIND OF CHURCH IN THEIR MIDST.

THE BEST THING WE CAN do for the poor is to plant the right kind of church in their midst. I am convinced of this. I say again: The best strategy for helping the poor is to plant the right kind of church among them. When I say "right," I mean this in both a theological (orthodoxy) sense and a practical (orthopraxis) sense.

This raises the question then as to what really helps the poor. Is the solution to poverty something that ought to be pursued solely by – or through – government? Should it be solely by acts of personal mercy, either through immediate charity or through individual or community development? Should it be to leave them to their own devices and use the incentive of hunger to make them change? There may be some who sincerely believe doing nothing is the best solution. Let us hope neither they nor their families ever have a need for mercy.

Macro-Solutions and Micro-Solutions

My answer to these questions is built from an acceptance of both the necessity and reality of macro- and micro-solutions. I think there will always be a need for individual-to-individual action (micro), along with institutional programs and government protection of the rights of the poor (macro). Yet, it is the space in between the two I feel offers one of the best (and most necessary) solutions, and that is: ***the creation of a local church within the poor or needy community***. Here's a good example:

Our church hires one of our young women to be a "children's missionary." She begins to walk around the neighborhood, hang around the playgrounds, and meet children. She meets a little girl and her younger brother. She finds out the mother is often drunk, not even knowing at times where her children are. I actually pull the mother out of the street one day as she lies drunk against the curb.

Our children's missionary begins to bring the kids to Sunday school, spending time with them, taking them with her to various church events and outings. She then suggests we scholarship these children to the local Christian school. With the cooperation of the school, both of the children are put through school. Eventually various families take the kids in a foster care arrangement, but never losing touch with their mother, who begins to go through a series of rehabs.

Both kids finish high school and get scholarships to college. The young lady eventually finishes at Covenant College, earns another degree from Covenant Seminary, becomes a staff member at several churches, and still serves and leads as one very dynamic Christian woman. It took a lot of people doing lots of different things to help them through, but what a privilege to be part of God's story in their lives.

A local church (and again, it must be the right kind of local church) is not a macro-solution compared to what government or economic systems can effect. (The poor absolutely need the economy of the country to be healthy and growing so jobs can be created in the general economy.) A local church seems pretty small compared to foundations and institutions that might have large coffers of money. Yet it offers more than the micro-solution of charity given from individual to individual.

The church provides a grassroots, community-based institution that becomes an engine of all kinds of mercy: encouraging mercy from person to person, as well as church to individuals or families, and from church to neighborhood. If planting the right kind of church in every community of need actually happened and became a movement, many things would begin to change in communities, cultures, and even nations. I think this is exactly what God intended for the church.

Positive Historical Impact

To some degree this has already happened historically in the spread of Christianity. I think history shows when the church has done its job Biblically and faithfully, the masses are affected for their good and well-being. Women are treated with dignity, children's lives are protected, humane treatment is provided to prisoners, the sick are treated in hospitals, slaves are freed, orphanages are established, and cultures of cannibalism and human sacrifice are ended. Cultures, and many negative things within them, have been changed because the Gospel has been planted in those cultures through churches.

Planting an effective congregation in a poor community does not deny the necessity for personal initiative and industry on the part of the poor, but it does in fact help instigate, support and reinforce it.

One day a couple in our church calls and says a woman they have known and ministered to over the years has told them she wants to come off crack cocaine. She has two young daughters and doesn't know what to do with them if she goes to rehab. "Can the church help us feed these girls if we take them in?" they ask. "Absolutely" is our answer.

So the church supplements our church members as they provide loving foster care for these girls. The woman finishes rehab and the church secures an apartment, pays the deposit and rent for her to get on her feet. Within a few months, however, she takes in a boyfriend and the church has to stop supporting her. Later she goes back on crack.

About two years later we get a repeat of the first phone call. "Yes, we will do it again." And we do. Some years later one of those young girls comes up to me in church ad asks the dreaded question, "Do you remember me?" "Ah, no, please tell me," I reply. She then reminds me of the story and how we had helped her and her sister, how they had come to church, and how now she was working and making it in life, despite the disadvantages she faced growing up. I like payback like that.

For those of you who are going into church planting, I would challenge you that you need to start thinking of mercy sooner rather than later. Some of you will not be going into communities of poverty, but that will not relieve you of being prepared to call your people into mercy ministry. Much of what I write in this book is particularly about ministries in very poor communities, that can be impacted by Gospel ministries that attempt to be wholistic in their approach, with good results if they do mercy well. The short "cheat sheet" that follows was prepared for the Global Church Advancement Conference put on by Steve Childers.

"Cheat sheet" for church planters on mercy ministry

1. Mercy ministry will be required in your church no matter what socio-economic group makes up your church or community.
2. It would be wise to plan for it ahead of time so that you will have some wisdom, mechanism, or personnel to rise to the situation.

3. Loving your neighbor or "doing good to all men especially to the household of faith" (Galatians 6:10) is not something you can put off until the 2nd, 3rd, or 5th year of the church plant.
4. It is not just the poor that have dysfunctional families, struggle with addictions, or have legal, medical, and death issues.
5. If you minister among the poor you will have more obvious dysfunctionality problems to deal with, with fewer resources.
6. The pastor and elders must protect their time of prayer and the Word, so they must delegate ministry to others so they can be free to do their primary work. Pastors should never be the "sugar daddy."
7. It is the pastor's job to "enable the saints to do the work of the ministry" (Ephesians 4:11-12). This means the pastor must teach, train, and target his workers for ministry. To preach the "weightier matters of the Law" you must preach on mercy and justice, and if you preach on them you must show your congregation how to practice them.
8. In Acts 6:3 we believe the first deacons chosen were men "full of the Holy Spirit and wisdom." Mercy is a spiritual work and it must be spiritually pursued.
9. To effectively change the lives of the poor mercy must be "accountable, returnable, developmental, and ecclesial." The local church is the community in which people can be discipled out of poverty.
10. To help your church be effective in mercy ministry the church must develop policies, priorities and process so they will know how to show mercy regularly, routinely and resourcefully without damaging the poor or the church (officers, members, and staff.)
11. Stop sending the poor away to other agencies and bring them into the Body of Christ.

12. Pray and plan how to increase the funds and personnel you will need to show and do mercy in ways that make a positive impact in your community.

Why is the church the right solution, and how is it the right solution? If the church is a key answer to poverty, then what kind of local church should it be? Is there any sense of reality to this solution, and should it be a substitute for government and for individual action? I will try to answer some of these questions, working backward in the order I have posed the questions.

Questions for Reflection and Discussion

1. What do you think the attitude is in your own congregation about them being a "solution to poverty?" Would this surprise them?
2. When you think of the history of Christianity, what models of mercy or justice do you know about?
3. What do you think would be the difficulties for a congregation that actually tried to establish an effective mercy program to really change the lives of the poor, whether within or around the church?

CHAPTER 19

Starving Souls: There Is a Famine

"The days are coming," declares the Sovereign Lord, "when I will send a famine through the land – not a famine of food or a thirst for water, but a famine of hearing the words of the Lord. Men will stagger from sea to sea and wander from north to east, searching for the word of the Lord, but they will not find it."

(Amos 8:11-12 NIV)

There is a famine in the land – and it is a famine for the Word of God. The poor starve in their souls because they don't know God, and if they knew God they would have hope. Hope is an engine that helps people to endure horrible pain and struggle; it will see them through when all those around them would surrender and give up.

Not only is hope an engine to help people keep going, even in the midst of poverty, but the Gospel message itself is life transforming. The Scriptures teach, *"Therefore if anyone is in Christ, he is a new creation; the old has gone, the new has come" (2 Corinthians 5:17, NIV).* If someone really comes to God, their character must change as a result.

Ephesians 4:28 says, *"Anyone who has been stealing must steal no longer, but must work, doing something useful with their own hands, that they may have something to share with those in need" (NIV).*

To end this widespread famine, the American church must again bring the Gospel to the poor. This was our heritage and this was the foundation of the Church begun by the Lord Jesus Himself. This also is the beginning of justice because it will involve our lives with the poor in their need, in their misery. When our lives are intertwined with theirs, we begin to see where and if there is injustice. Poverty stops being theoretical and becomes personal; we start thinking and praying about how to change the situation.

We are not messiahs, but we begin to jointly look to Jesus who is the true Messiah. He has the solutions, and with confidence in His power together we can begin to make changes. The simple fact is this: If we evangelize the poor, then they will be in our congregations – and then we will have no excuse for not helping to meet their needs. Otherwise, we are not true Christians.

Churches Among the Poor

Someone might point out there are many churches among the poor. Once at a conference I asked Dr. Ed Stetzer, who is a researcher on church planting, about this. He replied that although there weren't many obtainable statistics, there probably were more churches being planted among the poor than one might think. True, if you drive through most inner cities you will notice lots of church buildings and storefront churches. To me, this is both a good and bad indication of the plight of the poor in our cities.

The good indication is that there are Christians already present among the poor who love the Lord and study the Word of God. Some of these storefront churches help rescue broken people, give hope to the struggling, and point people to righteous and wise living. These are important building blocks for anybody coming out of poverty.

Some of the saints in these small churches have amazing faith and provide a mighty witness.

However, there are some bad indications, too. One is that many of the church buildings we might find in the inner city are not filled, and if they are, hardly ever are they filled with men. Quite a few churches in the inner city are commuter congregations where most if not all of the people drive in on Sunday and drive immediately out after services. Many of these congregations lack a holistic theology, and not many unleash their few resources to help each other economically.

I don't know if I have heard or read from anyone how it might actually be counterproductive to have "bad" churches among the poor. Let me say it plainly: Theology matters, and bad theology doesn't bring release to the poor. Just as purchasing junk food at a gas station is not healthy for the people of a community, getting half-baked religion doesn't help either. Lord, protect me from the knives that might fly from saying that!

Those churches that are filled with commuters that come to the community only for worship services, often not pursuing or showing any care for the community from which some of those very same church members have escaped. Sadly, some of these folks express rhetoric for justice and mercy, but often do nothing tangible for their own communities of origin. The presence of a crowded parking lot does not mean that congregation is doing any evangelism or discipleship of the poor people who live around the church building.

Without a doubt, many immigrant churches are being planted and growing in urban centers, and some provide real help to other immigrants experiencing various kinds of need. However, it is yet to be seen how many of them will handle the challenge of the wider diverse community, especially the poor from other ethnicities, in terms of evangelism, inclusion, and community development.

Have You Got Good Religion?

One might think this an arrogant assessment of inner city religion. People come to religion, use and hold onto it for various reasons. Some arrive at religious convictions by way of conscience. They believe what they do because in some way they think it is right or correct. Some come to religion because of how it makes them feel and what it does for them emotionally. Sadly we admit there are some preachers and church folk that plant churches and attend them because they see it as a way to make money, or get a financial blessing.

Though I might think that my view of the Bible and Christianity is mostly correct, I am not at this point seeking to insist that people believe exactly as I do. I have to leave room for the reality people have different beliefs, that other ideas might be valid, and there is still much for me to learn. I do think, however, what one believes or teaches does matter in terms of outcomes. Our faith beliefs have consequences in terms of morality, justice, personal industry, and community engagement. Again I must state – theology matters. It always matters!

It is the outcomes of religion, and how those beliefs and practices affect the poor, that are my concern. If religion is simply used to mask the pain of suffering, then it is a religion without a full understanding of the Bible. I am a Christian not because it is a drug to seduce me into an idealism that ignores the plight of the oppressed, but rather because it is the Truth that delivers people from oppression. Jesus loved me, I want to love people, and I don't love them if I see their need but refuse to help them. This message is inescapable in the Bible and is part of good theology. It is not paternalism to want the poor to have good theology. Nor is it paternalism to want the poor to have good churches planted in their communities.

It saddens me that some of those who confess the same theology I do, that have the education to think in theological terms, whose congregations are made up of middle-class folks and love to read and debate theology, usually don't plant churches among the poor. Middle-class people don't seem to want to live among the poor, and neither do they send their best church planters to start churches among the poor. Nor do they seem to have the will to financially sustain those pastors if they do send them. It is legitimate to ask, in that case, whether they actually have "good theology"?

Don't Worry About Competition

Sometimes I have heard criticism about sending someone into black, poor and urban communities to plant a new church, as if it was an insult to those Christians who are already there. While at first this objection might sound reasonable, it is actually as illogical as those in white middle-class communities who resist new churches being planted in their "area."

"Really?" I ask. Has there been too much competition for poor folks by a flood of church planters who proselytize in poor communities? While there are plenty of cults and false religions, I don't think there has been too much competition from Evangelicals. Are the churches that are already there in the inner-city using the power of the Gospel to bring positive change to those communities? Undoubtedly some of them are, but it seems obvious there is much work still to do. Are all those people in the inner city saved; have they all been discipled out of poverty? Are we all supposed to settle for the way things are because someone's feelings might be hurt if we suggest there is more that could be done?

There is sometimes resentment from established religious leaders about any newcomers into their community. We have certainly heard this kind of silliness from Reformed congregations against any other Reformed kind of church, as if one Reformed church in a city of over 100,000 souls was enough. Often they see other pastors as possible sheep stealers. This resentment flows among those of the same ethnicity as well as those who are not, although certainly if the new church planter is of another race or represents a "foreign" ethnicity, the race card might be played.

This is a shame and very sad, since my observation and experience tell me there is less church attendance in the poor black community than there used to be. If we were more focused on reaching out to the multiplying "goats" to see them saved and redeemed, we wouldn't waste so much time worrying about "sheep" stealing.

I confess to being irritated by those church planters who arrive in inner city neighborhoods assuming no saints are already present. I don't appreciate arrogance from self-styled messiahs who might presume there are still so many problems in the inner city because no resident pastor has had the skill or wisdom to make an impact. I certainly have met great men of God who have been struggling for years to affect their communities for good. Usually these men have been very welcoming of any reinforcements who come with humility, love, and a willingness to work together.

There are complaints about some white church planters who claim they want to do urban ministry, and some of these complaints are well-founded. They use terms that give an urban mystique to their mission while not actually meeting real needs. In my experience, all one has to do is identify a gentrifying neighborhood growing with hipsters and you will be run over by church planting networks that say they "love the city" and revel in an urban ambiance.

Sadly, these new "urban" churches still seem to avoid entanglement in real poverty. As long as the neighborhood is poor, violent, marginalized and without hope, we mostly leave the ministry to bi-vocational men who often have passion but not much education. God bless those sincere, faithful, and godly pastors and their struggling churches that have historically been present, and may God continue to use them. I believe they could use some help, however, both in terms of resources and reinforcements, and it is not wrong or presumptuous to bring more Gospel preaching and Gospel living churches to the poor.

Questions for Reflection and Discussion

1. From your own observations, are there many churches in the inner city? What kind of churches do you personally know about?
2. What should be our attitude toward churches that already exist within poor communities? How should we relate to them?
3. What would be some standards or criteria for a church planter to begin a spiritually healthy work in an inner city neighborhood?

CHAPTER 20

Which Poor Should the Church Help?

"Therefore, as we have opportunity, let us do good to all people, especially to those who belong to the family of believers."

(GALATIANS 6:10, NIV)

ONE OF THE QUESTIONS I am sometimes asked has to do with "which poor?" Is the Church obligated to help *all* the poor? Or is the Church obligated only to help the poor in the church? Sometimes it seems to me the same people saying the government shouldn't help the poor, because the Church should do it, are also telling me the Church should only help its own poor. So on one hand we are told the Church should be helping all the poor, but then we only have to help the poor in our own church. How convenient that sounds.

Preaching the Gospel to the poor makes this merely an academic question, one that should be fairly irrelevant. However, as long as we withhold the Gospel from the poor, and retreat into middle or upper-class enclaves of Christians and churches, we can maintain the luxury of not worrying too much about the unsaved poor – until they somehow find a way to cause us inconvenience, such as by panhandling and blocking intersections. The church in Jerusalem, as described in the book of Acts, would have had a lot fewer widows to feed if the apostles had just withheld the Gospel from them. But once these widows believed in Christ, the church was obligated to come to their aid.

'Spirituality of the Church'

I am a churchman, and I have an ecclesiology. That means I have a theology that informs me as to what the Church (capital C) is and what the local church (small c) are supposed to be and to do. I don't think my view of the role of the church is as limited as those that articulate the so-called "spirituality of the church" might demand. While admitting some adherents of this thinking are sincere in their opinions, I suspect some of that teaching was formed – and may exist today – as a way to retreat from social involvement, as well as a protection of the status quo. Historically, some of the formulation for this view was birthed in racism as an attempt to keep the church from interfering with the institution of slavery.

Some "spirituality of the church" adherents legitimately have a fear of churches getting caught up in tangential issues and missing their primary calling. For those "spiritual" churches, which are not located and not working among the poor, it might seem to be a stand they could easily maintain. If a congregation is made up of people that have no economic concerns, and face no threats to their survival, they may think they have the luxury of building a theology of church that divorces them from the physical struggles of the poor in the broader community.

I suspect some of these ideas come from the isolation of materialism. Yes, all churches are made up of people having spiritual, emotional and psychological issues with which they must deal. All churches have some families falling apart, and most churches have someone struggling with addictions. The insistence on a view that God doesn't want us to deal with social, economic, and community issues – outside of our congregations – makes me wonder if some of these congregations have gotten caught up in a self-focused and materialistic idolatry that fosters a refusal to learn and live out the Biblical demands of justice and mercy?

However, I do share a belief that some things belong to the individual church and other things don't belong to it. It is important for every pastor and session (or whatever the group of church leaders is called) to determine which theological and ideological boundaries should constrain their ministry. Some of these boundaries are imposed on us by government or tradition, but most important is what the Bible teaches us and what can be inferred from it.

We are brought together by the Spirit of God into our communion in Jesus Christ. We are formed to be a worshipping community. When each of us becomes a disciple of Jesus Christ, we are placed in a context of discipleship known as the local church. As disciples we are to learn and obey everything Jesus taught us, and through the church we learn it in a multi-generational, multi-gender, and sometimes multi-class, multi-ethnic and cultural environment.

A Balance – and a Tension

We pass the faith down from one generation after another, but also work as a community of faith to spread the faith to the lost. This calls for a constant effort to balance the tension in a church, to that of caring for the community of faith and our Covenant children, while at the same time bringing more "outside" individuals and families to the faith. We are bearing Covenant children, adopting children, and seeing the spiritual adoption of the lost, and are attempting to raise all of them in the faith.

As a worshipping and discipled community, we proclaim and teach the Word of God. The Great Commission calls us to be always in the act of going to the lost in order to make new disciples. Evangelism, or proclaiming the Evangel (the Gospel, the good news), without planting and building the church is an inadequate ministry because it misses the purpose of the New Testament, which is to disciple the nations, not just make individual believers. The local church is the context both for "teaching them to obey everything I have commanded you," and for "baptizing them in the name of the Father, and of the Son, and of the Holy Spirit" (Matthew 28:19-20).

The Bible is not written simply to individuals for helping them have faith, but to see individuals come to eternal life and live out their faith in the context of the community of the church. It would be hard to understand the ministry of the apostle Paul, and all of his instructions about how to be the church, if the local church is not at the center of things in Christianity. When we read the book of Revelation, we see Jesus being concerned for seven particular churches; He stands in the midst of them. Whether we like it or not, our Lord Jesus looks and judges us not simply as individuals, but as communities of believers. He watches and judges each local church.

Far too many Christians are in congregations that never see any people being converted and coming into the church family as new members. They see transfer growth, and hopefully see babies being born and raised in the church, but the utter, exquisite joy and experience of evangelism and hearing testimonies of the newly saved are being missed.

Evangelism and the Poor

I believe God wants us not only to do evangelism, but also to do it especially among the poor. To live a Christian life in a congregation that does not engage in evangelism, and never does it among the poor – especially if they are within reasonable proximity – is a completely artificial and foreign idea to the New Testament Church. The debate over which poor to help proves to be an artificial, intellectual exercise if we are in fact evangelizing them.

I am afraid we have taken the problem of James 2:1-9 – that of showing favoritism and deference to people of higher social standing – and solved it by not evangelizing among the poor. We don't have a problem of favoritism about people unlike us coming into the worship service because we are not intentionally reaching any of them. Okay, I admit some congregations still might have this problem. However, I think we mainly "insult the poor" by refusing to bring the Gospel to them in their neighborhoods.

If we indeed preach the Gospel to the poor, as Jesus did, we will constantly be in the communities of the poor. If that is our reality, we cannot escape caring for their needs as Jesus and the Jerusalem church did. As we read in the book of Acts, after the day of Pentecost, the poor were in the church. I marvel at the early Jerusalem church, where they were growing in numbers (and how difficult it can be to grow that fast), taking care of the widows by feeding them, and facing cultural division issues head on and resolving the problems (Acts 6:1-7).

Later in the New Testament we see the apostle Paul instructing Timothy to create a list of widows. Evidently the church was financially supportive of them, and in turn used them in its ministry (1 Timothy 5:9).

The Scripture does set priorities for the church, in both the Old and New testaments. It is interesting, however, that when Paul speaks to this issue in Galatians he begins the verse with *"...Let us do good to all men," and then "especially to the household of faith" (Galatians 6:10).* To "all" men is the direction of our good works. It is amazing how many pastors and churches seem to skip over this very small but hugely encompassing word.

It is proper for the congregation to set priorities in its benevolence and be a good steward of God's resources. Widows, orphans and aliens, along with any of its members who are in need, are proper concerns of the church, but it should not use this as an excuse to be hardhearted toward the people in its own neighborhood.

We have been amazed that some pastors, even in the face of natural disasters affecting their entire community, have closed their hearts to their neighbors. When we called them and asked if they needed our help to come and help them repair roofs, gut houses, cut fallen trees they said "no." This was because none of their members were in trouble. They had lost all concept of helping those around them.

Within and Without

As the church uses its resources to help the poor within its walls, especially if the congregation is evangelistic, it is almost inevitable this manifestation of mercy will affect the poor in the surrounding neighborhood, especially if attempts are made to attack the systemic causes of poverty that affect not only the church poor but everyone else in the community.

If one plants a church among the poor, and the poor in the area need work, who will provide it? Who trains the poor to do it? And who refers them to such work? This might be a ministry that encompasses the whole community. The church serves as an engine for such initiatives, and becomes a blessing not just to the poor within the church but to those outside of it as well – being a witness to the lost, and lending credibility to our statements of love.

I want to quote from Bryant L. Myers from his book, *Walking With the Poor,* where he lists three "critical contributions," he says, "only the church can provide."

"First, the role of the church in transformational development is the same as ours: to be a servant and a source of encouragement, not a commander or a judge....

"Second, the church can and must be the source of value formation within the community. While not an exclusive source of values, people who

are reading and living the Word under the discipling of the Holy Spirit should be a significant source of inspiration and perspiration working for life and shalom. When the church is its best, it is a sign of the values of the kingdom and is contributing holistic disciples to the community for its well-being....

"Finally, the church is the hermeneutical community that reads the biblical story as its story and applies this story to the concrete circumstances of its time, place, and culture. This is the community within the community from which the word of God is heard, lived, and revealed. This is the community that, because it knows the true story, can and must challenge the delusional assumptions and the web of lies" (Myers, p.127-128).

It would be well to notice that he says, "When the church is its best...." This is why we emphasize planting the "right" kind of church among the poor. We don't need any more irrelevant churches.

One of the things I really appreciate about Dr. Brian Fikkert of the Chalmers Center and one of the co-authors of *When Helping Hurts* is he, too, is a churchman. He believes ministries to the poor should be done through the local church. Sometimes I chide him with the impression I get – and that others sometimes get – from his book that charity (merciful relief) only hurts the poor, or that churches should stop helping with food or utility bills. Thankfully, I know he is not advocating less mercy but more of it – more wisely applied. In that (and in many other ways) we agree.

So how can things be done through the church, and done well? We will discuss these things in detail, but let me lay out a pattern, or if you prefer, a template for those trying to organize a ministry of mercy. There are several important components to keep in mind. I call them the "Five Components of a Congregational Mercy Strategy":

1. **Actually knowing and meeting the poor.** This is part of the "relocation" idea of John Perkins and the Christian

Community Development Association (CCDA) core principles. If there is no relational bridge to the poor, then the kind of help we provide will seem like what the military sometimes gives in times of disaster when it sends supplies out of an airplane by parachute. That might help save lives in time of disaster, but it doesn't change lives. We have found when we meet the poor on a spiritual basis, and in relationship, we have a far greater amount of influence in their lives for economic change.

Doing evangelism and outreach within poor communities is a way of building both spiritual and relational bridges. If your church simply makes itself an agency for the paying of bills or handling financial emergencies, then people will look upon your church as just another charity institution. The relationship will be impersonal, and to them you will simply be another resource to exploit for making it through the month.

If you are seeking to help the poor, I believe it will sometimes be necessary for your church to handle financial emergencies or offer monetary supplements for poor families. However, without a relational or spiritual basis for the help it usually will not result in any personal change. What makes churches different is that it is our role to go after the human heart and soul, and everything else can grow from that.

2. **Establishing a point of contact in your church structure that proactively seeks to help the poor**. We consider the deacons to be the ones best suited for this role. Please notice I used the word "proactively." This means deacons or mercy workers need to be trained to think "longer term" when seeking to meet emergency or relief needs. Creating structure, policies and programs are all part of this, but there needs to be a point of contact for the poor so they will know who to speak with and where to come for help.

3. **Developing the mentality that the church genuinely wants the poor to become part of the congregation – to attend, worship, and to join.** Jesus told us in His Great Commission (as we refer to it in Matthew 28:19-20) that as we go, we are to make disciples of the nations, baptizing them in the name of the Father and of the Son and of the Holy Spirit, teaching them to observe all things that He commanded us. The local church is the place of discipleship, so it is where the poor need to be in order to grow in the knowledge of the Lord and of His Word. Our goal is not simply to have the church minister to the poor, but that the poor should become an integral part of the Church. Then it becomes about us *together* – not "us" helping "them."
4. **Developing strategies, programs, spinoffs, and referrals: creating a mechanism for assisting the poor we have helped through relief to learn how to develop themselves economically**. In other words, move people to development. This is often unseen and unknown by prosperous churches. The processes of economic development, community development, and using appropriate technology for development are issues congregations within poor communities have to struggle with in seeking to help all of their people. Merciful relief gives the poor a bridge to reach the development process. But without introducing the development process, merciful relief can become a merry-go-round the poor can't seem to get off.
5. **Close the circle of ministry to the poor by discipling them into leadership so they can bless their own families and community, not simply escape it**. Many of the folks we help will not necessarily return to take part in our mission. Some will escape the "ghetto" through the education and jobs we help them to secure. Poverty makes people provincial by force, and when they have economic options they

will usually take them. And one of those options is to move to a better neighborhood. We share some success in the economic elevation of people with whom we work, but our aim is to create radicalized believers who don't live simply for themselves but for Him who died and gave His life for them. We want the poor to become the next deacons, elders, pastors and missionaries in our churches.

Questions for Reflection and Discussion

1. How did the early church deal with the poor in their midst? Look at Acts 2:42-47, 4:32-37, 6:1-7.
2. Think about the Five Components of a Congregational Mercy Strategy. Which of these is your church presently using, which do you need to add, and which ones do you need to improve?
3. Is the problem mentioned in James 5:1-6 – the rich oppressing the poor, the "haves" lacking any concern or compassion for the needy – present in the Church at large today? Explain your answer.

CHAPTER 21

What About Parachurch Ministries?

" 'Send the crowd away'...He replied, 'You give them something to eat.' "

(LUKE 9:12-13)

SOMETHING ELSE I HEAR IN discussions about helping the poor is, "Well, what about parachurch ministries? There are some that are very credible and devoted to this mission. Shouldn't they be the ones to focus on helping those in need?" These are good questions and discussing them also brings some important theological issues to light.

For instance, who is responsible to do evangelism, who is to carry out discipleship, and where and in what "wineskin" should people gather to worship? What are the limits to this thing we call "the local church"? In answering these questions, I will keep saying the church, the church, *the local church.* I also emphasize the role of the church in acts of mercy and specifically, in creating effective ministries of charity done from and through the local congregation.

However, to supplement the work of charity, and provide healthy and sustained growth from that charity, I advocate the use of parachurch development-type ministries. These ministries are usually outside of the direct supervision of the local congregation, its leaders and pastors. However, these ministries can be created, invented, supported and influenced by the local congregation and sometimes must be. Sometimes the church is the only stable and viable institution indigenous to a particular neighborhood.

Safeguarding Accountability

I am frankly jealous for the local church to be the one institution that pursues evangelism, ministries of discipleship, and worship. I don't want to give these ministries away to parachurch ministries or non-profits. I don't want to give the ministry of "accountable mercy" away to other agencies because other agencies don't have the spiritual clout to hold people spiritually accountable when they receive help.

When the poor come to Christ, they need to be discipled – and economic discipleship (personal financial stewardship principles) becomes a real part of that growth if their value systems are to be changed. Without that change of values, poor people still live only to survive, and not work to live for the future.

There are many models of how this can be worked out, and each congregation has to understand within their own context which ministries are best for them to own and what are best to give away. Some parachurch ministries are better than others in effectively working with the local church. However, I am not interested in supporting what become, in effect, substitute churches without the marks or components of a true church.

I have seen too much money wasted on these organizations in which they seem to say to the local church, "We can lead students to Jesus. We can lead children to Jesus. We can disciple men and women better than the local church can. We can give services to the poor. So give us your money and the volunteer man-hours of your members, but we won't demand any loyalty from the people we bring to Jesus to get involved in any particular church."

One of the marks of the church is a thing called discipline. "Discipline" is a much larger concept than the termination of someone's church membership when they refuse to repent of grievous sin. It begins with accountability though personal relationship. Without that loyalty, commitment, or accountability to the local church, discipleship is short-circuited. As a result, America continues on its slide into individual spirituality without building effective communities that can deal with local social issues.

Undermining God's Primary Institution

Foundations seem to love to support these non-church models, failing to realize they might share some responsibility for an undermining of the one institution God gave us for the spread of His Kingdom – and that is the local church.

Local churches can and have developed powerful learning centers, tutoring and mentoring programs, and schools. Local churches can and have developed housing ministries. Local churches can and have built clinics and hospitals. Local churches can and have developed job training and job placement ministries, savings and loan programs, and can certainly speak to issues of justice or injustice, all without becoming partisan political advocates and changing the true Gospel into a social gospel. I believe the implications of the Gospel among the poor are and must always have a social dimension. This is what happens when the community of love meets the community of need.

There is a time for the church to decide when to split these ministries off and make them self-governing, while trying to figure how to keep them loyal to their essential mission and not be competitors to the church. John Perkins told me once you should create separate 501c3 entities so they can sue or be sued, and you don't want the church involved in that. This seems like a sound, practical reason to me.

I am speaking here specifically about principles concerning relationships between churches and parachurch organizations, and not to the reality of good or bad management. Good management practices and financial accountability vary widely across the church and parachurch spectrum. Good and bad examples of management, however, aren't the thing that should sway us on the principle of whether we should create parachurch ministries.

At New City Fellowship we have spun off various non-profit parachurch ministries over the years. At first we created them and watched some of them break away from the spiritual and ideological control of the church. This often happened for funding reasons. The idea was that if you create wider governance, then more church, individuals and funding organizations would be able to support it. You can find some ideas as to what programs or ministries might be possible for a parachurch organization to pursue in Chapter 28, as well as some principles in development-type ministry.

Avoiding 'Ideological Drift'

New City could not possibly financially maintain by itself all of the ministries it created in such a way that they all could do an effective job. We clearly needed outside support. However, we also witnessed theological and ideological "drift" in some of those organizations. One problem was they had no outside referee or broker when there was conflict between their board and the director, or a means of appeal for their staff and leadership.

A faith-based non-profit that is not a church is constantly in a fund-raising life cycle. It has no natural support base, so it must find and maintain loyal donors. It has to spend a lot of energy on fund-raising. One of the easiest things for a non-profit ministry to do is "ministry." I am contrasting ministry activities here with actual life-changing development. Programs, "giveaways" and other one-time events that do things for lots of kids or people attract "funders." Non-profits need those funders if they want to survive fiscally and thrive as an organization.

My opinion is that a great deal of Christian money is wasted on helping non-profit ministries do "ministry" that will have no long-term results. Ministry within a congregation, however, is different because it is meant to be part of a lifestyle, a lifelong discipleship process (in short, life-on life-accountability). Planting a relevant and community-loving congregation might be harder, but it is a far better, more effective and, most important, a more Biblical strategy.

The Bible doesn't speak to or about parachurch or non-profit ministries. Obviously the institution that is mentioned in the Bible is the local church. This doesn't mean these organizations are sinful or wrong. However, from my experience I have heard too many founders and leaders of such organizations speak very cynically about the local church. I admit there are plenty of bad churches, but across-the-board criticism is not warranted and usually self-serving.

These non-profit ministries want support from local churches, but at the same time some of their leaders badmouth the church. With that kind of attitude so prevalent, it is hard for me to believe they really encourage the folks with whom they work to become part of a supportive and caring local church. If the church is the bride of Christ, then I don't think we should insult Christ by running down His bride every chance we get. If you love a man, don't diss his wife!

Non-profits can and ought to do meaningful economic and community development and stay away from the easy choice of "ministry activity." The problem is the Christian funding population thinks ministry is more Biblical than development, and to some donors it doesn't matter who does it.

Funds Spent to Raise Funds

Non-profit ministry activities certainly can create more splash and generate more publicity photos than the necessarily longer process of development. This in turn brings in more money, so a lot of non-profits are caught up in the money game, the never-ending cycle of raising funds. I am not accusing them of lacking integrity (although, along with some local churches, some do), but simply expressing concern about using funds that could be better spent.

Our New City Fellowship congregation eventually decided on a model whereby we would create separate legal entities but have 51% of the appointed board being NCF members. The directors would be members of the church and stay in close communication with the pastor and elders. Because of their unique relationship to the church, and without the leaders of the church engaging in any management of the organization, we were at times able to help these non-profits settle disputes, and even bail them out financially when hard times came.

We have never been embarrassed to ask for outside support of these non-profits since these ministries are not about enlarging New City or supporting its ministry as a congregation, but about helping the poor and the broader community. We knew our investment could be multiplied if we could recruit others to help in community ministry. This is something potential donors don't always understand right away – this might be because they are not accustomed to seeing congregations helping the broader community even when it doesn't directly benefit the church.

Missing Grassroots Opportunities

For a funding institution, such as a foundation or private trust, to declare they never give to local churches or even to the non-profits a local church has created, seems to be an admission of ignorance that they can't see differences between such organizations and how they operate. This may be a convenient excuse to step away from helping congregations active in their communities, but this also results in preventing the funding institution from helping the most grassroots of all organizations.

I'll admit it seems most churches exist for themselves, with their programs being built for their own people. This isn't to say such ministries are wrong or evil in any way, but most churches don't seek to build programs that reach out and minister to the broader community of the poor. Congregations loving their communities tend to bless the poor no matter where they go to church, even if they don't go anywhere.

We never felt NCF had a right to ask foundations or other churches to help us pay our pastor's salary, or pay for our chairs, hymnbooks, choir robes, or even help us in buying or enlarging our building. In principle, we felt these were matters for the members of the congregation to seek to pay for and support.

As for helping the poor, children, the youth, the sick, and immigrants in the broader community, however, we felt we not only had a right but also an obligation to ask the larger community (Christian and non-Christian) to help us. If another church became jealous of this initiative, they were welcome to establish their own programs (and we would have been glad to help them) or share in ours. I make no apology for inviting the poor to my church, since I know the Gospel they will find there is for their ultimate good.

It takes leadership – leadership that seeks wise and godly counsel – to know what, if and when such parachurch ministries should be created. This leadership has to hear and want to respond to the cry of the people, and not simply be building a personal empire for the pastor or director.

Sometimes these ministries begin because the Lord brings a gifted and burdened individual or couple that sees an area of need and wants to champion its cause through a congregation. At times these folks get frustrated with the slow-moving wheels of a church and choose to launch out on their own. We stress the need for accountability of leaders, and a good church provides that.

Leadership Mixed with Passion

Every community needs leadership and people of passion who will respond to the real and felt challenges of a neighborhood. Helping such leaders to receive the accountability and spiritual oversight they will need is important. If you are going to create a non-profit, we encourage you to do it right, with competence, and proper governance. There are many non-profits (probably too many), and some do not have good leadership, good management, or attentive and engaged boards to provide oversight. Many times these ministries seem to exist only to give the director a job or feed his or her ego, and as we have mentioned, they are constantly in need of funds.

Sadly, sometimes we see charismatic and gifted individuals who have no skill in administration or fund-raising that lead non-profits. This can be frustrating for them as well as for those who want to see them succeed. If they are humble enough to receive help, other gifted individuals can be brought alongside to give them the management and accounting help they desperately need.

If a church is going to create such an entity, it needs to make sure the director is not only competent but also has integrity; that board members will be well-trained and will be diligent in their oversight responsibilities; and that the church will help this new director and the board members to police the vision of the organization. "Policing the vision" means to keep the organization on track and stay in its own lane, and not to experience "mission creep," moving into competition with the ministries and purposes of the local church. Often this happens because someone thinks some new program will attract funds, but if it is not consistent with the purpose of the organization, it's a distraction.

Organizations created to help the poor, or deal with some challenge in the community, must always guard themselves from paternalism. The only effective way to do this is to make sure indigenous people from the community, acting as champions for the community, are full voting members of that board.

Wary of the 'Politics' Trap

Let me give a warning: If and when churches become "players" in their communities, by making an effective and positive economic and social impact, they can and do in fact become political. Even if they may not seek as an institution to sway politicians or government offices, politicians know which people and institutions carry weight and influence in a neighborhood. This is a byproduct of making a tangible impact in a community, of loving all the people. This kind of success speaks loudly to policy makers. It can also be a point of temptation that leads to various kinds of personal and organizational compromises.

Churches can protect their mission, integrity and prerogatives while being allies, partners, or merely co-belligerents with other organizations. It can create dependent or independent ministries to carry out works of mercy. This requires wisdom and skill, but there are many models of church-based, church-connected ministries from which to learn.

Some non-profit ministries have become very large, and sometimes it seems as if the "tail is wagging the dog" instead of the other way around. Often this happens because a non-profit might have a very charismatic spokesperson able to raise lots of money, or once the parachurch entity has been created it gains the ability to create income and become economically powerful through its programs.

Size, power, and money should not exempt individuals or organizations from accountability. Let me put it like this: The more charismatic you are, the larger you are, the more powerful your organization might be, then the more important it is for you to humble yourself to other leadership. We have seen examples of spokesmen becoming somewhat famous, well-known, and starting to pull away from local accountability. This can become spiritually dangerous for the individual – and the organization he or she leads.

Opportunities for Doing Good

There are many ways church members can do "good" in their communities. They can create, join and supervise any number of parachurch ministries. They also can deploy volunteers to all the social service and other Christian ministries in the community. Let me give an important caveat here: Lots of volunteer man-hours do not necessarily mean anything long-lasting has been accomplished. Churches and parachurch organizations should find a meaningful way for evaluating the quality, depth and longevity of their impact.

Church members can pursue employment in various social service or government agencies that affect their neighborhood, and strive to work unto the Lord in those settings. Individuals can become entrepreneurial and create businesses that in turn create jobs in marginalized communities, committing to give their employees fair and just wages.

Individuals can follow through on their commitments to the poor and the oppressed through political involvement by letting a Biblical worldview and life perspective direct them in their thinking and actions, as well as attempting to influence political organizations with those values. Church-created non-profits are one way the local church can stimulate and coordinate economic impact, and show tangible love to their communities.

Questions for Reflection and Discussion

1. What are some "church-connected" non-profits that you know about?
2. Which parachurch ministries are engaged in your community? Have you been involved with any of them?
3. What do you think should be qualifications for board members of parachurch non-profits?
4. What significant economic or social needs are not being met in your community, or in the community of need about which you are concerned?

CHAPTER 22

Who Is the Ministry For: Them, or Us?

"So when you give to the needy, do not announce it with trumpets, as the hypocrites do."

(Matthew 6:2, NIV)

A good pastor, I believe, should want to mobilize his people into ministry. Unfortunately, many churches only mobilize their members for congregation-focused ministries (the choir, parking volunteers, ushers, youth group, Sunday school, etc.) I concede as a pastor these are important and helpful. But if that is all the people of a congregation do, it can become irrelevant to its community and make it seem self-focused and hardhearted toward the poor.

One of the conflicts in Reformed churches today involves the passion for family ministry and the raising of their own children versus ministry to children from non-Christian homes. Many of these poor families from the community are single-parent led, or blended with various stepfathers and mothers. If a church is planted among the poor it must take for granted that it can no longer simply focus on its own children from Christian homes – not if it wants to reach the lost and impact its broader community. This inevitably creates tension, but one that some either overcome, seek to avoid, or let become divisive.

Many new church plants, especially those that have grown quickly and large, seem to want an image (if not an identity) that reveals they care about their city, community, and the poor. Many talk about "loving their city."

Some of these new churches have created very effective mobilization strategies through small groups, ministry teams, Sunday school class projects, missional communities, and other initiatives. Some of them have exhibited strong leadership in finding areas of service or places of need these teams can focus on. The question still remains, however, as to whether the activity is directed toward the discipleship of the poor, or simply a ministry opportunity for the volunteers?

It is important for all Christians to learn to serve, but it is far better for that service to be directed toward some specific goal rather than simply helping us to feel better about ourselves. It certainly seems a waste of time for church members and attendees to do lots of "ministry" while in reality deceiving them into thinking they are bringing about actual change.

We need to mobilize the Church—our church—into effective ministry. One of our goals in this book is to help you learn how to *mobilize* a congregation in the work of mercy ministry. This is always a challenge when the leaders of congregations sense the will of God and want to move a church in a new direction or renew an existing direction.

> ***Mobilization: Energizing a group to pursue a certain goal and helping them to put into action the people, plans and resources needed to accomplish that goal.***

It is important for the pastor and the leadership of a congregation to know that their ability to frame and express their vision, create a sincere desire, and inspire the congregation into the practice and ministry of mercy is crucial to success.

If there is no real vision for an effective practice of mercy, this will be just another item on a long list of items that we "should do, ought to do, and hope we get to do someday." Without a committed vision for mercy, it will not be something that changes the character of a congregation. We are writing with the expectation love and mercy ought to be part of a Christian's character – and the character of every faithful and true church of Jesus Christ.

We should want this mobilization to result in *effective* mercy ministry, not just a new organizational chart, new pamphlets, or new and catchy slogans. Effectiveness implies actually solving a problem or meeting a need.

Far too often we engage in producing repetitive activities that don't seem to move us very far ahead in accomplishing anything. Church activities often take lives of their own, becoming perpetual motion machines, typically with specific individuals and personalities that seem tied to them and insist on their continuation. They may have been started to accomplish a good purpose that might have become irrelevant or forgotten, but are now perpetuated because, "we have always done it that way."

Mercy seeks to eliminate the real need of hurting folks – healing the sick, feeding the poor and helping them to feed themselves, housing the homeless, giving hope to the hopeless, and not keeping people in perpetual need and dependence. Experience shows this is not easy. In fact, it is hard to do and will require *wisdom* from God to carry out properly and effectively.

Mobilization techniques are a beginning, but not an end!

If you are planting a church, or beginning a new emphasis on mercy, you might be wondering how to get all of your people into mercy or at least exposed to it. One way is to ask each small group or Sunday school class (if you have them) to adopt a mercy project one to four times a year.

The pastor, staff member, or church planter should research and suggest doable projects; such research should definitely be community-sensitive in understanding what the community thinks it needs. It would be good if each group can do the planning and preparation themselves, giving them the opportunity to buy in to it. Teach them to pray and work as a team to successfully pull off such a project.

Unfortunately, many churches end up simply letting their folks become "mercy tourists" without any long-term or effective involvement. So-called vision trips on the mission field are okay, but not good enough to accomplish missions in depth (which is to raise up indigenous leadership). Neither is allowing our members to cruise through a slum or ghetto, paint a house or two, and think we have accomplished anything of lasting value.

We need to move people from "mercy exposure" through "mercy tourism" to "mercy involvement," and eventually to "mercy accomplished." One the strengths of the modern Western (especially American) church is the ability to mobilize many of their people for mission trips or service projects. There are innumerable opportunities to help out parachurch organizations that are always in need of manpower, or even connect with a church in a distressed area both here in the United States and overseas. Youth groups and mission committees are able to generate thousands of dollars for these trips. For some people this is a once in a lifetime event; for others, it becomes something they try to do every year.

While this strategy can be helpful for exposing our church members to needy people, neighborhoods or even countries, the question arises as to whether this is an effective strategy to change the lives of the poor for the better? There are those who absolutely despise this strategy as wasteful, patronizing and confusing to the poor.

At the same time, it is not realistic to think sending churches are just going to simply write checks and forward the money to indigenous pastors and missionaries that are on the field for the long term, although some may have done that. For that kind of support to be sustained, there must be some personal involvement, some exposure to the work or the workers. An axiom of ministry says money follows people, and people will support what they are interested in and those with whom they have relationships.

If our ministry to the poor is to be more about them than it is about us, how do we get church members interested without causing disruption to those that will be recipients of their ministry? How can we help our members understand their few days of service are usually not going to make a significant difference while not discouraging their interest?

Yes, sometimes relationships formed on a service or mission trip prove to be life-transforming. There will be realizations and understandings about need, poverty and affliction that redirect a career path or vocation, or even the level of charitable giving toward significant development. The challenge is to approach these events as part of a process rather than as ends unto themselves.

It is imperative that we rely on indigenous leaders, on the wisdom of those who live in the places we think need help. It is important that churches, organizations, and ministries that receive outside help know how to control this outside invasion so it doesn't overwhelm or destroy their ministry and integrity. The money might look good, but sometimes it is better to refuse it than to be compromised, abused, or patronized by those who bring it.

There are those who teach that the poor, whether in the West or in other parts of the world, don't really need our money and probably don't need us either. Instead, they say, what they need are learned techniques, changes in values, maybe training in self-organization. While I can agree with some of these concerns, I am faced with the reality this is not primarily what Jesus teaches when talking about mercy.

EVEN WHEN IT IS COMPLICATED, we are not exempt from responding. Jesus seems to really go after all of us in our personal refusal (or simply neglecting) to help those in need. His teaching and rebukes come because of the neighbors we see who are in trouble that we simply pass them by. Whatever we do, we cannot escape Jesus' scrutiny in how each of us personally deals with the poor and the needy.

Does showing mercy to the poor profit us, or should it ever? Of course it profits us – and profits our churches when they show mercy. It profits our children in gaining a fuller understanding of their identity. Proverbs 19:17 says, *"He who is kind to the poor lends to the Lord, and he will reward him for what he has done."* There ain't nothin' wrong about being rewarded by the Lord!

Questions for Reflection and Discussion

1. How would you define "effective mercy" or "mercy accomplished"?
2. Is it ever right to "use" the poor, treating them as object lessons to help middle-class people learn about poverty? Why or why not?
3. Can poor people be effective teachers for Christians desiring to learn how to do mercy? If so, in what ways?
4. What would be some practical events or steps you can think of for mobilizing the people of your congregation into direct ministry to the poor or for them?

CHAPTER 23

Some Things You Are Going to Need

"Brothers, choose seven men from among you who are known to be full of the Spirit and wisdom. We will turn this responsibility over to them."

(ACTS 6:3)

TO DO MERCY WELL WE need wisdom, and this is one of the main qualifications for a deacon. When you go to select a deacon make sure you don't just ordain a "doer," someone who is always willing to set up chairs and lock the doors. That is the gift of "helps." That is a great gift and we need lots of helpers in the church. To do mercy well, let me say it again, we need wisdom and especially wisdom from God. Praise God, He invites us to ask for wisdom when we need it.

Our suggestion in this book is that wisdom in the ministry of mercy can be developed through learning some basic ***principles*** from Scripture and experience, then learning and studying ***methods*** to apply those *principles,* and then growing in ***skills*** to do mercy well. We also highly recommend ***prayer.***

Principles are the reasons you do things. Mercy ministry often exposes us to recurring or similar types of situations, even those often presented to us that seem to be unique problems. We can develop policies and guidelines to direct us, especially in recognizing and responding to typical kinds of situations.

These policies need to be based on some set of principles that will help us in becoming consistent and even-handed. We also need principles that align with our congregation's beliefs and standards, and protect the welfare of the church.

We shouldn't have to face each new situation with panic or subjective emotional responses (see chapter 23). We shouldn't have to keep responding to requests as if we were starting from scratch.

Methods are the strategies and organization we can develop to solve problems. These enable us to create solutions that are both proactive and programmatic.

Skills are what we need to develop in our officers and members so they can help people effectively without burning themselves out while helping others, or leaving them feeling frustrated. God-given spiritual gifts can be used in the ministry of mercy, but training and practice can help greatly in making us become more and more effective in this ministry.

Prayer. Scripture teaches us, *"If any of you lacks wisdom, he should ask God, who gives generously to all without finding fault, and it will be given to him" (James 1:5, NIV).*

We take it that the first deacon prototypes were men "full of the Holy Spirit and wisdom." So if our deacons or mercy workers need wisdom, they also need to learn to pray. I would hate to see someone read this book and think they could adequately deal with the poor and those in distress, or live in and minister in neighborhoods with lots of poor people, without praying and actively seeking the wisdom of God.

Without prayer being a part of our mercy ministry, we are declaring we can do it without God – and that would be a tragic mistake. Mercy is a spiritual work and must be spiritually pursued, which means it cannot be done without prayer.

For what should we pray? Pray for yourself; pray for your mercy workers; pray for the people to whom you extend mercy; pray for the positive impact of your deeds. Pray for your motives not to be misinterpreted, and pray for the right words to say – as well as the knowledge of when to keep quiet and listen.

We need to remember the more God-honoring our work and the more effective we are in proclaiming and living out the Kingdom of God, the more intense the spiritual warfare is going to get. The more we go into neighborhoods where real evil has had a long-time grip, the more opposition we are likely to experience, as we see in Ephesians 6:10-20.

This truly is spiritual warfare, so we must pray against the Devil and evil. We must pray for justice, and pray for hearts to be opened to understand the Gospel. Pray against your own pride and glory-seeking; pray against weariness in well doing; pray for the glory of God to be revealed by the good works of the Church.

For Reflection and Discussion

Make a prayer list of mercy concerns. Pray for:

- Poor people you know;
- Mobilization of your own congregation to be engaged in mercy ministry;
- Protection and blessing of deacons engaged with the poor;
- Creation of effective mercy and development strategies to really bring the poor out of poverty;
- Establishment of justice against the forces of oppression and injustice;
- That the people might see the love and glory of God.

CHAPTER 24

Principles of Effective Mercy Ministry: Know Why You're Doing What You're Doing

"The righteous care about justice for the poor,
but the wicked have no such concern."

(Proverbs 29:7, NIV)

We have already discussed the concept of mercy in Part Three of our book. We will review some of those principles here, as well as attempt to present some guiding ideas for establishing an on-going, effective work of mercy.

Mercy is our foundation for doing mercy.

Mercy is one of those attributes of God for which all Christians are and will be eternally grateful. It is what brought each of us into the Kingdom, and it is what restores and heals us.

Being a Christian means we are to be imitators of God – and that means for us to be Christ-like. To do that we cannot simply ask ourselves, "What would Jesus do?" This desire to imitate God cannot be accomplished by willpower or human effort, but as a result of saving and sanctifying grace – God's power that works within us.

God gives the supernatural power to walk and live like Christ, as well as the appetite for it in the heart of the true Christian. This transformation comes from what we call being "born-again," and happens only by the mercy of God. Our eyes are opened to see our need of a Savior, and by faith we come to Christ. All this is a work of God's mercy in us. We realize God loved us and gave Jesus to die for us, and His dying in our place is definitely a work of God's mercy.

Once we believe in Jesus, all our sins are forgiven, and the act of being forgiven is a work of God's mercy. Every time we fail to live as we should, we as Christians are able to come back to God and be forgiven, over and over again. All believers live constantly in the fountain of God's mercy. Mercy is the constant hope and sanctuary of the believer.

We are in constant need of mercy.

Who among us does not need forgiveness on a constant basis? If you are one who answers that question as if you were an exception, I suggest you run to God and ask Him for mercy so He won't kill you for your self-righteousness. In the parable of the Pharisee and the publican, Jesus wants us to be aware – like the publican – that we are people in need of constant mercy, "Lord, have mercy on me a sinner." My joy and hope in the midst of my personal need is the assurance God never, ever runs out of His divine mercy.

Mercy from us – evidence of a work of grace.

Every Christian is by definition someone who needed forgiveness and has received it. How dare we not offer mercy to others? Remember the parable of the unforgiving servant that I cited in chapter 15 (Matthew 18:21-35), as well as Matthew 25 (a passage we looked at earlier in a different context), which speaks of the separating of the sheep from the goats? These passages speak of the reward based on a lifestyle of mercy that is directed to Christ.

"Then the King will say to those on his right, 'Come, you who are blessed by my Father; take your inheritance, the kingdom prepared for you since the creation of the world. For I was hungry and you gave me something to drink, I was a stranger and you invited me in, I needed clothes and you clothed me, I was sick and you looked after me, I was in prison and you came to visit me.' Then the righteous will answer him, 'Lord, when did we see you hungry and feed you, or thirsty and give you something to drink: when did we see you a stranger and invite you in, or needing clothes and clothe you? When did we see you sick or in prison and go to visit you?' The King will reply, 'I tell you the truth, whatever you did for one of the least of these brothers of mine, you did for me'" (Matthew 25:34-40, NIV).

It is important to understand that Christians interpret this passage in view of the theology of the New Testament, which teaches salvation is by grace through faith and not by works. Notice this passage is not simply a list of duties that if you fail to do them you will be judged, though it is about judgment. The righteous response from the "sheep" is because they are doing something unto Christ. The whole passage assumes a relationship to Jesus. However, the theology of such a salvation is always evidenced by works. The notion that we can have a faith that produces no love or mercy in our life and practice leads to a self-justifying hypocrisy. That kind of religion is foreign to Jesus and the Bible, and it would not be wise to base your hope of salvation on it. I ask you to notice it again – Matthew 25 is a description of the coming judgment.

Mercy takes action.

You can't just feel mercy without showing it, or else it does no one any good:

"What good is it, my brothers, if a man claims to have faith but has no deeds? Can such faith save him? Suppose a brother or sister is without clothes and daily food. If one of you says to him, 'Go, I wish you well; keep warm and well fed,' but does nothing about his physical needs, what good is it? In the same way, faith by itself, if it is not accompanied by action is dead" (James 2:14-17, NIV).

Nice-sounding words, even an attitude of good intentions, but without action leaves the poor still hungry and cold. But at the same time, acts of mercy without love profit you nothing, the Scriptures teach:

"If I give all I possess to the poor and surrender my body to the poor and surrender my body to the flames, but have not love, I gain nothing" (1 Corinthians 13:3).

Mercy has an attitude.

Romans 12:8 teaches us to show mercy with cheerfulness:

"We have different gifts, according to the grace given us. If a man's gift is prophesying, let him use it in proportion to his faith. If it is serving, let him serve; if it teaching, let him teach; if it is encouraging, let him encourage; if it contributing to the needs of others, let him give generously; if it leadership, let him govern diligently; if it is showing mercy, let him do it cheerfully" (Romans 12:6-8, NIV).

It is interesting to me to find this passage in the Bible. I mean it seems intriguing to find "cheerfulness" being important for showing mercy. It seems obvious if we give charity with a spirit of bitterness, or feel like we are coerced to do it, then the recipient may be injured in their spirit. Poor people are still people, which means those in need have a God-given dignity, even though at the moment it may seem they are below us. This, of course, is an illusion:

"The poor man and the oppressor have this in common; the Lord gives sight to the eyes of both" (Proverbs 29:13, NIV).

"Rich and poor have this in common. The Lord is the Maker of them all" (Proverbs 22:2, NIV).

We are all created in the image of God, and therefore are all equally valuable to him. Many people find it difficult to receive help even when they absolutely need it. Some may even die before they ask for it. The part of their dignity that gives them a sense of shame because they can't make it by themselves can also make it hard for them to receive help from others. Some may call that pride, but sometimes it is a legitimate kind of self-respect.

It is wicked to purposefully make people feel bad when we deliver charity to them. I tell people not all of my deacons have the gift of mercy. Some are better at the role of administration in the overall scope of extending mercy. Those not gifted with mercy are not the ones I want to send to visit the sick in the hospital, as they just might make people feel worse. If you have the gift of mercy, the spirit in which you show it is very important.

Mercy is the credibility of love.

Love is the mark of the Church, and mercy ought to be our consistent response to need. We need attitude along with action, since both are important.

One of the accusations made by enemies of Christianity is that our acts of mercy are simply bribes to induce people to turn away from their traditional religion. Some Christians have seen the distribution of food or other acts of mercy only as a "door opener" to get to preach. Rescue missions have used this method for ages in getting people to listen to a Gospel message before receiving a meal.

It is important for us to understand mercy is valid in and of itself. It does not need to seek validation by accomplishing another goal. We don't show mercy to "bribe" sinners into listening to our evangelism. Mercy in Jesus' name, such as a simple act of giving someone a cup of cold water, gives *glory to God.* This means some of our ministry of mercy will never give us an opportunity to explain the Gospel. We might never get to take a person to the Scriptures and share the Gospel message. We may simply have to trust God to take our actions and use them as a conviction there is love on earth, there is goodness, and therefore we should give mercy freely and share it with freedom.

The ministry of mercy is not in competition with the ministry of the Word.

I am not attempting to diminish the need of everyone to come to faith in Christ. And I don't think deeds of mercy can ever replace the ministry of the Word of God. Yet we need to realize this: Mercy is mercy only if it is freely given – and not given with a price tag.

For me, this is explained by using the word "tension" more than the word "balance." I want to always feel the tension of wanting to explain the Gospel to someone, even if the circumstances dictate that what I have time for right now is only a material or physical response to their need. I have to trust God to create the timing and the right opportunity. We do believe the poor need to saved, as do all people. We do not believe, however, that mercy should ever be manipulative.

Gospel mercy does have a goal.

The ministry of mercy shows people the love of God. The ministry of mercy shows people our words of love have actual meaning. Since we pursue mercy as part of our respect for human beings as "whole beings" (not as either a body or a soul, but both), we care about the physical needs of folks and also care about their eternal destiny. The ministry of mercy ought to *seek faith,* since ultimate eternal benefits are impossible without faith. We never need to apologize for calling people to faith, but ought not to use mercy as a means of extorting faith or commitment.

The poor need faith if they are to do the hard work necessary to improve their economic condition. And they certainly need faith if they want to make it to heaven. There ought to be healthy tension between our concern to be merciful, and desire to be evangelistic. These things together, the showing of love and the preaching of love, ought to always be in our minds and hearts.

When congregations disperse all their people and resources into a community to "love the city," but never seek a return from mercy, never seek to bring people into the faith or into the church of Jesus Christ, then they do not fully love people.

Mercy responds to real need.

Mercy must respond to real situations and actual *circumstances of need.* Our churches need to know where our mercy programs or activities are leading. Are we clear on what are we trying to accomplish, or are we just doing things randomly, always *reactive* but never *proactive?*

Our goal should be to help people become *self-sufficient,* not dependent. This ought to affect our methods and policies. So as the leadership of the church begins to move toward doing something about the poor, reaching out with mercy to the community, it should be thinking in advance about how far, how much, how long, how intense, and for whom it will pursue this ministry.

What is the scope?

In analyzing what our church is going to do about mercy ministry, we must ask ourselves some questions: What is the *scope?* In other words, how broad an area or population will we seek to do mercy ministry in? When our NCF congregation finally acquired a church building, it was in a neighborhood new to us. We had been doing ministry throughout the inner city in

Chattanooga for years. We had concentrated work in the area near the old YMCA building where we had worshipped in for about 13 years, but now we were in a totally new neighborhood.

By this time we had realized we needed to concentrate our efforts if we wanted to make more of an impact on the community. Our leadership decided to focus on the census tract area surrounding our church building. We would focus evangelism and ministry programs there and make the people around the church building a priority for both mercy and development ministries.

What is the intensity?

What is the *intensity*? How much effort will we put into mercy ministry as a church in terms of money, time, personnel and resources? Since we started our ministry as an inner city Sunday school, we already had a commitment to poor people. We knew we could not operate the way many congregations did, where our focus would be on ourselves – *our* building, *our* music ministry, and so on.

We began with an outward focus (long before the word "missional" became popular) and have never wanted to surrender that attitude and spirit. This meant we would put money in the budget to help poor people in the community – and not just for those who were in our congregation. We eventually created the position of Full-Time Deacon so we would have a staff member who could focus on mercy needs. In doing this, we determined our ministries of mercy would need to have certain level of intensity if we were going to be fruitful in our ministry to the poor.

What is the depth?

What is the *depth*? How far will we go, and how long will we work with individual cases? It quickly became obvious how each case needing help could lead us into a labyrinth of complex need. Some poor people are generationally poor; their needs are deep and as a result, cannot be solved quickly or easily. People coming in for help present a varied set of challenges: illiteracy, brain damage, addiction issues, legal concerns, multiple relationships of parenting and children, transient in housing, indebtedness, chronic illness, and other problems.

The cultural value system of many poor people resists simple middle-class slogans and concepts about how to plan for tomorrow, save money, or delay self-gratification. Some people haven't figured out that one key way for not going deeper into a hole is to stop digging. We had to come up with policies that would protect our deacons, staff and church resources from simply enabling people in their bad habits, or depleting our resources so quickly we couldn't help other folks.

Strategic innovation is required.

One of the wonderful things about poor people coming into the church, becoming regular in worship and becoming members, is they become real members of the Christian community. We get to know them, and they get to know us. We observe their character and begin to see their potential.

Drawing from personal relationships that begin and grow is the opportunity for wealthier members of the church to funnel resources to individuals in order to make a strategic difference in their lives.

One of the first men in my life that I knew to be an elder (Mr. Ferguson) came up to me in church one day and handed me a bag of books. They were Christian books designed for youth and captured my imagination. (I believe it was a series called the "Sugar Creek Gang.") A few years later, another elder came up to me and said one day the following week he would come by my house to give me a bike, the first I ever had. I had to learn to ride it, having never been on a bike before, and used it to get over to the church quite often. This same elder would often give me new clothes from his men's clothing store and actually gave me my first real part-time job in that store.

I received a college education through the generosity of a wealthy man. I was given my first two cars by another wealthy man, and my tuition for seminary was paid by yet another wealthy man. All of these were "strategic interventions" in my life. Since then I have tried to pay it forward, buying the first suit of clothes for several young men; raising money for various African and African-American students to go to college; trying to open a door of opportunity for various people whenever I could. These all came about due to relationships in the church. And because they were personal, all those involved could see and measure the results. Their investments paid off.

Questions for Reflection and Discussion

1. From this chapter, what are some of the principles of mercy mentioned?
2. What is the "scope" of your own church's mercy ministry?
3. What does "strategic intervention" mean? How would you define it? What does it look like?
4. If you had $100 right now to use for mercy, how best could you use it?

CHAPTER 25

The Decapitated Chicken

"Good will comes to him who is generous and lends freely, who conducts his affairs with justice. Surely he will never be shaken; a righteous man will be remembered forever. He will have no fear of bad news; his heart is steadfast, trusting in the Lord."

(PSALMS 112:5-7, NIV)

FAR TOO MANY TIMES I have visited congregations whose deacons felt each time a person presented a need, they (the deacons) were running around like a chicken with its head cut off. Decapitated chickens still running around are a sight to behold, but they don't accomplish much. Poor people often present themselves to us as having an emergency, and this starts the deacons running: This person needs to pay their rent or they will be evicted. Their lights or heat are about to be shut off. They are out of food. There's no gasoline to get to work, on and on. The feeling is that we must hurry to meet this immediate need.

Some churches seem to act as if these problems have never occurred before and as a result, have no preset ideas for how to deal with them. Usually this means the few deacons available are asked to figure out solutions quickly, usually "off the cuff." Inevitably, they get caught in situations where they don't have the checkbook, the key to the pantry, the knowledge, authority, or time to provide help.

If this happens enough times it leads to resentment from those leaders who seem burdened with the responsibility but who have no plan. They begin to feel guilty, angry for being interrupted in their schedules, and then the blame-shifting begins.

Having a 'Go-to Guy'

Sometimes churches have a "go-to guy" who always handles things. Then he dies, moves, or gets disgusted. In any event he is no longer there to solve the problems. One way many churches have decided to deal with these things is to just say "no." They either consciously or unconsciously make the statement, "We don't help with those type of things." Other churches have tried to always say "yes," and then simply become yet another agency that habitual beggars learn to manipulate to keep themselves going. Unfortunately, this kind of benevolence seldom leads to any permanent change for the poor. One of the most effective things a mercy committee or group of deacons can do is to create an *SOP* – a Standard Operating Procedure. A set of policies that serves as a guide for decision-making is very helpful to the church secretary, the pastor, and the deacons. (We will give more details on this subject in Part Five of this book.)

To establish these policies, it is necessary to agree on what the church is trying to achieve in its mercy ministry. This takes us back to what we discussed earlier: Intensity, Depth, and Scope. It is also necessary for the deacons to know how much money they have to spend over the course of the year, as well as a sense of what kind of help they can provide in each given month.

Deacons, please ask yourselves some questions! Who will handle walk-ins? How will you direct inquiries when someone asks if you can pay a bill for them? Who is prepared to move to (or discuss) the spiritual need of people when they present a physical one? These are all important questions, so we suggest those in leadership of the church decide in advance what you will do and will not do, for whom, by whom, and how it will be done.

Some good things you may decide not to do because some other agency or ministry is available to do them, or because you are going to focus on what no one else is providing. We believe in working cooperatively, but not in such a way as to deprive us of direct witness and ministry to poor people who come to us for help.

It is so much easier to do the work of mercy as a congregation when these questions have been thought out and prayed over. In this way, when a case seems overwhelming you already have some boundaries regarding how much, how long, and how far you can go. There are always exceptions, and this is why the deacons work as a group. When one person or situation seems like an exception to the stated policies, then the whole group of deacons, or a designated committee, should help in coming to a solution together.

If exceptions are needed, let the group pray over it and arrive at a group decision. Many problems are repetitive, however, so a good set of policies protects deacons from having to call a lot of unnecessary meetings. Deacons can and should refer to the pastor or elders whenever they need additional help.

Understand Your Limits

Remember this: It is self-defeating to assume you have no limits for how many people you can help, or how big an area you are responsible for serving. This is just not wise. Agree on your area, select your target, and do something meaningful within those boundaries. You can always enlarge as you get better at doing the work of mercy, and if your available resources increase. It is better to be successful at something small and limited at the beginning than attempting too much too soon, resulting in feeling overwhelmed, eventually leading to failure.

Our prayer ought to be for our people to be ready to move when a situation of need comes before them. We need to be like the Good Samaritan who, when he saw a need, took action. *Readiness* is affected by good preaching, by good training, and by a clear vision of what is possible. The vision of what is possible should be something the congregation's leadership can articulate.

We can want to be "ready," but without training we cannot rise to the occasion. One of my favorite quotes comes from a film character portrayed by Denzel Washington: "There is no such thing as tough. You are trained or you are un-trained" (from the movie, "Man On Fire").

We may want to do the right thing but sometimes pursue it in the wrong way and end up doing damage. We may want to be generous, but handing out cash to alcoholics and crack addicts really is not helping them. We have even learned giving a box of groceries to known addicts is not very helpful, since we found them selling the food we just gave them in the alley behind the church.

Not only is the right desire necessary, but also the right method, with the right skill, performed in the right Spirit. All of these are important. The *Holy Spirit* can give us the *wisdom* that we need, and we should ask Him for it.

Questions for Reflection and Discussion

1. Who in your congregation is designated to speak with and handle those coming to the church for financial help?
2. Is there a known or posted schedule for when people needing assistance may come to the church?
3. Are your church officers and members ready and willing to pray with folks who come by and need help, even if they can't give them financial help?

Part Five:

Building A Working Framework

CHAPTER 26

Developing Policy

"Suppose one of you wants to build a tower. Will he not first sit down and estimate the cost to see if he has enough money to complete it?"

(LUKE 14:28, NIV)

HERE ARE SOME QUESTIONS TO ask yourself as you prepare policies and programs to help the needy. Some of these may sound really basic and simple, but they might help reveal what your church actually believes as expressed in and through its present policies:

1. Will we provide help to our own members when they ask for it?
2. Who can they go to with their requests? Do they know whom to ask?
3. Can we meet a need even without someone asking for help, if it comes to our attention?
4. Will we help walk-ins, relatives of members, or neighborhood people? What is our defined area of neighborhood and where does it end?
5. Will we provide emergency food, have a food pantry, or give out food vouchers to an area food bank? Do we provide

food for those in the congregation that are sick, injured, or recovering from childbirth?

6. When can requests be accepted? Will we take requests at any and all times, or only on Sundays, during office hours, after business hours, or on designated evenings?
7. What staff will handle those requests? What processes will they use, or do we refer them to the deacons for another appointment or visit?
8. Who will have the ability to pay these bills – the church secretary, full-time deacon, or volunteers on certain days and at specified hours?
9. Will you hand out cash? (The answer to this should be "no.")
10. Will you use an application process? Will you maintain a database?
11. Can you do background checks or research for determining whether this is a scam, or a request that has already been met by another church or agency?
12. Will you create institutional relationships to expedite solving problems, such as an arrangement with a local grocery store, gas station, utility companies (where you can just make a call and promise to pay a bill, or prevent a shut-off or have service restored), or emergency housing shelters?
13. How many times a week, month, or year will you give the same kind of help to a person?
14. How much money will you spend on a member each year, or on a non-member?
15. What is your "next step" when you begin working with someone who needs your help? Will you refer them to worship services, Bible studies, job training, job opportunities, social worker counseling or other helpful resources?
16. Will you commit to supplement persons that will never be able to fully support themselves, such as a widow, elderly or disabled person? How often and how long will you commit to do this?

We suggest you answer these questions and write them down. These then can help create your policies. We suggest you train on your policies, and that each officer of the church have a copy and review them at least once a year. Policies are not good at all if you refuse to refer to them or won't use them once you have created them. It is amazing how things smooth out once everyone knows there is a routine that can be followed. Not every "emergency" presented by someone in need has to become *your* emergency if you are prepared to solve such problems.

What follows are some of the policies written for and by the Deacons of New City Fellowship.

PRIORITIES OF ASSISTANCE (FROM FIRST TO LAST IN ORDER):

1. Church members who are in regular attendance.
2. Church members generally.
3. Regular attendees.
4. Families of church members.
5. Involved or associated with a specific ministry of New City, e.g., Hope for the Inner City, Sunday school, Bible studies, Youth Group, Children's ministry.
6. People who live in the neighborhood of the church.
7. Neighbors of our members.
8. Sister churches, either through Presbytery or local church associations.
9. Referrals from supported urban ministries of the church.
10. Referrals from Christian or government agencies.
11. Call-in or walk-in requests. (Set limit of assistance, screened for need, exceptions can be made to policy by a vote of the Deacons.)
12. Providential encounters – members meeting someone in distress.

DETERMINE THE LEGITIMACY OF NEED, QUESTIONS THAT NEED TO BE ASKED AND ANSWERED:

1. Who is asking for help? Are they eligible under our policy?
2. Is this a real emergency? Is there an underlying problem that will make it happen again? What is the best way to help them?
3. Will helping the immediate problem create more problems for them, or for the church?
4. Is the problem self-induced? Is it better for them to bear the consequences of their behavior?
5. Is intervention necessary no matter whose fault it is?
6. Can we help enough to make sure the problem doesn't keep happening?
7. Does this person have their own resources, or other options? Can they get help from family, their home church, or another agency?
8. Are they telling the truth? Can we verify it?
9. Is the person hostile or threatening?

NOTE: Hostility or threats are grounds for immediate denial of help; intimidation, coercion, or manipulation should be confronted and rejected. Please be wise in the context of the confrontation. Speak gently and sweetly, but firmly. Call the authorities if you need to do so to protect yourself or the church.

CONFIRMING LEGITIMACY and preventing duplication in services: Some cities and communities are tied together in a sharing of data to prevent people from going from one church to another to obtain the same kind of help. There are various kinds of computer programs or networks to help churches and agencies link up when providing help to people. Obviously if our attitude is more fear than faith, we become obsessed with protecting ourselves from ever believing the lies of a con artist. However, it doesn't really help the truly needy if those who are thieves and liars are getting all the resources because they know how to con the system.

If your community has an area Food Bank or some kind of link system, we suggest you tie into it. This only works if you use it when people apply for help, and if you add data to it. So if someone is told they can get a food voucher from your church or site, but nowhere else in town during that month, then this helps prevent a duplication of service. At New City we use a voucher system with the area Food Bank so people can get a substantial amount of food, and then our church pays into the system for each person we send with a voucher. We also have a food pantry so we can give food to anyone at any time if the situation requires it.

To use these kinds of systems, people usually have to present some form of identification. If you have a relationship with people over a period of time they may very well need a regular kind of supplement to their resources. We strongly suggest you combine continued counseling along the way with these folks to see how you can move them to self-sufficiency, although for some folks the economy, their abilities, or circumstances may make them eligible for your continued help for a long time.

We have spoken of the need to have policies. Policies help to move the ministry of mercy in a congregation from simply reacting to thinking proactively, and creating programs that consistently help in meeting needs. There is more discussion of policy principles in Chapter 27.

Another reality of the dynamic of church life is the turnover of personnel that carry out various functions. Sometimes when ministry is simply "personality-driven," the history or memory of how things have been done leaves with the "personality" when they leave. This is why formal policies need to be written down.

To train new leaders and ministers and channel the energy of workers in effective ministry, it helps to have stated and proven policies. It is good to develop "continuity books" so future deacons will know how things get done. You might want to store these in the church office. Every time there is a change in leadership, make sure the new leaders get to read them and add to them as needed while they are doing ministry.

We have shared some policies that were developed by New City Fellowship. However, each congregation is unique; some policies are probably already in operation in your church, even if they have not yet been written down.

As stated earlier, policies keep you from facing each situation as if it were the first time you have ever encountered this question. It protects the pastor and deacons from panic or confusion, trying to come up with quick, spontaneous solutions. There are such things as emergencies, but is interesting to see how good policies make such emergencies less frequent and easier to deal with. Hasty reactions can sometimes create more problems than they solve.

There are many things to learn in helping people cross-culturally, especially when the help will involve economic aid. Poverty has a culture and value system all its own, one that is important to understand so we don't waste time condemning people because they don't think and act as we think they should. Even though they may not always be obvious, there are reasons for their behavior.

Questions for Reflection and Discussion

1. In reading over the "Priorities of Assistance," which of those would seem to be applicable to your congregation, and which should you eliminate?
2. Are there any priorities you think you should add, and if so, where would they fit?
3. What "next steps" could you plan, organize and offer to someone who comes to you for assistance again after you have already provided help for them?
4. What process can you implement to train and retrain your church leadership in assistance policies?

CHAPTER 27

Analyzing the Need

"Elisha replied to her, 'How can I help you? Tell me, what do you have in your house?' "

(2 KINGS 4:7)

CHURCHES NEED TO DEVELOP TOOLS by which they can *analyze* and even foresee what kind of economic problems folks will have. If we keep giving groceries when people need jobs, we are missing the mark. Soup kitchens feed people, and hungry people need to eat, but we should not be feeding the same people year after year if we can help them feed themselves.

Churches can help themselves if they can analyze folks as groups, because different categories of people tend to have common needs. Widows are a category, as are single-parent moms, fatherless children, unemployed men and women, the physically disabled, mentally challenged, refugees, undocumented immigrants, illiterate individuals, folks returning from prison, and those struggling with addictions. These are all categories of folks for whom programs and strategies can be created.

We need to know what is really going on around us if we want to help in the most effective ways. Do we know very much about our own members, or about the community that surrounds the church? A good *demographic study* from census statistics can help us. The local government usually has marketing data and other facts they use in city planning. Some criminal justice agencies actually have a count of how many prison inmates return to a community every month. Some city governments have departments designed to specifically help neighborhoods. They usually are pleased to help a church that is active in its own community.

You need *data.* Do we know how many widows are in our congregation, who they are, and what their needs are? Are there any single-parent families in the church, and do they have any special needs? How are we dealing with the disabled? We need good information and ought to be asking these kinds of questions. Members often assume the pastor knows all this, but usually he doesn't. He needs help, so if he does ask these questions he needs to know whom to ask and what information will be available.

If you have a full-time mercy worker, full-time deacon, or a church social worker (I love the idea of churches having trained Christian social workers that can work with the deacons), hopefully they will have a database. A computer will help, and new data needs to be entered consistently so the mercy worker will know how often a certain person has come back for help. It might even be necessary to follow a person's case over several years.

As you pray for them, providing help when you can and denying help if and when you must, you should still encourage them and invite them into the body of Christ. Over the years you will see a profound Gospel impact among some of these folks.

Building the Data

You will need information from both the neighborhood and the congregation. It might help to do a survey to gather data. Before you begin to do this, try to think through what you need to know and why you need to know it. If you are not going to do anything with the information, then you probably shouldn't even begin to take a survey. Tell the people why you are asking for information and what you hope to gain from it.

Ask yourself, "Will people actually answer these questions?" If you simply hand out forms and ask people to turn them in, your response will be fairly low. It is better to personally ask people, do a phone survey, or spend a class time where you all work on it together. Select a few reliable people who will collate the responses. Have a group analyze the questions before writing them so you can avoid confusion and incoherence. Once you gather the answers, have a group collectively look at the answers to see if you understand what the people meant when they answered.

Try to use several methods for gathering information in your survey: Questions requiring yes or no, multiple choice, and sentence answers that together will give you a reasonable chance at knowing what people are saying. It is amazing how difficult it can be to achieve clear communication. You do not want to communicate negatively by asking silly, misleading, or nosey questions. Don't imply world change or even a complete neighborhood makeover with your questions. The act of surveying itself can be a form of community building if done in a positive manner.

Community Survey

In the very first data block, decide if the respondent to a community survey should be known or anonymous. For some neighborhood surveys you don't need names, just general information. If you are using the survey to identify specific household needs, then of course you will want the names and addresses of the people who live in the house. Tell them why you want to know about them, assuring them that you are deciding on how best to help the community.

Get opinions on what the people of the community think is needed, as well as what they think the church should do about it. Ask what they would be willing to do to help the community, and ask what community resources they think are available. Even poor neighborhoods can have pride and do have community assets, even if they are limited. You can build on those assets.

Follow up and share results. They might be interested to know what others in the area think are the needs. Be certain to keep an individual's answers and their needs confidential.

Congregational Survey

In conducting a congregational survey, the question arises again: Should people providing data be known or anonymous? Usually, for the church you will want to know the names of those who turn in the survey.

Look for information such as: Are they a widow, single parent, have no father in home, or low income? Do they need employment, transportation, handicapped access to church, care for elderly family members or children, medical insurance or preventative care, repairs to home, appliances, knowledge or where to go for certain kinds of help, or supplemental food?

Also, ask respondents for information about their own resources: What can they do to help others, what do they have to share, both materially and in terms of skills and talents? Use this information to create a resource bank, to create care committees, and to create targeted programs.

Church members may have specific concerns for the neighborhood of the church because they live in it, or because of things they notice. This may be the beginning of an idea about what needs to be done and will signal the willingness of someone to take action on it.

Questions for Reflection and Discussion

1. Can you define what the phrase, "felt need," means?
2. What do you think "asset-based development" means?
3. How many widows do you personally know in your congregation?
4. Can you list the names of any fatherless children in your congregation?

CHAPTER 28

Creating Structure To Meet Needs

"We want to avoid any criticism of the way we administer this liberal gift. For we are taking pains to do what is right, not only in the eyes of the Lord but also in the eyes of men."

(2 CORINTHIANS 8:20-21, NIV)

A CONGREGATION CAN *STRUCTURE* AND *program* ministry under officers or committees to meet the needs of these groups of people. If they have the resources, they can hire staff for mercy ministry – and the more impoverished the community is that surrounds the church, the more I encourage churches to staff for mercy ministry.

New organizations can be birthed out of churches (as we spoke about in Chapter 19 concerning non-profits and para-church organizations), such as community development or economic community development corporations. In addition, churches can expand their resources through coalition building. They can use their denomination, local networks, foundations, even government as coalition partners.

We recognize there are different views of church government. No matter what your congregational organization is, you can plan and develop instruments – such as teams, committees, staff – for mercy.

In the Presbyterian Church in America (PCA) we have a Book of Church Order that directs what our officers are to do. This does not mean our officers always do what our standards direct. Pastors need to be trained in how to train deacons. (Remember that quote from the movie, "Man on Fire": "There is no such thing as tough. You are either trained or you are untrained.")

One of our deacons gets a call in the middle of the night that one of the families we carry to church on Sunday just had their pipes break over a cold winter's night. The pipes are under the house, and the slumlord is indifferent. The deacon gets the tools, along with a portable light, and in the freezing cold crawls in the mud to repair those pipes – in the name of Jesus.

For Presbyterians, deacons have a different ministry than elders. We have Teaching Elders that people usually call "Pastor" (or Reverend, minister or clergy). We have Ruling Elders, usually laymen, who are to govern the church. The elders are to spiritually govern the church, and if there are no deacons, then they must do the ministry of mercy as well.

In the PCA, deacons are described and given their task in the Book of Church Order. I want to list some of the sections of Chapter 9 that apply directly to this discussion of structure for helping the church to do mercy. Notice especially the first lines of 9-2:

Chapter 9
The Deacon
9-1. The office of deacon is set forth in the Scriptures as ordinary and perpetual in the Church. The office is one of sympathy and service, after the example of the Lord Jesus; it expresses also the

communion of saints, especially in their helping one another in time of need.

9-2. **It is the duty of the deacons to minister to those who are in need, to the sick, to the friendless, and to any who may be in distress.** It is their duty also to develop the grace of liberality in the members of the church, to devise effective methods of collecting the gifts of the people, and to distribute these gifts among the objects to which they are contributed.

They shall have the care of the property of the congregation, both real and personal, and shall keep in proper repair the church edifice and other buildings belonging to the congregation. In matters of special importance affecting the property of the church, they cannot take final action without the approval of the Session (board of elders) and consent of the congregation.

In the discharge of their duties the deacons are under the supervision and authority of the Session. In a church in which it is impossible for any reason to secure deacons, the duties of the office shall devolve upon the ruling elders. (Notice here what I said earlier – that if there are no deacons, the ministry of mercy must be picked up by the elders.)

9-3. To the office of deacon, which is spiritual in nature, shall be chosen men of spiritual character, honest repute, exemplary lives, brotherly spirit, warm sympathies, and sound judgment.

(I have omitted paragraph 4 as it is not necessarily relevant to our discussion here.)

9-5. Deacons may properly be appointed by the higher courts to serve on committees, especially as treasurers. It is suitable also that they be appointed trustees of any fund held by any of the Church courts. It may also be helpful for the Church courts, when devising plans of church finance, to invite wise and consecrated deacons to their councils.

9-6. The deacons may, with much advantage, hold conference from time to time for the discussion of the interests committed to them. Such conferences may include representatives of churches covering areas of smaller or larger extent. Any actions taken by these conferences shall have only an advisory character.

9-7. It is often expedient that the Session of a church should select and appoint godly men and women of the congregation to assist the deacons in caring for the sick, the widows, the orphans, the prisoners, and others who may be in any distress or need. *(Note: Some congregations call the women who help the deacons, deaconesses.)*

Deacons Address People's Needs

If there are deacons, like the example of those seven men in Acts 6 who were chosen to help widows and serve tables, then the deacons can serve the needs of the people. Far too often, deacons have been left to worry about cutting the grass and turning off the lights in the church building while poor people have no one to care for them.

Mercy is an important assertive arm of the church in terms of being proactive in our communities. Too often we have left this service to personal choice, chance, and charisma (giftedness). The church can use this great office of deacon (and the members of the church whom they can mobilize and lead) to make a powerful social impact for Jesus Christ and demonstrate the love of Christ in a very personal, practical way.

Guidelines for Meetings

Meetings are both the worst and (I almost said "best") things about being a church officer: the actual getting together to discuss issues, make decisions, and hopefully, pray over things. What ought to be a joy, however, can become a joy-stealer, and sometimes a cause for real discouragement and an inhibitor to the retention of qualified leadership. I don't think anyone becomes a church officer because they like going to meetings.

It gets worse when meetings are boring, dominated by one or two personalities, filled with argument and contention, and never seem to end. It is ironic that some of the people who actually do most of the talking and make meetings difficult are the first to complain about them.

Among Presbyterians, the problem of misusing meeting times is a concern for both elders and deacons. The genius of the system of Presbyterianism is that lay people get to hold power and make decisions. Another positive aspect is officer groups are supposed to get a lot of their work done via committee, or subcommittee. Many churches never seem to grasp this concept, however, and make every meeting a "committee of the whole" for every issue. This is a waste of time.

I am afraid some very good deacons and elders have found their wives and children really don't appreciate how much time is stolen from them due to "church business." It is important for church officers to have the enthusiastic support of their families in what they do, or else they won't do it for very long.

For this reason I would like to give a few suggestions about meetings:

- Keep meetings SHORT, SPECIFIC, and SPIRITUAL.
- Have absolutely no more meetings than you actually need.
- Always start a meeting on time, rewarding those who show up on time and not those who are late.
- Have someone assigned to prepare an agenda, think through the time commitments to actually fulfill the agenda, eliminate or postpone what will exceed your budgeted meeting time to accomplish, and stick to the agenda.
- Try to assign detail work to subcommittees, commissions, or a task force.

- Try to have subcommittees or moderators present items for decision in written form, or even introductory discussion, prior to the "decision" meeting.
- Try to never have large, expensive, or large-impact decisions made in the first meeting in which they are introduced. If they are, the meeting will usually take too long in order to come to a wise decision.
- Large groups of people are better at making a "yes" or "no" vote, if they have been given previous time to consider things and pray.
- When doing business, officer groups should be asked to make a "yes" or "no" decision and not to mull, ponder, or think out loud about an issue on the spur of the moment. Try never to have the entire officer group prepare a decision from scratch.
- If you want a theological or substantive discussion, put that on the schedule without the pressure of a decision to follow immediately after.
- Moderators should make sure that during a discussion, once an opinion has been given and someone else begins to echo the same opinion, let the group know that idea has been heard and move on.
- Establish end-of-meeting times, or "order of the day" as it is sometimes called, and be diligent in keeping the promise to end each meeting at that time.
- Deacons should attempt to have charity or mercy decisions about individuals or families made primarily by subcommittees. Once a financial level is reached where the whole group must act, have the subcommittee prepare a briefing sheet and arrive with a specific recommendation. Don't simply engage in freewheeling discussion. Instead, move toward a decision.

- If assigned deacons say, "We don't know what to do," create an ad hoc committee to consider the issue and come back with a recommendation. Recommendations for decision are what make meetings function well.
- Seek to have someone always follow up on action decisions to see if the action was taken, and mark deadlines by establishing dates. At the next meeting, announce when the action was taken. I believe this is what "Old Business" on the agenda used to mean, a report of what action was taken from a previous decision.
- Try to have regular joint meetings with elders and deacons to consult on ministry activity, or at least written reports from the deacons to the elders.
- Don't use meetings to complain about the other officer group. If you need communication ask for it, but don't let individual officers use meeting times to vent their frustrations.
- Always seek to have "spiritual" meetings. This means having times of prayer, personal sharing, devotion, and encouragement.
- Make sure all officers are presented with opportunities for training and re-training. Holding an office for years doesn't mean you are being re-trained. Having the humility to receive additional training periodically will keep you from being proud or lazy about your responsibilities.

Creating a Deacons Bank

When New City Fellowship was still fairly small and meeting in an old YMCA building, it became obvious we had more mercy needs to meet than we could handle. Many of these were for people within the congregation, and at times we simply ran out of benevolence funds. It occurred to me then we were in partnership with other congregations in our city that had a lot more money than we did. Their pastors were my friends and gave every indication they approved of our work.

I am a Presbyterian, but at that time our regional governing body had no structure for helping various member congregations unless it was a direct appeal to the Presbytery. They had no funds set aside for mercy purposes, either for pastors who were members of Presbytery, congregations, or other kinds of needs. Several of the congregations in Chattanooga began to discuss the rolc of deacons and how we could help the poor. This included one or two congregations that were not in the PCA.

I proposed we create a "Deacons Bank" that would allow congregations to withdraw funds as needed to help with mercy situations among their church members. I remember speaking to one leader of a wealthy congregation on Lookout Mountain, Tennessee. I told him, "We have something you need and you have something we need. Maybe we could make a deal?" He asked, "What do you have that we need?" I responded, "Poor people." We made the deal.

It was set up so that any member congregation could have their deacons make a request in writing to the bank administrator, who then would ask the other churches to honor that request. Eventually a bank account was set up so the administrator could write a check up to a specified maximum amount to any church in the Deacons Bank that asked. It was stipulated each church had to spend their own funds first, and never ask the Bank to do something they wouldn't first attempt to do on their own.

Inter-Church Cooperation

This was really an amazing example of inter-church cooperation. Eventually this Bank was assumed into a new Permanent Committee of the Tennessee Valley Presbytery. Permanent committees are, as they sound, permanent – a fairly limited group of committees that regularly report to Presbytery.

In the Tennessee Valley Presbytery, the Mission to North America Committee got tired of me asking them to stretch their mandate from church planting to help those churches ministering to the poor. They suggested I ask to start a new permanent committee on mercy and establish our own budget. I have a great Presbytery, and they didn't hesitate a moment in creating this new committee. We tried to find examples to model after, but only one or two Presbyteries in the PCA had anything like it.

To my surprise, one of the first requests for help from that committee was not from my own congregation. I fully expected New City to make good use of these mercy funds, and surmised most of the other Presbyters thought that was my scheme. However, one of the teaching elders in our Presbytery had fallen into huge debt from medical bills. The Mercy Committee was able to help him get out from under that debt.

The Mercy Committee, like the Deacons Bank, never allowed itself to usurp the role of an individual church diaconate (board of deacons). Each church first had to do its own ministry, and then it could ask us to supplement or continue what they were doing through their agency.

This committee went on to create a matching fund for adoptions. Any member congregation giving one of their member families a grant up to $500 for an adoption would have it matched by the Presbytery. They would also come to "license" mercy ministries within the bounds of the Presbytery for member churches to support. The committee also gave annual support to the widows of teaching elders and retired ministers in need.

During times of natural disaster, this Mercy Committee has helped mobilize our Presbytery for significant responses around the country. It gave our Presbytery a personality of compassion and readiness to respond in times of need. I am so very thankful and proud of them.

Constant Battle With Dysfunctionality

As we were developing New City Fellowship, it was obvious we were interacting with children from very dysfunctional situations. Many families were broken, with only a mom, maybe having had children by several different men, or the kids being raised by a grandmother. Sometimes there was a "live-in" boyfriend in the home, and sometimes these were very temporary relationships.

Some of the children we met had moms that were drunks, and later more and more women and men became addicted to crack cocaine. It is hard to adequately describe the devastation caused by the crack epidemic in the inner cities of America, not only from addictions and the extremes people would go to feed their habit, but also by the prison sentences that deprive children of their parents.

This reminds me of an article I read from a book series in my seminary library. It was the history of missions and described urban missions in the slums of New York City at the end of the 19th century. It especially described urban missionaries going upstairs in tenements in an Irish ghetto where drunkenness was prevalent. Violence and domestic abuse were widespread.

Today this is mirrored in the "meth" (methamphetamine) epidemic in the poor and rural white community. Abuse and neglect created by addictions placed members of our church in situations where we didn't know if it was better to call Human Services and ask them to take the kids, or try to be available for rescue when needed to take in children, get them to school, or just show them some love.

Over the years we have hired staff to help us in our outreach to children. We have had children's missionaries and many volunteers that wanted to make a positive impact on the lives of these kids. We have had families adopt children, become foster parents, or pick up kids on Sunday for church and be their "church parent" for the day.

Getting to BASICS

One of the structural things we saw created came from one of our staff in the children's ministry when Paul Green was directing it. He hired a young woman, Debbie Hawkes, who attracted a group of volunteers that really pursued inner city children. Mrs. Jenny Head was one of these faithful volunteers, and she and her family helped create something we at first called, "the Head Project," and later BASICS (Brothers and Sisters in Christ Serving). Over time this ministry was integrated with Chattanooga's Big Brother-Big Sister organization.

We have always had some families that developed ministry relationships with inner city kids, but this program gave us a significant structure to develop deeper relationships. Debbie Hawkes was instrumental in helping us build a neighborhood house (we called it The Lighthouse) and she worked actively to sustain relationships between "Littles" and "Bigs."

Some of these relationships actually outlived the program for positive results. Sadly, others revealed the power of the inner city to devour the lives of kids who at one time were bright-eyed, receptive and involved. When I use the term "devour," I think about how many of these kids grow up in homes where every single young girl gets pregnant out of wedlock, every boy fathers a child with a woman he will not marry, and far too many of them will go to jail, be shot, or get hooked on drugs.

This is part of the challenge of discipling the poor out of poverty, establishing long-term, loving relationships that act as a lifeline for helping children and families climb out of the mess. We have certainly failed many times, both in those personal relationships, maintaining effective programming, or sustaining significant staff to carry them on. Yet because there is a church planted in this community, relationships are able to continue, programs can be renewed, and we can try again, hoping and praying to help some.

I mentioned Jenny Head. Recently a young man she worked with for years, praying for him and trying to help, returned to church when I was preaching. Seeing him reminded me of one time when his home had been invaded, his father was shot multiple times, and he was shot as well. I remember him coming to church the next Sunday with an IV pole and bag still in his arm.

On this day he was with his present girlfriend, still trying to remain connected to the church community that had been there for him when he was a young teen. We are still hoping God's grace will own and be revealed in his life. Relationship discipleship is a lifelong affair.

Questions for Reflection and Discussion

1. How are your deacons organized and functioning to effectively minister to the poor, or people in need?
2. What connecting relationships with agencies (like a presbytery) can you approach and utilize for additional resources and help in mercy ministry?
3. What community outreach ministries has your church established for seeking to meet with and evangelize poor people?

CHAPTER 29

Developing Proper Leadership

"When the princes in Israel take the lead, when the people willingly offer themselves – praise the Lord!"

(Judges 5:2, NIV)

Without pastoral leadership it is difficult for a church to become mobilized for mercy ministry. Pastors need to examine how much they emphasize *mercy* and *justice* in their preaching and teaching. I am afraid many pastors rarely speak to these issues, and when they do sometimes it is only because they have become angry about something political.

Moral issues have political implications, and pastors should not hesitate to preach the whole counsel of God. However, they must refrain from being partisan and preaching from anger or to arouse anger. Discerning real issues of justice and giving a firm Biblical basis for evaluating them, as well as articulating a Biblical strategy for dealing with them, takes wisdom from the Holy Spirit.

Pastors often need attitude and behavior adjustments of their own in living out Micah 6:8, which states:

"He has showed you, O man, what is good. And what does the Lord require of you? To act justly and to love mercy and to walk humbly with your God" (NIV).

The example set by pastors in their spirituality and life behavior leads the congregation. Does the pastor show he is a man of compassion for poor folks? Does the pastor spend time with the poorest members of the church: Does he visit them in their homes? Does he ever have them over to his house? Does he share his money (his personal assets, not those of the congregation) to help them? The people of the church – and not just the poorer members – are watching to see how and what to imitate from their pastors and all their leaders.

Pastors Must Be Trainers

Pastors need to *train* deacons and other practitioners of mercy in the congregation. As with evangelism, this is often better caught than taught. To effectively train deacons, as well as other members in mercy ministry, the training must be more than theology and church government. Those things need to lead toward actual hands-on skill development for showing mercy and leading the congregation in mercy ministry. The pastor should take deacons with him on home visitations, or have them sit with him as he listens to someone that is asking for financial help from the church.

The training of deacons in mercy ministry is usually an area of weakness for most pastors. It is rarely something they know much about, since it is seldom addressed in seminary. Pastors can discern the theology readily enough, but typically have not had much practical experience in serving or doing ministry to the poor. This is just as shameful as the inadequate preparation for evangelism that many pastors have received.

I believe seminaries, students preparing for ministry, church planters and established pastors can do much better in learning new skills of mercy, as well as being able to teach others as well.

I repeat this for emphasis: Our seminaries aren't doing a good job of helping pastors know how to train deacons. Church planters are often sent out to start a new church with absolutely no knowledge of what deacons are supposed to be doing, and as a result, this church plant will be full of new Christians who have little background in the role of deacon or mercy ministry.

Learning from Others

If a pastor doesn't know how to train a deacon, or isn't sure of what they should be doing, he should consult with a pastor who does know and whose church has an active and effective diaconate. I suggest pastors take some deacons with them and visit a church that has a good track record of deacon ministry so they can learn and observe firsthand.

Eventually, once deacons are trained, the pastor can give the ministry of mercy totally over to the deacons. Just as the early apostles and elders realized they needed to focus on prayer and the ministry of the Word, the pastor needs to give mercy ministry away to qualified men and women. However, he must have a heart for those in need; if the ministry of mercy is not being handled well, he will need to devote time and attention to reviving it.

Here are some very general things for which a deacon should receive training:

1. Biblical guidelines for qualifications for church officers, as found in 1 Timothy 3:1-13, and Titus 1:5-9.
2. The Biblical priority to help widows, orphans, and strangers, as stated in James 1:26-27 and 1 Timothy 5: 3-16.
3. The principle of the division of work in the ministry: Elders to the ministry of prayer and the Word, and deacons to service, especially to the poor (Acts 6:1-7).

4. The concept of servant leadership (John 13:1-17). No one should personify servanthood more than a deacon.
5. How to work as a team with the proper division of work, based on giftedness. (1 Corinthians 12:7)

It is important in congregations for deacons to meet with the elders and pastors from time to time to discuss whether everyone is working toward the common mission of the Church and if there are areas of stress or friction in the work. Deacons should be careful to never let their meetings turn into gripe sessions about how the elders or pastors are not showing them respect for their office. Deacons need to be proactive and ask the leadership where their service is needed.

Saints in Action

As we have mentioned earlier, I strongly suggest deacons not be worn out by meetings, either long ones or frequent ones. If ministry can be delegated, subdivided into committees or teams, more time can be spent in conducting actual ministry rather than in attending meetings. This may seem anti-Presbyterian, but wouldn't it be great to give new definition to the term "Presbyterian" as "saints in action," rather than "saints getting sinful in antagonistic meetings"?

Sometimes the pastor becomes the bottleneck for mercy ministry because pastors often don't know how to delegate. This may occur simply because the pastor has never received basic administrative and management training. A failure to delegate may also be due to the pastor's own insecurities; it may be threatening for him to empower other people. Yet this prime pastoral skill must be developed if ministry is to distributed to and shared with the congregation.

We as pastors must give the ministry away to our members so they can do the work. As Ephesians 4: 11-13 says:

"It was he who gave some to be apostles, some to be prophets, some to be evangelists, and some to be pastors and teachers, to prepare God's people for works of service, so that the body of Christ may be built up until we all reach unity in the faith and in the knowledge of the Son of God and become mature, attaining to the whole measure of the fullness of Christ" (NIV).

In the area of mercy ministry, it is not helpful for a pastor to be a "sugar daddy" where everyone must speak to the pastor to get any help. This not only overburdens the pastor, but also deprives the members of opportunities to learn how to minister in the name of Christ.

Make sure to spread out the work and not let too much fall on any one person. Some churches have only one employee, the pastor. Even if this is true, he needs to give away the work to the members. Often folks think the only person to see is the pastor. If the pastor gives no one else the authority to make decisions, especially decisions involving money, then everyone will want to see him and only him. This might make the pastor feel important, but over time will drive him into the ground.

The pastor should *cast a vision* for the entire congregation regarding mercy concerns. He ought to emphasize mercy, but certainly not as a work to earn God's forgiveness, nor as a legalistic obligation. The pastor should not fall into the trap of using guilt to manipulate people into being merciful. Sometimes pastors that use guilt or browbeat their members into mercy ministry have this backfire on them, making their people angry and resistant.

Encouraging a Gracious Work

Mercy ought to be a gracious work graciously encouraged. In fact, it ought to be fun, something that gives joy and warms the heart. Most people legitimately want to see good come out of their acts of service and don't want to see their time or resources wasted with no apparent result. Many people, as I do, take delight when they are able to help someone that is really hurting and in great need.

We have spoken elsewhere about how God calls us to do good works. The pastor is a key player in helping the people to observe this being modeled in his life, and hear from him in his teaching what doing good looks like. The apostle Paul, in the book of Titus, really goes after this idea:

"Similarly, encourage the young men to be self-controlled. In everything set them an example by doing what is good" (Titus 2:6-7).

"Jesus Christ, who gave himself for us to redeem us from all wickedness and to purify for himself a people that are his very own, eager to do what is good" (2:13-14).

"Remind the people to be subject to rulers and authorities, to be obedient, to be ready to do whatever is good…" (3:1).

"This is a trustworthy saying, and I want you to stress these things, so that those who have trusted in God may be careful to devote themselves to doing what is good. These things are excellent and profitable for everyone" (3:8).

"Our people must learn to devote themselves to doing what is good, in order that they may provide for daily necessities and not live unproductive lives" (3:14).

Isn't it interesting how many times the apostle comes back to the idea of doing good, and emphasizes the pastor is the one supposed to be teaching the people to do good? We are not just talking here about *being good,* but *doing good.* This is a pastoral epistle, meaning it teaches what pastors are to both do and teach, just as Titus was supposed to do in Crete.

You might say, "But the people of Crete were really bad people and needed this kind of help." Certainly they did, but if you are a pastor and don't realize how bad the folks are around you, you either don't understand depravity or aren't paying attention. The pastor should be an example of a "doer" and a teacher of the doing of good. Our ministry is not just for the head, but through the head, to the heart, into behavior. Grace and performance are inextricably mixed, never enemies unless performance seeks to earn grace.

Possible, Practical and Profitable

Pastors need to help their people set good targets for ministry. By this I mean identifying opportunities for service that are at once possible, practical and profitable in actually helping individuals in their physical needs, while also making a spiritual impact on them. The pastor often has opportunity to see and realize first-hand the needs of people in the community. It would be good for him to pass along ideas for projects or activities to the deacons of the church.

At the same time, it is important not to make the people who have been shown mercy a public spectacle of pity or condescension. While taking care to guard the confidentiality (and dignity) of individuals and families, stories and generalized examples of mercy practice can (and should) be celebrated by the pastor from the pulpit.

At one of our first mercy conferences a church was asked to give a "mercy testimony." They spoke of a homeless family they found near the church building. The church organized to get this family new clothes, they purchased a used car for the father to get to work, they helped in several material ways. Then, within the second week or so of this relationship, they invited the family to church and had them sit in the front row. By this time everyone in the congregation knew what was happening, knew that this was the poor family they were all trying to help. As I listened, I squirmed in my seat since I guessed what was coming. "They never came back after that," the speaker said.

Please don't embarrass the people you help.

The pastor can deflect many situations presented to him as "emergencies" (again, we realize there are true emergencies) by telling folks his deacons or the mercy committee will be here at such and such a time, or take an address and let them know the deacons will come to visit. Remember the apostles and elders in Acts, chapter 6, who figured out they needed to spend time in the Word and prayer, so they chose others to do the ministry of mercy. If you say someone will come to visit, make sure that is what happens.

When you have volunteers doing mercy work, make sure you encourage them. The pastor must be a cheerleader for practitioners of mercy. Pray for them, *praise them*, tell them they are doing well at doing good. Send them to training seminars (preferably to the most stimulating training in the most exotic and luxurious place you can afford).

It is good to set smaller and measurable goals so mercy teams can see direct success, which will inspire them to do so much more. This is why we encourage churches to become proactive and programmatic in their approach, not just reactionary to problems.

Even if you can afford to hire someone full-time for mercy ministry, it still remains an important principle not to let them do all the work. Make sure they take part in the task of multiplying the work force by *mobilizing* others. They should develop a mercy apprentice, have a list of volunteers to call, and mentor those who want to learn about ministries of mercy.

Questions for Reflection and Discussion

1. Who trains deacons or mercy workers in your church?
2. What method is used to re-train or give continuing education to your congregation's deacons and mercy workers?
3. What sermons have you heard or given, if any, that deal with the subject of mercy ministry?
4. Does your church provide a Sunday school class or another training class for mercy ministry?

CHAPTER 30

Programming For Ministry

"...so that the church can help those widows who are really in need."

(1 TIMOTHY 5:16B)

TIMOTHY WAS INSTRUCTED BY PAUL to put widows on a list (1 Timothy 5:3-16), and these widows were to be active in ministry. It seems the description of those widows qualified to be placed on a "list" also is a job description for what they should be doing. The widows that were to be supported evidently were known already for doing acts of mercy. Wouldn't it be wonderful to see more churches use the resource of widows for ministry to the poor?

"No widow may be put on the list of widows unless she is over sixty, has been faithful to her husband, and is well known for her good deeds, such as bringing up children, showing hospitality, washing the feet of the saints, helping those in trouble and devoting herself to all kinds of good deeds" (1 Timothy 5:9-10, NIV).

Pastors should – in fact, must – be mindful of the widows in their congregations, enlisting them (even employing them) into mercy ministry. A pastor should visit widows and, if he can recruit his wife to go with him, host them or take them out from time to time, as individuals and as a group. These women need to be celebrated, appreciated, and loved on. Usually they wind up giving much more back to their churches than they receive.

Hopefully the leadership of your church has begun to articulate a vision for what they want to be, and what they want to do, as a church. Congregations have reputations, for good or ill. Some are known for their great preachers, massive buildings, extensive mission programs, strong theology, and wonderful children's and youth ministries. These things, however, may be completely unimpressive to the community surrounding the church building.

Building a Reputation Among the Poor

Many congregations have no idea what the neighborhood around them thinks of them, and sometimes they don't care. Unfortunately, it seems to be true that if some church buildings burned down, no one in the community would even know they were gone. What is the identity and reputation of your congregation when it comes to the ministry of mercy?

Mercy ought to be a part of our life as a congregation, both within and outside of the church. If this is not articulated, it tends to fall to a small number of people who seem to have that interest. If this is a ministry just getting started, one very practical thing a pastor can do is to take some of his leaders with him to a seminar or conference on mercy ministry, or to have such a seminar offered right at the church.

For congregations wanting to reach out to their neighborhood, and desiring to do it proactively, they need to think through what the community already has to offer (existing assets), and what it feels it needs. This knowledge and information usually come through talking, interactions, and relationships. Sometimes a simple question to city, community and neighborhood leaders and members can be, "What do you think a church could do for the community?"

Launching Into Community Ministry

Here are some things to think about:

1. What educational needs are present for children in the neighborhood or the local school? Do they need tutors, help with uniforms, shoes, glasses, or other essentials?
2. Could our church help the local school by encouraging their teachers with special coffee days, encouragement, messages and various kinds of support?
3. Do young people from the community, especially from single parent homes, need decent clothes? Can the deacons help them to "dress for success"?
4. How about fire safety? Do the homes of the people have smoke alarms? Fire prevention programs can be a great outreach approach for your neighborhood, with deacons installing alarms free of charge to your neighbors.
5. What about auto maintenance for single-parent moms? Having a monthly car rodeo with oil changes and maintenance checks for single parents can be extremely beneficial.
6. Do widows or elderly need help with lawn care or house cleaning? Would shut-in elderly folks be blessed with home Bible studies during the Sunday school hour?
7. Is there an apartment complex that could be adopted by your congregation? Is it possible to meet the manager and ask what help is needed, and whether the church would be welcome there?

There are some significant challenges for a local church when ministering to the poor. One of these concerns the local church located in a poor neighborhood that directly ministers to the poor. Should poor communities only be ministered to by their own people and/or by professional Christian workers, such as urban missionaries or development workers living in the community? Should *wealthier* (always a relative term) Christians be invited into the poor neighborhood to become part of the church? What if they commute in, not living in the neighborhood or area of the poor?

The Christian Community Development Association has some core principles it teaches to assist people in ministries of mercy. These are not without debate or controversy. Sometimes their application varies depending on the circumstances on the ground, which are not the same in each place. This is why they are principles and not laws. Wayne Gordon, pastor of Lawndale Community Church in Chicago, has articulated them. These are:

8 Core Principles of Community Development

1. Relocation – living among the people.
2. Reconciliation – being among and between the people.
3. Redistribution - a just allocation of resources.
4. Leadership Development
5. Listening to Community
6. Church-Based
7. Wholistic Approach
8. Empowerment

John Perkins, who has taught the "Three R's" (the first three core principles of Relocation, Reconciliation and Redistribution) for many years, calls on believers to identify with the lives of the poor by relocating and living among them. Sometimes implementing this is difficult, especially when raising children in a place becomes too dangerous. It becomes limiting when it simply cuts off folks who really have an "incarnational" spirit but who can't or haven't moved in yet. Or, relocation stops being that and makes a transition into gentrification, as a result actually hurting the very people we want to help.

The word "redistribution" often raises eyebrows, but the reality we seek is the active presence of middle-class people who become part of a poor congregation and immediately make their education, skills, networking, and resources available to the church. This assumes they are there to give and share those things as they normally would in any church. It is not that poor churches don't need outside resources, but we are not simply advocating the transfer of money – although sometimes, if done with transparency and integrity, this can be very helpful.

'Radicalization of the Middle Class'

We stress the "radicalization of the middle class" as part of an effective mercy ministry. We call on those who have achieved a piece of the pie, attained some of the American dream, to willingly give some of it back by being part of a church in a poor community, as servants to that community.

It is so important to ask the people of the community what they want, what they need, along with what hopes and dreams they have. Unfortunately, poverty has a way of screwing things up in terms of people even knowing what is hurting them. When Joan and I came back to Chattanooga from seminary, we developed a questionnaire and Joan spent some time going door to door (mostly in a local housing project) to take a survey.

This survey included two questions about education. One asked, "Are you satisfied with your child's achievement in school?" The next question was, "Are you satisfied with the job the local school is doing in educating your child?" We were surprised when most answered they *were not* satisfied with the progress of their children, but *were* satisfied with the job the school was doing.

I believe middle-class parents would have answered this question differently. They would have blamed the school, and fought to make the school and school system do right by their kids. I mention this because there is nothing absolute in terms of truth when it comes to a community knowing what it actually needs. They need help with research and assessment as well, but in no way should solutions be imposed upon them without involving them in a discovery process, if not in final approval of strategies to change things.

Sometimes when a local church has no internal resources it looks to sister congregations for those resources. How can wealthier churches be motivated to help their sister congregations in poor communities? 2 Corinthians 8:13-15 gives us the Biblical challenge for wealthier congregations to assist other churches needing help. One might hope this could happen automatically, but even the apostle Paul had to write, had to communicate, and took pains to give good accounting. Mercy between churches takes work.

Creating a Plan – and Working the Plan

If the church actually has a will to help, they need to create a plan to put aside funds to help the poor. They may be willing to rise to meet emergencies but fail to get prepared to be generous. There are various ways to put aside money for the poor and manage it, and it needs to be done intentionally.

How does your church do it? Does your church put an amount in the annual budget your deacons or mercy committee can plan to use and allocate each month? Does your church take a mercy offering every time there is communion? That is how some churches raise that money. Or does your congregation just put out an appeal when there is a need and then sees what comes in to know what and how much they can do? Once your congregation gains a reputation of mercy, especially within itself, it is interesting how many folks are willing to specifically designate money for mercy ministry.

Programs are only limited by our imaginations. Our imagination is sometimes limited by our lack of vision, along with not training ourselves to look for needs and seeing need as an opportunity for ministry.

We challenge you to start asking questions, then add your ideas to the lists above and below. Match them with your given sets of opportunities and problems, as well as with people who are gifted or willing to do some of these kind of things.

Here are some other types of programs:

- Big Brother-Big Sister programs in coordination with the local church. (Mercy funds can be used to help administrate or staff this or in ministering to families in program.)
- Scholarships to a Christian school program or "exodus" program to send inner city kids to Christian boarding schools. Creating a Christian pre-school, or urban school. (Mercy funds can be used to help provide scholarships for some kids to this program.)
- Matching grant for adoptions, especially special needs adoptions. This is a great program for presbyteries to match a grant when a local church gives to one of their own families toward an adoption.
- Prison halfway or re-entry house.
- Men's or women's shelter, drug rehab program.
- After-school tutoring program, summer-long enrichment camps and programs.
- Mom's day out – making certain to include community moms.
- English as a Second Language (ESL) classes.
- Legal aid and immigration counseling, and similar assistance.

- Medical fairs or clinic days for the community, creation of community dental or medical clinics (with free service if necessary).
- Information festivals to bring together community social services and introduce them to the neighborhood.
- Sexual trafficking relocation program.
- Urban gardening and farming programs to help residents in planting, growing and eating their own food. Food co-ops and cooperative buying plans are very helpful.
- Employment training programs (such as Jobs For Life), job referrals to employers, particularly small business or industry start-ups to create meaningful jobs.
- Moving teams to relocate people, or load and unload trucks.
- Work response teams of craftsmen to build wheelchair ramps, redo roofs, replace decayed floors, and make other repairs.

Here's a quick picture of how such an integrated approach geared for helping the poor can look:

We meet some young boys in the projects. They love sports, and our youth worker begins to hang out with them, takes them to games, and gets games going. We begin to think about how we could help them and their families with some income. We start an urban farming program. Our summer youth intern secures several empty lots for gardens, he acquires tools, watering buckets and a pickup truck. We get help from the 4-H club and the state extension agent. We raise funds to pay a weekly stipend to about half a dozen teens to clear, plant, cultivate, weed, water, harvest, pickle and can the produce. It is a hot summer, and they work hard. One of those young men eventually joins the church, gets married and has kids, and is now a regional manager for a fast-food chain. He still works hard.

Throwing a Block Party

Block parties are one particular kind of ministry that can establish for you a beachhead into a neighborhood. Throwing a block party for a nearby apartment complex can give incredible name recognition for your church, allow you to meet your neighbors, see and hear about their real needs, and offer your church members something tangible they can do. This is suggested as the beginning of a community effort, not simply as a "one-shot" event that doesn't lead to relationships with people in the community.

At New City we developed a pattern in which every Memorial Day we would hold a block party at a nearby apartment complex. We would follow that up with Bible clubs held in the complex through the summer. We then recruit children into our middle school soccer programs, summer day camp and annual tutoring programs. At the end of the summer we would take them to a week of urban camp.

Bible studies were started for mothers in the complex, families came to the church with mercy requests, and some of these folks began to come to Sunday school and joined the church. A few even joined our church staff.

To start off the planning for the block party, we requested the management or tenant association for a day when the church could come and throw the neighborhood a party. It is good to do it on a specific holiday, such as Memorial Day. (Chances are the people you desire to serve will not be away on vacation.)

Gather a leadership team from the church. As the years go by and you continue the programs, you can add neighborhood folks to the leadership team. Build sub-teams for various activities, such as buying and cooking food, children's carnival, repair projects, visitation and prayer team, choir and band, logistics (cook tent, sound system, children's games, chairs, tents, garbage, portable potties, and so on.)

Make the event a low-key, fun day, visit every apartment, and simply ask the residents if there is something the team can pray about for them, invite them to the free meal, and give them a brochure about the church. Witness evangelistically only if questions are asked and an opening is given. Just tell them you are throwing the party as an expression of the love of Christ.

Plan well, let the block party teams function, have fun, clean up, watch for safety, and get out before dark. Think of other evangelistic or ministry initiatives you can do in the neighborhood at other times in the year.

A Matter of Show-and-Tell

Obviously, each church can develop its own scheme of organization depending on the gifts and skills of volunteers in the congregation. Authority, responsibility and accountability need to be taken into account in whatever scheme you use. Spread the ministry to the people, give them something to do, show them how to do it, encourage them in the doing of it, and pray for them. Give God the glory, and give honor to those to whom honor is due.

Mercy ministry can take place in various intensities, as well as different sizes and depth. It can be personal, relatively small in scope or effort. It can be very large, and even impersonal. There are many resources a local church can utilize from within itself or by appealing to the broader community.

The local church should not allow itself to be taken out of direct action in ministry to the poor. I believe the local church must be a player because it is God's organization, and at the same time it is one of the most grassroots of all organizations.

As we wrote in Chapter 26, it is a good idea for a church to have written policies for deacons to use as reference for knowing what to do in specific cases. When new, unique situations arise, the deacons or church leaders can meet and figure them out. Most often, however, the same kinds of things will reoccur. Principles help create policy, and policies give operating procedure for knowing how to respond.

There are some principles to keep in mind in framing your policies. One is to protect the family. Don't circumvent parental authority, especially male authority. Our goal should be to reinforce it, not weaken it. So in giving toys at Christmas, it is better to have something like a Christmas store and let parents come and shop, paying a small amount, so we are able to guard their dignity. Let the parents give toys to their own children so they can be the heroes. We never want to replace their role.

Dignity – the Most-Prized Possession

You need to treat the poor like you would your best customer: You need to ***guard their dignity***. In fact, treat them as if they were Jesus (Matthew 25). It can be very humiliating to ask for help. If deacons treat people like they are beggars, it will alienate them from the church. Again, be careful not to embarrass people you help by making them a public example at a church service. Tell stories of the kind of assistance your church provides, but keep the names of those you help confidential.

Deacons are to be stewards of the resources of the church. They should set limits of assistance, especially for strangers. The church should protect deacons and members, being careful to whom you give home phone numbers. Home visitation should be done by teams, not by individuals.

It is not some Utopian ideal to seek to move a person, or a family, from whatever tragic circumstance you find them in to self-sufficiency. This eliminates the need they have, and that is what we want to do – eliminate need. We don't merely want to make poverty easier to endure; we should try to build our mercy strategy so eventually it will end someone's poverty.

Ending someone's poverty is dependent on many things, such as their own response and effort, and the blessing of Almighty God. Yet much of what poses for mercy ministry has no ultimate objective, so it continues to do the same things for the same people time after time with no measurable result. When we help people, we need to provide them with something they can use to leverage their lives into more stable situations.

Capitalize people by giving them capital (financial resources) or skills, or an asset they can use to improve their lot. For example, Habitat for Humanity is a good way to help a poor person acquire and enjoy their own home and property. Tuition to a training course, giving a single-parent mom a workable car, or creating training programs for getting and holding a job (like Jobs for Life) all are means for capitalizing people.

If you have a church team working with a needy person or family – with their consultation and agreement – you can develop a plan that can move them toward self-sufficiency.

Devising Policies According to Context

The questions above are meant to help you in writing your own policies. Those will be different for each congregation based on resources, the social-economic context of your neighborhood, and frequency of acts of mercy in your daily or weekly ministry.

Some churches have no college students, so when you get one who asks for it, help with tuition might be appropriate. If you live in a college town and dozens, if not hundreds, of students come to your church, you may have to decide tuition assistance is not something you will give. This decision rests on your resources and your mission. We have found food is usually the easiest help to give to anyone, and can usually be given without too much concern over whether someone is getting it falsely. Food will usually be eaten by somebody.

However, protecting alcoholics and drug addicts from themselves by not giving them a resource they can sell and turn into drugs is a good idea. If someone is hungry, you can always buy food or cook a hot meal for them, and sit with them as they eat it. Some churches might not pay a phone bill, especially not for "call waiting." Yet in the case of a handicapped person, providing a phone might be a very practical, valid and important act of mercy.

Helping church members can sometimes be difficult since they don't always ask for help until things turn desperate. Their lifestyle might be producing debt and financial crisis, or their need may be chronic, making them feel embarrassed to ask again. Referring them to the pastor or the elders for counseling when spiritual issues are involved in their struggle might be helpful. Budget counseling is a consistent need among many American Christians.

Questions for Reflection and Discussion

1. Which of the questions from "Launching Into Community Ministry" caught your interest or intrigued you as possibilities?
2. Do you have a problem with any of the CCDA core principles? If so, which ones – and why?
3. In this chapter we listed numerous possible programs for church ministry to the poor. Does your church have any of them? If so, which do you have? Which ones do you think might be possible to start, or should be started through your congregation?

CHAPTER 31

Unwrapped Gifts

"Now to each one the manifestation of the Spirit is given for the common good."

(1CORINTHIANS 12:4, NIV)

GOD HAS GIVEN HIS CHURCH *gifts.* People may not look like a Christmas present, but God has given each of us to each other to be used to build up the Body of Christ. These gifts help that body to function. The gift of *mercy* is a wonderful gift, and most of our deacons should have it, but not necessarily all of them. For example, someone might have the gift of *administration,* but not mercy. All effective committees of mercy or boards of deacons need good administration.

Let administrators administrate, but sometimes you have to protect the poor from direct contact with them. That may sound strange, because many of our people want to see the poor and needy helped. They want to see suffering alleviated. The only problem is some, due to their personalities, are not very good at "people skills." This doesn't mean they shouldn't be involved in the ministry; just find the right place for them. They may be much better at working the details, at getting things done behind the scenes. God bless them for that ability, as those skills are desperately needed.

Deacons and mercy committees also need *leadership*, someone who keeps the vision before the people and in their consciousness, who inspires and motivates, who knows how to make decisions – hopefully, the correct decisions.

The gift of *encouragement* is so needed in the life of poor people, the sick, or someone suffering from a disaster. Mercy can sometimes be nothing more than a personal visit letting someone know you care. Many times the gift of encouragement is exercised by simply listening, being there in times of grief or trouble. Showing up during times of trouble is a powerful ministry, and we don't have to know or provide all the answers to make an impact.

The gift of *helps* is invaluable in a church. This gift is found in people who just do things to help others or the church organization overall. These are the "doers," and we need to set them free to do things. Tell them what needs to be done, set the standards, and let them do it. They are often unnoticed, so praise them and let their efforts be used as examples to others. Some people have told me directly, "Pastor, I don't want to be in charge, just tell me what to do."

The gift of *discernment* is very important, especially for anyone who does intake, or who interviews strangers coming to request help. The church needs someone who can ask good questions and see past the presented problem to deeper, root problems. We need people who can spot phonies and con artists, and can even look beyond a scam to the person's need for Jesus. Look for this gift in your potential officers. We are often limited only by our imaginations in how to use people in the church for ministry. I always yearn for several Master of Social Work (MSW)-qualified types to come on my church staff.

Questions for Reflection and Discussion

1. What do you think are your spiritual gifts?
2. How do you use your gifts faithfully in your congregation? If you are not using them, why not?
3. Is everyone required to have the gift of mercy to participate in mercy ministry? Is everyone required to show mercy when it is needed? How are these two questions different?

CHAPTER 32

Developing The Needed Skills

"Do you see a man skilled in his work? He will serve before kings; he will not serve before obscure men."

(PROVERBS 22:29, NIV)

ONE OF THE THINGS MERCY committees and deacons need to do more is to train themselves in people skills. Some folks naturally seem to have these traits. It helps to highlight the need for good "people skills" so mercy workers will begin to think about how they are communicating when doing mercy work.

TQM – *Total Quality Management:* I was told this means treating customers as if they were what your business is about. It is really just a way of loving people by making them feel valuable and important. This is essential in mercy ministry. *Be cheerful* when you visit and interview people, *listen to them* and ask questions without a suspicious attitude, and interact with them. Show some compassion as you hear their story. I have seen social workers, and mercy workers in the church, be flat-out mean-spirited to people because they have grown cynical. You need to get your "love face" on when you do mercy ministry.

We can always offer to pray for folks, even if we can't give them money or solve their problems. If it was possible for us to solve all their problems, then neither we nor they would need God. But we do need God, and it is good for us to admit our own limitations.

'Can You At Least Pray?'

One of my most memorable moments of doing mercy ministry was the day when I couldn't help a lady who called the office. All my staff was gone for the day. If I remember correctly, I had no transportation so I couldn't get to where she was. As I listened to a list of all the problems she was facing, I felt so badly for her and a little ashamed as I told her there was nothing I could do for her. She suddenly asked me, "Are you the pastor?" "Yes," I meekly replied. "Well, can you at least pray for me?" she responded.

I confess it was hard for me not to be weeping as I prayed for her over the phone that day. I was embarrassed she absolutely had to push me to do what I should have offered to do in the first place. I hope God blessed her faith.

It reminded me of a time I was doing mission work on the islands of Lake Victoria in Uganda. During our trip to the Buvuma Islands, I had to use my first-aid kit to help someone who had cut himself. Immediately I was surrounded by folks from the fishing village asking for medicine. The Anglican priests who were with me set up an impromptu clinic at each island as I handed out vitamins, Band-Aids, malaria pills, whatever I had. I cleansed wounds, gave out aspirin, told some of the villagers they needed to get to a doctor fast.

After the third island I was out of everything, but people were all still gathered around me. I looked aghast at the Anglican priest. "I have nothing left to offer," I admitted. "Well," he said, "can you at least pray for them?" Why do I have to keep learning this lesson? Since that time we have maintained monthly prayers for healing in our worship services at New City Fellowship.

When people come to get help at your church, I encourage you to use interviews as chances to *teach*, but *be humble* about it and don't lord it over people. Don't act impatient; hear them out. If you know immediately you can't help, it is a good idea to let folks know quickly. Don't lead them on as if you will help them when you know you can't. Be honest, but gentle. It may be they have more problems than they are presenting. When you give people some time to talk, other things may come out in the open.

It is always good to look for ways to help people earn something for themselves, so if you can supply work around your church, do it. This often requires some supervision, especially if the worker is not a church member. Single men who ask for help are often willing to work for the assistance you might give them. There might be some elderly person who needs their lawn or yard taken care of, and might even have money to pay for it. Organize to provide for lawn care: the deacons can pay for the men to work on the homes of widows, and then two problems are solved at once. *A problem thus becomes an opportunity.*

The ministry of mercy requires good administration to be effective. Set up a useful method for analyzing what someone needs. This usually involves some kind of *interview.* It needs to be fairly quick and as non-threatening as you can make it, yet complete enough to give you the necessary information. Let people know you want to respond to their requests quickly, and let them know whether you can help them. We don't want to come across as an impersonal, bureaucratic agency.

Anticipate Next Steps

One of the important things to know before you interview is what are the next steps you can and will most likely recommend. Will you refer them to a budgeting counseling session? Will you send them to a practical training course, such as Jobs for Life, or Faith and Finances? Do you have a list of possible job openings or an employment agency? Do you have a list of apartments or houses for rent? Do you have a professional that might be able to give them some free services, such as a dentist, doctor, lawyer, or counselor?

One of the key skills that can be learned, especially by someone skilled or gifted by God in administration and/or organization, is the ability to do research. Many of us can pick up information intuitively. The danger of relying on this is unless you study your community and congregation systematically and formally, you will miss many things. Even though you might think you know everything, believe me, there is always something hidden under a rug somewhere.

Someone on your mercy team needs to *know what resources are available*, both through the church and in the community. There are many agencies and ministries that can be a great asset to you in your attempt to help someone. Much of this assistance is free. Collect all the manuals and books you can about resources available in your community.

Add data from situations so you can track people. This allows you to build a history so you can see where people have been, and where they seem to be going in their struggle against need.

Here are some questions that might help you and those deacons who want to pursue mercy ministry:

1. What categories of people can we identify in our congregation or community that need help? (Widows, single-parent families, homeless, refugees, handicapped, unemployed or under-employed, poor, and debt-ridden are some categories.)
2. What people in our own church are already engaged in a mercy effort of some sort? Who seems to have the necessary gifts and interest? Who could do the necessary research?

3. Is our pastor, or church leadership, behind the idea of building mercy ministry? Will they support it?
4. What kind of money are we as a church presently spending on mercy?
5. Given our present resources, how much could we be spending on mercy?
6. What organizational changes need to be made to launch or improve mercy ministry? What kind of training is needed?
7. What one thing could we do that would get us started, something we could do well and see some success that would encourage more and deeper involvement?
8. Who will assume leadership roles to start things in motion?
9. With whom, and when, can we gather to pray about making this happen?
10. What resources are available to provide us with demographic data on our community?

Delegate different tasks to others so a team is built around a specific "case." This *protects the members* from burnout. Don't always go back to the same church members for every situation.

Evangelize by training deacons and mercy workers in how to share their faith and present the Gospel. Jesus is looking for disciples, and being discipled means your values and lifestyle will change. This is one important way for helping the poor to change.

When people are hurting and need help, they are often very timid and sensitive about asking for assistance. One of my personal heroes is our full-time deacon at New City, Mr. Gene Johnson. He says if someone has no problem asking for help, then they probably do it a lot and this usually means it is a con. If the person coming to you is not a con artist or a professional beggar, they probably are finding it difficult to ask you for assistance. This is why it is so important to not be impersonal and rude when people ask for help.

Responding to a Spiritual Moment

The moment when someone comes asking is a spiritual moment. Matthew 25 reminds us we should think in terms of showing mercy to Jesus Himself. Being gentle with people doesn't mean we are going to be able to meet all their needs, but gentleness is a mercy in and of itself. I have seen from personal experience that being gentle with people in times of need is extremely important.

As we have said previously, one of the greatest things you can do for people is to offer to pray for them. Sometimes you can't solve their problems, but God can. When you interview it is important to ask questions to find out why and how they got into this mess. Sometimes the mess is pretty deep. They may only want help with the immediate problem. However, you can assume they probably will need assistance next week or next month, too, if they don't solve the real issue. These root causes can include needing a job, a cheaper place to live, to have leaky pipes fixed, or even obtaining medical insurance.

Pray and think about both immediate and long-term answers for the problem. They may not be ready to attempt the long-term solution you propose, and that may hinder your ability to help them in the future, but you still might be able to solve their immediate problem.

The Importance of Preparation!

***Prepare* policies, *prepare* people with training, *prepare* resources** such as a food pantry, a mercy fund, and skill banks. Have a list of relevant phone numbers and build relationships with agencies where you can refer people.

One very spiritual method of preparation is **prayer,** and here I speak of your own prayer preparation, as well as the preparation of the congregation.

Some folks find themselves in situations when they think their need should be obvious to everyone. They think the church ought to be doing something about it, but the need doesn't seem obvious to the leadership of the church, or the rest of the congregation. If you are someone close to the situation, this might make you feel frustrated.

It should not be our approach to be self-righteous about mercy ministry. Be patient. Pray for the Lord to open the eyes of the church's leadership. We need allies and support in this kind of work, not enemies. To build a base of mercy concern within our churches we need the work of the Holy Spirit in the hearts, emotions, minds and wills of God's people – and this requires prayer.

Plan Resources and Responses

Make a list of resources; prepare a template for usual responses to typical and recurring needs, and have tangible resources for meeting needs, such as food, accounts at gas stations, and helpful contacts at utility companies.

There are skills and principles that can be taught. Churches and Christians that are committed to loving, evangelizing, and changing the lives of the poor are not supposed to be unique, nor should they be exceptions to our faith. They ought to be the norm. Toward that end, much of what is already happening – things that are good and working – can be reproduced within other congregations.

There are models, examples, literature and trainers available to help you if you know where to look. One good source might be *www.Fastennetwork.org*. Dr. Amy Sherman has much helpful information to offer in knowing how to help poor communities. "The Welfare of My Neighbor," with a workbook and supplemental guide by Ms. Sherman, could be an excellent resource for a church that wants to make an impact.

It's worth repeating that we do suggest setting aside money each year in the deacon's budget just for mercy. Some churches take a special offering on communion Sundays for this, others make it a part of the general budget, and still others have formal endowments for mercy. Depending on how you budget your church's mercy funds, you should keep track of how much you are spending on each particular person or case that needs help. This is where we need to be wise in the ways of this world, especially in regard to money.

Know when to say "enough." Know when to buy a house rather than help someone rent; buy a car instead of just continuing to fix a bad one; relocate someone when the landlord won't fix up or repair the apartment, or send someone for vocational training if that would make them employable. These are all forms of "capitalization." At times, if we give only a token amount, it doesn't effectively change anything other than to prolong the problem.

Budgeting instruction and financial counseling and training should become ministries consistently offered by the deacons for everyone, but especially for those in financial difficulty.

We suggest when there is a complicated case – such as a single parent mom with lots of little kids that need a place to live, employment, child care, and help with legal problems – you can build a team around that person. One deacon can't handle this much trouble alone, but Jesus can. Building a team of church members with various skills and energy can help protect one person from being overwhelmed. It can also bring creative ideas for solutions.

Deacons should recruit others in the church to help, and give them an apprenticeship in mercy ministry.

Ideas for plans, preparation, and policy:

1. Food distribution: Some churches have food pantries, others are in a Food Bank system where vouchers are used.

Food is the easiest thing to give. However, the way you give food is important. Even drunks can be fed a meal, but it is not wise to give them bags of groceries or something they can sell to get another drink or drugs. If possible, have deacons take the groceries to people's homes.

2. Families are encouraged to take people in for housing, especially if there is no security threat. People that seem to be a bit scary, or are totally unknown to you, might best be put up temporarily in a shelter or hotel. Deacons can provide supplemental funds to households that host guests. Shelters, missions and hotels can be used according to need, convenience, and the strategy adopted by the deacons. For example, the deacons can pay the Salvation Army for a few nights for an individual to stay in one of their shelters.
3. Meals should be arranged for the sick, or homes with new babies. If you have a women's organization in the church, they should be consulted and coordinated with in providing this ministry.
4. Deacons should never give loans – only gifts. Loans make poor people resent the lender since they struggle to repay. If they want to repay, tell them to put it the church's general offering. (This in no way precludes a church from setting up or participating in a credit union or community loan fund.)
5. Anonymous gifts designated for mercy cases are encouraged, but follow IRS guidelines.
6. Generally, tuition will not be the deacons' priority. Set up a separate ministry to give scholarships. Phone bills are not a priority, unless for someone that is disabled or homebound. Cash grants are to be avoided. Checks written directly to landlords or utilities are safer and more likely to be used properly.
7. It is good to offer work to people, especially single, healthy adults. Temporary workers will need supervision.

8. Deacons are allowed to spend *a fixed, predetermined limit* out of their own pockets. A suggested limit could be $100. More than that should require consultation with the other deacons. Deacons should be encouraged to try to make sure all situations and needs can be verified. Then the church should reimburse the deacons.
9. There are always *con artists*, and they often target churches. If your church building is located off an interstate exit ramp, or your congregation has become known for helping people, you may become a target. The church staff and deacons can try to learn and recognize individuals who are hustling, but the average church member usually won't. So it is important to train and remind everyone about the strategy the church is taking for helping people.

   Some needy individuals may begin attending the church and start asking for loans from various members (without letting it be known they are asking more than one person). It is important for members to refer needs to the deacons, or ask for advice. Deacons should be a point of reception for funds to assist with specific cases.

   It might be a good idea to develop a casebook of "cons." This will help new deacons recognize typical scenarios, such as showing up as a church service is ending when people are in a rush to get home. There is almost always a request for cash, and a need that cannot be verified.
10. *Keep records, and keep confidential* those you help and what kinds of help you give. You can share types of cases you have dealt with and statistics, but be careful not to embarrass people by identifying them to the congregation.
11. Think *security*: There is safety in numbers, so visit homes in teams. Don't endanger your members in their attempts to do good for others.

Assistance Grants for Adoptions

At New City Fellowship, member families may request the deacons for help in adopting children. This is a positive step in fighting abortion. The church deacons then decide if they wish to use their resources to help meet this request. If they choose to do so, the deacons write a letter to the Mercy Committee of Presbytery and request a *matching grant.*

Presbytery always sends mercy funds through the local church, never directly to a person or family. The local church can then give the family, or the designated agency, the total of church grant and matching grant (at this time up to $1,000) toward an adoption.

At New City we encourage special needs adoptions, especially of African-American or biracial children, since many of them wait a long time for adoption. This would be a worthy program for endowment, either through the presbytery or the local church. Deacons should help church members leave their money to worthy ministries as they prepare their wills and inheritances to be left behind.

As bold as it may sound, New City wants to eliminate poverty and its horrible consequences from the lives of the people that are recipients of its ministry. As the church preaches the truths that help people change their value systems, and the poor come to faith, it gives them hope so they can become productive people.

Strategies for Helping People Make Progress

The church must also help create strategies for moving people toward economic progress if it is to make a lasting impact in a poor community. One strategy for that is creation of a development organization that specializes in attacking the systemic issues that hold people back. The two areas that usually need change the most are in a person's personal value system (which the local church can help to do) and the systemic context where a poor believer is found.

Some years ago I asked one of our young men, Chris Hatch, to come on my staff and do the preparation work to create a new 501c3. For two years Chris worked to form an initial board and create the structure for a ministry that came to be known as Hope For Glenwood. Hope was launched and became our facilitator for the many urban mission teams that come every year to help us.

Later, Paul Green moved from the church staff to become the new director after Chris went on to be a missionary in London, England where he planted New City-London. Eventually Hope merged with Inner City Ministries and became Hope For the Inner City.

Some of the systemic areas that typically need to be changed are illiteracy (so we established tutoring programs and scholarship programs); unemployment and underemployment (so we have a Jobs For Life program); and a lack of labor-intensive entry jobs (so we have tried to help in setting up small businesses, such as a lawn care company and a barbecue shop). Another problem area involves inadequate job mentoring (which should have come from good parenting). This can be provided by a jobs training program, or apprenticeship jobs in companies overseen by supervisors with a commitment to disciple and mentor employees.

Equipping Others to Help

New City and Hope for the Inner City host teams of young people during the summer to help us in urban ministry. Hope For the Inner City also brings in many suburban church teams to do and learn urban ministry. This in turn helps New City to do service projects for widows, the elderly, single moms, and to evangelize inner city children.

These outside church teams give us the additional manpower to repair, paint and renovate homes. We train them in cross-cultural and urban ministry skills. Summer-long internships for college students are used to train young people in more intensive mercy and urban ministry, and to help us administrate the ministry. These internships are also available to community young people who have grown up in the church.

It is obvious some churches have lots of resources but not much direct access to the poor. We have previously referred to passages in the Bible that teach us in regard to need there is to be equality between the churches. This concept is emphasized in 2 Corinthians 8:13-15:

"Our desire is not that others might be relieved while you are hard pressed, but that there might be equality. At the present time our plenty will supply what they need, so that in turn their plenty will supply what you need. Then there will be equality, as it is written: 'He who gathered much did not have too much, and he who gathered little did not have too little'" (NIV).

This kind of mercy cooperation between churches is biblical, but unfortunately a practice that is not as common as it should be.

Creative Approaches to Mercy

There are congregations actively trying to reach out. Some have become "bridge churches." These are middle-class congregations that seek out other congregations in poor communities close by and build cooperative ministries of mercy. This mobilizes their own people and brings help to communities and other churches that do not possess the same resources.

Redeemer Presbyterian Church in Manhattan has created an organization called Hope for New York, which mobilizes and places many of their members in various kinds of ministry throughout the city of New York. Sojourners Network out of Louisville, Kentucky has done wonderful work in mobilizing their members to take part in many acts and programs of community ministry, medical clinics, and mercy work.

John Perkins has been a pioneer in the work of community development. We recommend any of his books to you as a resource. He has helped to found an organization called the Christian Community Development Association (CCDA). You can find out more concerning that organization at www.CCDA.org.

CCDA sponsors an annual conference that usually provides many workshops and ministry tours to help churches and ministries learn how to do urban, cross-cultural, mercy, and development ministry. This would be an excellent place to send your mercy workers to get an abundance of information and training.

It is in the direction of development that mercy workers need to be thinking: Helping families to acquire their own homes, have skills for jobs, or create their own businesses. Mercy workers ought to be thinking about helping the poor create platforms from which they can help themselves. Neighborhoods and poor communities can organize and learn how to gather resources and use the assets they already possess or have readily available.

Churches must learn how to mobilize their communities and stop being seen as merely self-focused institutions. This carries with it certain theological and ecclesiastical implications. The local church obviously has ministry in two directions, one to care for the discipleship of its members, and the other to be salt and light in the world, a city set on a hill, a platform for the evangelism and discipleship of the nations.

One of the great challenges congregations can face is ministry to the disabled. Joni Erickson Tada, herself a quadriplegic who has accomplished much despite her disability, has been not only a great inspiration but also a tremendous leader and innovator in showing how to minister to physically challenged people. From the building of wheelchair ramps, to offering handicapped bathrooms, to making available deaf interpreters, there is so much that can be done to include these folk in worship.

Home visits for the sick, care for AIDS patients, and the historic ministry the Church of Jesus Christ has had for orphans, as well as the creation of hospitals, are all things deacons and ministers of mercy can be involved in.

If We Don't See Them, Where Are They?

Churches often need to ask questions about things they can't see. The unsaved are sometimes not visible in the congregation (due to their absence), but if we don't make the conscious effort to think about them we will fail to reach them. When we look out on our congregations, if we don't see the handicapped, then where are they? Why do they not come to church – or better yet, why do we not go to them? If they came, would they feel welcome among us?

The very little step of providing handicapped parking spaces can be a big help to those who would come to worship. The use of handicapped vans to transport people for worship can be helpful. This service often can be provided by other agencies if necessary.

We keep going back to this word picture: Many poor people are in the situation of being in a hole and continuing to dig deeper. A good rule of thumb is that if you don't want to go deeper into a hole, then stop digging. One of the ways that hole of poverty gets deeper is unscrupulous lenders, check cashers, title loan companies and negligent landlords conspiring to make the lives of the poor harder. If the poor were treated with justice, they would need less mercy. Sometimes a city government, public school system, even a large, powerful church can be oppressive toward the poor.

Christians should first treat others with justice, especially those who work for us. We may desire personally to keep the Sabbath or the Lord's Day, but then make the poor work on those days to serve us. That is unjust. We should pay a decent wage so someone can afford to live on it. We should not exploit people because they are desperate and willing to work in unsafe and unsanitary places without having decent protection.

Champions for Justice

Since the poor are not politically organized, we have to be extra protective of their rights. This may mean exposing what is going on, appealing to the conscience of the powerful and decision-makers. Sometimes it might mean advocating for just laws, or reforming or replacing systems that thrive on and produce injustice.

Part of the struggle in achieving justice for the poor is simply opening our eyes toward how they live their lives, trying to understand what affects them. They are affected by so many things we take for granted. What if there is no grocery store in their neighborhood, or a medical clinic, or government services? How do they gain access to those things?

Is racism a factor in keeping people poor? Are people denied jobs, or denied the chance to sell their products? Americans live in a capitalistic system, and an open and free market is one of the great values of a capitalistic system. However, racism can deny access to that free market – and that is injustice.

Remedial justice is helping poor people get the leverage needed so they can take advantages of the opportunities that do exist. If the educational system perpetuates the graduating of illiterates, how can the church bring remedial justice to bear? Perhaps through adult literacy, tutoring or G.E.D. programs we can remediate justice. Maybe through advocacy of good education, or creation of Christian schools for poor children in poor neighborhoods, we can move back to the balance of equity.

Earlier I commented on Graham Scharf's book, *The Apprenticeship of Being Human*. I have become convinced part of the intransigence of inner city illiteracy arises from the damage done to fatherless children from birth to three years of age. This is the period where parents should be cuddling their children, speaking to them, starting to read to them, and helping them with their first vocabulary words, syntax and conversation.

This dynamic is woefully inadequate in the homes of the single-parent poor. As we have mentioned, these families have no books or very few, and inadequate verbal interaction for development. These children are already behind long before being introduced to pre-kindergarten or Head Start programs. I would love to see more churches tackle this problem head-on by mentoring pregnant women, prior to birth, in how they could work to develop their child's ability to learn right from birth.

Divorce laws have created fast and easy destruction of families. The church has been most often silent, when the protection of the family is a moral and Biblical concern. Divorce leads to the impoverishment of children. We need every program we can think of that can slow down divorce, marry only people given pre-marital counseling, make divorce very expensive, and make certain that fathers pay for the care of their children.

How About Individuals?

There are many just and righteous individuals who have done good things, and the poor have been helped. The Bible speaks of how Job made the widow's heart to sing. I think this should be the ambition of all just men. Proverbs 31 speaks of the virtuous wife who extends her hand to the poor and reaches out to the needy. I think this should be the ambition of all just women.

There are individuals who have accumulated riches and resources, and they have in turn created philanthropic institutions or taken philanthropic actions by which the poor have been helped. Both person-to-person activity and personal initiative to create new institutions are necessary. And they are often effective and beautiful. Most often it has the effect of supplying a missing piece in someone's life, to be that one key element to move a person from a desperate situation to self-sustainment.

Unfortunately, most of us cannot (having neither the means nor the ideas nor the skill) or will not (having neither the compassion nor the obedience nor the leadership) to attempt to pull the chronically or generationally poor person from the culture of poverty. For this reason, there need to be other pieces supplied before the puzzle can be solved.

I absolutely endorse and encourage individual acts of charity, along with individual acts of philanthropy to develop others. I wish with all my heart that young people would be creative and successful in business and then take those resources to create new strategies of development that allow poor people to solve their own problems and take ownership of their own lives.

Yet, individuals can be as stupid in their philanthropy as government has been, and their well-meaning actions can be no less damaging. Not only that, but well-meaning "do-gooders" also can get burned and might develop calloused hearts as a result. Once the wealthy become hardened, not only are the poor not helped, but the wealthy are spiritually hurt as well. There are always dangers in doing good, and that is why it is so important to do it with wisdom and Biblical boundaries.

Part Six:

What's Our End Game?

CHAPTER 33

Can We Really Change Communities?

"Your people will rebuild the ancient ruins and will raise up the age-old foundations; you will be called Repairer of Broken Walls, Restorer of Streets with Dwellings."

(Isaiah 58:1, NIV)

The question is sometimes asked, "Can we really change communities?" Yes, I believe communities can be changed, although when you are living in the inner city some days it seems you take two steps back for every one forward. Where you live can mislead you with a perspective that is not always accurate. Sometimes it gets hard to believe the sun will ever shine again if it rains for more than one day.

This is one reason I trust neither myself nor those who live around me, or those who live in beautiful and safe neighborhoods to give the best assessment of life or progress. It is the Word of God that gives us hope, and only the Word that gives us an honest critique. I live in a beautiful city surrounded by hills, with a mighty river flowing through it. There is a lot of money here, some great companies, large churches, and wonderful people. Yet that is not the whole story of Chattanooga, Tennessee.

Chattanooga has a hard core of poverty, some failing schools, and depressing statistics for infant death. It has too much obesity, diabetes, too many low-income jobs, and way too much violence. Some poor neighborhoods are built on or near industrial waste and pollution.

All of this trouble and mess is surrounded by what looks like progress and affluence. It is a good place to gain a new perspective by simply driving a few blocks. This can help you realize no one place sums up all reality in Chattanooga. Viewing some communities of poverty can overwhelm you with a sense of hopelessness, while looking at other areas can deceive you into thinking there aren't any problems. The Scriptures give me the perspective to believe communities can be changed for the better.

Market Forces for the Good

Communities can sometimes be changed by market forces taking advantage of opportunities, such as reinvesting in immovable urban resources such as proximity to downtown, a river, or some positive infrastructure or historical place. This can be considered urban reinvestment or gentrification. Sooner or later developers will realize where money can be made, and if there is potential they will then reinvest in places where previously money had fled. However, this is not always helpful change for the poor.

In the past there were "urban renewal" programs, some of which were the brainchildren of city fathers that simply wanted slums torn down and moved. This was sometimes done without much of a plan for helping the poor to possess their own homes and businesses, or even being relocated to adequate housing. As a believer and someone who wants to help the poor, not just move them around, I want to change communities by looking at things holistically.

I am not opposed to all aspects of gentrification. I don't know if there is much we can do to stop it anyway. I do want those Christians involved in it to pursue it with justice, ensuring the poor are not displaced. It would be wonderful if developers could provide affordable housing options in the neighborhoods where some elderly and poor have lived their entire lives.

My hope is for people to be able to live in a decent home. I also want them to have pride in their property, neighborhoods, local schools and every cultural institution within their territory. I would love to see all children grow up in a home with both their mother and father.

Changing Values

To make this happen among the poor, and for the poor to have a role in their own positive transformation, a change in their values needs to take place. This is why I think preaching the Gospel makes sense – it is God's power to change people. If we are properly discipled, every aspect of our lives must begin to change as well.

Someone might think I am not respecting the poor, or that I am trying to impose my own religious and cultural values upon poor communities. Yes, you would be right, except for the respect part. I am attempting to impose the Gospel on people who do not yet have it, have not asked for it, and do not know it or practice it. This is what missions is all about and I make no apology for it. We never seek to do this deceitfully. It is never done in a coercive manner, as 2 Corinthians 4:1-2 instructs us.

I don't think you can take what is broken and fix it simply by renaming it. I grew up in a "broken home," not an alternative one. I needed a resident and active father in my life, not a redefinition of the word "family" to make me feel better about myself. An exchange from the movie, "The Princess Bride," comes to mind at this point: "What do you want?" "I want my father back…."

Why wouldn't I want to help people by giving them the engine to change their own lives? The Gospel is the engine of hope and truth, and the poor need those things desperately. I am not blaming all of the poor for their poverty. I am also trying not to steal their dignity by treating them as if they were powerless. They are not powerless if they are walking in the way and will of God, and it is liberating for them to realize that they are not.

Questions for Perspective and Discussion

1. What statistics bother you about the economic and social condition of your city or community?
2. What difference is your church making in any of those social ills?
3. Are we arrogant to think our religion is what people need?

CHAPTER 34

God's Vehicle for Social Change

"His intent was that now, through the church, the manifold wisdom of God should be made known to the rulers and authorities in the heavenly realms, according to his eternal purpose which he accomplished in Christ Jesus our Lord."

(EPHESIANS 3:10-11, NIV)

I WANT TO SPEAK OF the necessity of the local church as a significant and, I believe, indispensable strategy for helping the poor. As a student of the Bible, I realize of course the local church is not primarily about helping the poor. God did not introduce us to the idea of the gathering of people into congregations as an economic and social revolution through which to end world hunger. Then again, maybe He did have something like that in mind if we really practiced what we preached.

Maybe I could describe the role of the local church as being about three W's – Worship, the Word, and Welfare. If the word welfare scares you, you might be able to substitute "Works." The word "works" is also scary to many evangelicals, but if it is understood in its proper Biblical light it should not be scary at all. I use welfare because it includes what to me is a proper and wonderful function of the local church.

God loves me, and is concerned with my welfare. He wants me to know Him and pursue Him and be my joy (my welfare), so He puts me into a worshipping community. He wants me to know His will (His Word, my welfare) so He puts me in a teaching and learning community.

God wants me to grow and mature as a Christian (my welfare), so He puts me into an accountable community. He knows I need to be loved and to love people (my welfare), so He puts me in a loving community. He knows I need to be cared for physically when I can't do that myself, and to learn to be generous to others (my welfare), so He puts me in a community of good works.

The local church, the right kind of local church, planted in the midst of the poor is what we are advocating. This doesn't sound very revolutionary, does it? Yet, it is absolutely personally, socially, and culturally transforming. This is the main strategy we as Christians should be pursuing if we care about social justice. I am not saying there are no others, but I am saying the church is and must be the main thing. I think this quote sums it up well:

"It is impossible to imagine a transforming community without a transforming church in its midst. Such a church is in love with God and with all its neighbors, celebrating everything that is for life and being a prophetic voice, telling the truth about everything that is against or that undermines life." (*Walking With The Poor,* Bryant Myers, page 115)

During most of my life I have heard people speak about the failures of the Church. I have heard this from both non-Christians and Christians. Some of the worst criticism of the Church has come from Christians that seemed embarrassed by the lack of everything from evangelism to justice, lack of openness toward the different, alienated and ostracized, and the absence of acts of mercy for the needy. This is not to mention the criticisms of hypocrisy, self-righteousness and irrelevance.

I certainly could admit most of these criticisms at times have been truly deserved. And there is no doubt in my mind some churches should not be simply criticized but condemned as "synagogues of Satan" due to their racism, and/or simple but depraved immorality.

Rotten Fruit Doesn't Represent All Fruit

How repugnant it is to come to a beautiful-looking piece of fruit or loaf of bread only to turn it over and find it rotten and filled with mold. So it is when we look for what ought to be life and life-giving, and all we see is hardness of heart, meanness, and self-centered obsession. Nevertheless, I still love fruit, still love bread, and can't condemn the idea of the local church because I've found some have turned rotten.

Thankfully, the right kind of local church is not just an idea. It is being realized thousands of times every day over the entire planet. Although each one is imperfect, (since there is no place here like up there, no place on earth that is yet heaven), still we pray to God, "Thy kingdom come, Thy will be done on earth as it is in heaven." Certainly the churches I have pastored have been imperfect and had an imperfect pastor. At the same time, we do see goodness lived out, church by church, person by person, story to story.

Personally I don't engage in much church-bashing. I don't find it an effective way to evangelize, and believe it is to some degree dishonest. Do you preach the Gospel by ridiculing the Church to lift up Jesus? As I have asked previously, how can you insult a man's wife while you are praising him? Isn't the Church the bride of Christ? And if in fact you do lead someone to Jesus after mocking the local church and emphasizing that the church is not Christ, do you then tell him he must now join a church? This seems sort of self-defeating to me.

Maybe you don't believe in joining a church, but then you would be failing to accept the church as the bride of Christ and also failing to do the very thing Jesus was about, which is the gathering of a people. "He who does not gather with me, scatters," Jesus said (Luke 11:23). I will not quibble over the word "joining," but whatever kind of associating you do, in whatever way the congregation chooses to describe it, all believers must be in the orbit of an accountable, supporting, worshipping and teaching local congregation.

We must plant local churches – the right kind of churches – among the poor. We must plant these churches because this is the community, organization and organism described throughout the New Testament. Are we not the body of Christ?

How can one read the Bible and not notice the care God takes to speak through His disciples about the organization of local congregations, the way they should worship, the qualities and duties of their leaders, the support we should give them? This individualized, independent, spiritual self-fulfillment seeking, unaccountable religion practiced by so-called Christians (especially in America) was never endorsed by the writers of Scripture.

Planting the 'Right Kind' of Church

We must plant the right kind of churches among the poor and the "right kind" of church takes the totality of a human being into consideration when loving them. We do this because Jesus said He was anointed to preach the Gospel to the poor. So, evidently the poor are a priority with God. I am, of course, amazed at justifications I have heard from the non-poor to spiritualize this word (poor), as if God didn't care about the physical realities of suffering, hunger, homelessness, exposure, sickness and alienation.

In America, as I have visited many congregations and tried to teach strategies for doing mercy in and through the local church,

I have sometimes heard church members tell me they had no poor in their own church. This could be the sign of an awesome material blessing – or it could be used as an excuse to do nothing.

As we have discussed earlier, some try to make arguments that the church should only care for the poor in their own membership, and churches have no responsibility for the poor around them, or in the greater city or the world. If no one is poor in the church, then of course someone might think this to be a good excuse and that there is nothing for them to do. If they think they have no responsibility for their community, they might feel they are "off the hook."

But even the wealthy leave widows behind when they die, get divorced or abandon their children, have their houses catch on fire, or see their businesses go bankrupt. Sooner or later, trouble comes even to those that are well off in the church. The need to show, practice and receive mercy will come sooner or later to every one of us.

The question I would like to ask such churches (the ones that think they have no community responsibility) is, "Do you assume that because you are middle class and enjoying a material blessing that the Lord Jesus has exempted you from preaching the Gospel to the poor who might be around you, that He has allowed you not to gather them into your own congregation?"

Raising Objections

I have no objection to middle-class people preaching the Gospel to middle-class people. That should happen. However, there are some things I do find objectionable. One is establishing demographic class targets that might allow some church planters and pastors to think the parts of the Bible talking about preaching to the poor, giving justice to the poor, and caring for the poor simply don't apply to them.

I also object to the idea that the poor should only be preached to by super saints, that professional missionaries are what the poor need. The idea that selectively gifted individuals, whom we look to as "heroes" because they will go to neighborhoods the rest of us won't even drive through, are the only ones that should seek to preach to and plant churches among the poor is a limiting strategy.

For many years people would say things to me such as, "You are unique. It takes someone like you to reach people in the inner city." At first I owned that view. I liked it because it fed my ego. But it was wrong. It meant this is not a reproducible concept, but one that had to wait for uniquely gifted or contextually prepared folks.

Wrong! This is the duty of the entire church. The poor in this country need the middle class, and they need to be incorporated into communities of the middle class through honest and genuine relationships, or middle-class people need to be incorporated into them. That happens when a local church is the right kind of local church, located in the right place.

Communities of need are desperate for role models – people that know how to function, are literate and economically astute. When a church is planted among the poor, this does not have to mean only poor people go to that church. Christians in this country need to be radicalized about what *being* the Church means.

Many local churches are simply not radical communities of selfless, generous, faithful, merciful saints. Too often they are just the opposite. So when we think of those churches that are full of people who go to church because of what's in it for them, of course we don't want that monstrosity among the poor. God doesn't even want it among the middle class. We have had enough of that.

We will have the poor among us if we put ourselves among the poor. If we go to the poor and proclaim Jesus, we are going to have them in our congregations. We will have to take loving action to help them, and will need wisdom to do it right. I am happy for heroes, the exceptional people. They give us all inspiration. But I would rather have an army with me to get the job done than send one altruistic soul that gets burned out and bitter after the first few years of ministry in a poor neighborhood.

Giving Away to Gain

Here is the counterintuitive truth of discipleship: When we give ourselves away, we gain. *Dying for Jesus means gaining our life.* It has always been that way. Spiritual math always has the same conclusion: If you live for yourself you die; however, if you die to yourself for Jesus, then you live – abundantly.

If you grow up in a large city with a concentrated population, established political forces, religious leaders and institutions, school and other municipal systems that engage in patronage and cronyism, it can be difficult to imagine things ever changing. Into that seemingly impervious wall of vested interests might enter a tiny little church plant, with a young inexperienced church planter. But we know "little is much if God is in it." God can and does use little people to do amazing things for His Kingdom and His glory.

Hopefully, that young church planter will have tons of optimism and idealism, because he will need an abundance of it if there is to be something still remaining after reality beats him up.

It is certainly easier to have a theology that teaches our only goal is to snatch a few from the fire, to get a few people saved out of the quicksand of cities that seem to give no access for the poor or the politically unconnected, and to have no compulsion for changing that community. Racial politics also plays a role in this, and if you are not the right ethnicity in some cities the door remains closed, even if altruistically you desire to serve.

Why bother then with a theology of justice, a theology of renewal and transformation, or even a theology of vocation that says work can be fulfilling, meaningful, and bring glory to God? Why bother with that kind of thing when the job you have drains life out of you, providing you with no fulfillment other than what little you can earn? Why bother with city fathers and powers, trying to influence or work with them when all they seem to want to do is hold onto power for self-centered reasons?

Here is why: Because Jesus is bigger than any city. Besides that, Jesus loves the people of the city and has all the power we need to change institutions, schools, city halls, universities, cultural institutions, and other social constructs. He can do it through us, and civilization is changed (even realized) by people living out a theology that is active, believing, hopeful and engaged. It may have to start out on one single block, or a part of a neighborhood, or through some kind of employment network, or maybe even through direct politics. But it has to start somewhere.

Making a Difference Together

Good ideas do make a difference, and there is no doubt we will have to be wise as serpents and harmless as doves. It means we will sometimes have to work together with people that we don't agree with on everything. Alliances will shift, but our commitment to live our lives with love, honesty and integrity for the defense of the weak must never change.

The "Social Gospel" of the early 20th century tried to replace the blood of the cross theology with a positivism that implied somehow, if we were civilized and could civilize the savage, we could bring in the millennium. The "Great War," World War I, destroyed that fantasy. On the other hand, the cynicism of the Second World War, the prior embarrassment of the failure of Prohibition for socially minded Christians, the psychological sense of security found in Fundamentalism, and ambivalence about racism led evangelicals to retreat from social involvement.

Evangelicals largely stood on the sidelines, or even the wrong side, during the Civil Rights movement. In its fear and lack of faith in an all-powerful sovereign God, many in the evangelical Church sought refuge only in personal conversions as the answer for the world. I have even heard evangelists teach that if enough people got saved, everything would finally start getting better.

I think such thinking is fantasy. Without a comprehensive theology of culture (the world, beauty, art, justice), then a world full of "saved" folk with bad theology simply perpetuates unjust systems, although probably with a troubled conscience. The antebellum South might be such an example – at least of a nominal Christian culture without a sound Biblical understanding of justice. Churches with bad theology, full of saved Christians, can still be very imperfect places, perpetuating and supporting injustice.

We pursue societal transformation with the understanding everything we do can be swept away by the rise of the wicked, by war, and by our own hypocrisy and immorality. We know "the Kingdom of God is neither meat nor drink." In other words, its manifestation is in the intangibles that affect the tangibles.

So all the institutions we create, all the reforms we establish, all the material progress we make even in the name of Christ, can be swept away in the unfolding of history. What cannot be swept away is the work of God in the hearts of His people, along with the eternal value of every act of justice and mercy.

Perspectives on Progress

It is interesting to me that sometimes unbelievers – non-Christians – can have more optimism about positive change than we do. Theology that dismisses all human social progress as merely things that "will burn" doesn't understand or recognize the impact of the Kingdom of God upon the earth, its value, or its necessity.

We ought to be optimistic without denying the reality of fallen human nature, the rebellion of unbelieving man against the lordship of Christ. And we should never give up standing for justice and the poor. We live in two worlds as it were, the City of Man and the City of God (thinking of Augustine and his book, *The City of God.*) Everything done for Christ in the City of Man pays eternal dividends in the City of God, even if it is only temporary in this temporal world.

One time in the early 80's I was studying Saul Alinsky, a writer and the one considered the founder of modern community organizing. I tried to take some of his lessons on improving living conditions of poor communities and apply them in Chattanooga to organize the neighborhood around the old YMCA building where our church met. I had never tried to organize non-Christians before, and just because I was a pastor, that didn't mean anybody automatically trusted me. Black folks in the room had been cheated out of their homes before in other urban renewal programs, and they suspected I was an agent of just that kind of thing.

It proved to be hard to do a simple thing. We wanted to get our streets paved, repair the broken sidewalks, and rebuild the walls on our street that had been there since the Civil War but now were crumbling. We would have to cut down some trees whose roots were breaking up the sidewalks. The neighborhood residents couldn't afford to repair their own sidewalks, which the city said was the owners' responsibility. They continued to say it until our Fort Negley organization was founded. As small as it was, this counted in the eyes of City Hall.

Two years later I returned from a pastoral stint in Nairobi, Kenya. As I entered the neighborhood I walked down level sidewalks, stared at stone walls that stood up straight, and marveled that somehow, somewhere tax money had been found that was designated for community development. I knew it wouldn't last, of course. Time and weather would take their toll, as they had before, but our lives were better for the time being. A touch of beauty had come to the neighborhood. For that, I felt very thankful.

Would Your Church Be Missed?

In some of my speaking engagements I have asked congregations, "If your church moved tomorrow from this neighborhood, would anyone know it was gone? If it burned down, would anyone care?" It seems to me if our congregations were really loving our communities, making the widow's heart sing, standing for justice, caring for the orphan, and loving the broken, neighborhoods ought to weep if we left.

It is true Satan opposes us. It is true that even if we do everything right and well in a neighborhood, there will possibly come those who hate the Gospel and hate us. Non-Christians sometimes oppose and attempt to persecute us. But I think our acts of mercy and justice should make it hard for them to have a case against us.

I have been reading some things written by Ed Stetzer concerning the word "missional," including his article, "What Does 'Missional' Mean?" in the June 9, 2014 issue of *Christianity Today*. I was intrigued to hear him cite Jaques Matthey using the term "ecclesiocentric," that the mission of God was larger than planting churches. The implication (not from Stetzer, but from those he quoted) was that to really be part of God's mission in the world, we had to have a bigger picture of justice and not be so focused on the starting of churches – that the Church wasn't really necessary to bring in God's mission.

Without question the Kingdom of God is larger than the local church, and the creation of things in the world like righteousness, peace and joy in the Holy Spirit are to be evidence of the presence of the Kingdom of God. While these very things might not exist in some local churches (since such a church might be no true church at all), I see no other corporate strategy directed by Scripture for creating those things in the world other than through the Church.

I believe communities can change for the better. Thank God for all aspects of God's common grace that enables a thriving economy to give more jobs for the unemployed. Usually there are less poor people when the economy improves because there are more jobs and more money for paying workers. I am glad for newer housing, improved streets and sidewalks, more public art, along with better architecture to create human and pedestrian spaces. Many of these things can happen without Christianity, and often do.

One Powerful Force for Change

Yet for human life to flourish in communities of poverty, where there are not clean or safe streets but rather crumbling sidewalks, failing schools, no jobs, high rates of violence and crime, and too many broken families, I see one powerful force that can begin to turn things around. It is a vibrant church on a mission to love the people of that community, lead them into a discipling relationship with Christ, and gather them into a worshipping, loving and supportive body of believers.

So I confess I am "ecclesiocentric," seeing the local church as a primary means for bringing people to become Christo-centric, so that the poor especially might see His Kingdom come.

If the poor are merely victims produced when there is injustice, they either have to wait until the powers that be decide to give them justice, or must somehow rise up and gain justice for themselves.

The Scriptures give us another model, one very different than simply revolution or community activism. That is in the creation of a self-conscious community that practices love and values not only for their neighbor but also the neighborhood. This model is centered on the church – the right kind of church. The poor do need to rise up, but with values that enable their rising to be without a consequential regret from the use of evil means or the idolatry of materialism.

I can hear some pastors responding to these urgings with despair, feeling it impossible to get the members of their church to do any kind of evangelism or outreach, let alone to do it holistically among the poor. I am sure some are wondering what they can do or teach to get anyone, just someone, to show some love even within their present congregation. I hear you, brothers.

Some churches are in drastic need of revitalization, and let me assure you with God all things are possible. If this is not possible, we might as well stop preaching because we would be admitting the Word of God has no power to change people. But the Word of God *does* have power to change people. So whether we send out new church planters to poor neighborhoods, or raise the bar for the folks in our present congregations, we need to engage in the discipleship of poor people so their lives, their children, their neighborhoods – and our country – might be changed.

Questions for Reflection and Discussion

1. What is your definition of the local church? What do you think should be going on in a true or real church of Jesus Christ?
2. What is your definition of the Kingdom of God, and where in the Bible do you get that idea?
3. What do you think a healthy community or city look would – or should – like?
4. What is one thing your church could do to bring beauty to its community, and in the process, instill a sense of hope?

CHAPTER 35

Panhandling, Scams and Con Artists

"But seek the welfare of the city where I have sent you into exile, and pray to the Lord on its behalf, for in its welfare you will find your welfare."

(Jeremiah 29:7)

I want to discuss several corresponding issues about mercy ministry and helping the poor, ones I am often asked about. One of these is the problem of panhandling, and I want to separate this discussion from another about homelessness.

We have fallen into a plague of begging in many of our major cities. Most churches involved in extending mercy to those that walk in and ask for help encounter numerous scam and con artists. Christians face a struggle whenever they are suddenly asked for help on the street. If we are reading our Bible, we know Jesus told us, *"Give to the one who asks you, and do not turn away from the one who wants to borrow from you" (Matthew 5:42).* So what should we do when we know someone is lying, being lazy, or addicted and seeking money from us to support a lifestyle of dissipation (wasted living)?

"At what point, then, do we begin to set conditions? What is the guideline? It is this: We must let mercy limit mercy." This is the observation of Dr. Tim Keller in his book, *Ministries of Mercy: The Call of the Jericho Road.* Dr. Keller points out mercy should be the thing that limits mercy. If our generosity hurts people, we need to have some wisdom in how our good intentions might result in harm. That is a good principle, but we also need a theology that helps us to interpret Scripture with Scripture.

The apostle Paul says, *"For when we were with you, we gave you this rule: 'If a man will not work, he shall not eat'" (2 Thessalonians 3:10).* Obviously the context of Paul's admonition is for those in the church, and he is concerned about idleness and its dangers. We do not have a contest between Jesus and Paul, so we need to attempt to heed the Holy Spirit as He speaks through both the Son of God and one of His apostles.

Do professional beggars and con artists deserve our continued generosity if it helps them continue living lives where they avoid responsibility and discipline, the very things they will need to actually change their condition? Should our kindness enable them to continue a life built on deceit?

Helping Without Being Exploited

How do we stay close to the heartbeat of Jesus, which to me is acting with quickness and sacrifice in responding to those who need our help, even to the evil person who is trying to abuse us? How can we do that and at the same time help those who simply want to use us – and even use our Christianity to exploit us?

The well-meaning generosity of some churches among the homeless has frustrated various city governments. Sometimes well-intended ministries have carried out food distribution in the center of cities, creating an attraction for homeless people. As a result, some of these go on to scare tourists and tick off the business owners. Some churches have resisted city leaders' requests for them to simply move their distribution sites to a different place.

I think our churches can do better – and our governments can do better – in how we minister to the homeless, and how we deal with begging. Here again is a guiding principle I have found helpful: *No cash, ever!* With that one rule, so many issues disappear. We can learn to be discerning in what people actually need. If someone asks you for money for food, then buy them a meal and sit with them while they eat it. If someone asks for work, then have a list of places that will provide it, or ask your congregation to be ready with day jobs for those who need it. If someone needs bus fare, take them to the bus station and put them on the bus.

One thing we could do a lot better is to have small cards on hand with information about available shelters. If the shelter costs a nominal fee, either be ready to go and pay that fee for the person asking or have your church set up an account with the shelter. Carry water in your car, beef jerky, crackers and cheese, and similar food items so you can respond quickly.

I can almost guarantee that most people who approach you will immediately dismiss you and move on the next victim to get the cash they desire. If they really need what they are asking for, your positive (alternative to cash) response will actually help them. Our continued subsidizing of a begging lifestyle will not.

Cities should have tourist booths where someone accosted by beggars could go to find references for all kinds of help to offer persons asking for help. Often our ignorance, being in a hurry, and a false sense of guilt make us continue to keep these folks on the street. It is ridiculous, in my opinion, for Christians to be reduced to lying, "Uh, I don't have any money," in trying to get past the beggar.

Panhandling as a Lifestyle

Unfortunately, for too many people panhandling has become a lifestyle and a source of income. Some of the most consistent beggars I know get a check from the government every month, have a place to live, but use panhandling as supplemental income. Many panhandlers are not homeless. Those that are quick to ask strangers for money, who have contrived stories, and use guilt to manipulate, are quite used to doing this sort of thing. In short, they are professionals.

They often present themselves as if this is an emergency. For instance, their car has broken down, they are stranded without bus fare on their way to another city, or they could buy a certain car part for $19.67. Sometimes they actually name pastors or prominent people, even asking what church you go to and naming the pastor, as if they also were members.

I must confess – I rather enjoy those who just say, "Look, I need money for a drink." At least the honesty comes through. I get weary of different sets of people using the exact same "Will work for food" sign. Once I saw a man so drunk he held the sign upside down. Seldom will these folk do any work if you offer it to them.

Jesus does not ask us to give "alms" to the poor, as if that would help us get to heaven. He does require us, however, to respond to those in need, love mercy, and preach the Gospel to the poor. I find I am often caught off guard when approached, although my wife says I must have a sign floating above my head that seems to say, "Ask me for money!"

That is not true: I've looked, and have never seen a sign over my head. But for some reason I am often a target of beggars wherever I go. And I confess that sometimes I still go against my own policy and give something.

So I suggest we all need to do a better job of being prepared to respond, even to hustlers. Obviously, if we refuse to give cash many hustlers will move on, but often we are left with a sense of guilt if we don't do something. This is why it is important to think about how you are going to respond to panhandlers before they accost you. Ladies, don't ever open your purse or pocketbook in public to help someone; in the process you may be tempting them to just grab it and run.

Hustled in the Church Parking Lot

If you are in a church where hustlers seem to show up in the church parking lot asking for help, just as you get ready to go home, then you should be prepared to refer them to a deacon on duty. In your hurry to go home and your guilt in front of the church, you are a perfect victim for a hustle. One of our most consistent hustlers has even told people, while she gives them her various and imaginative sob stories, "Don't tell Gene Johnson I am out here." Because Gene, our full-time deacon, knows this lady and her many stories quite well.

We would love to help this lady and truly see her life changed. The problem is she enjoys what she does, is good at it, has an income and a place to live, and uses religious talk to convince others of her sincerity. Church members that subsidize her hustle are not really helping her.

One of our deacons became fed up with being propositioned by a man who lived in a nearby halfway house. The man had mental problems and was brazen enough to ask this deacon if he would give him money for sex. After another disturbing encounter, when the man suddenly asked for money to go to Florida, our deacon decided, "That's it, if that is what you want, I will buy you a one-way ticket out of town."

The next day we started receiving irate phone calls from a city in Florida asking why we had sent this disturbed man down there. Later we found out the person most angry was his own sister who had not expected to see him bothering her again. I'm sure the halfway house had no idea where he had gone.

Of course we had to buy a ticket for him to come back to Chattanooga. Although we had to have a frank discussion with the deacon, we understood his frustration and anger. (He did wrong, but it was pretty funny.) Sometimes we don't get it right.

During the winter months it can be good to have wool caps and gloves available. These can be purchased cheaply and handed out to the homeless on the street. Be proactive rather than reactive. If you get taken, pray for the person and don't let the Devil push you into anger because you resent being a sucker. There is no sense getting angry for being compassionate. Thank God you still have a heart, and pray for Him to give you a mind of wisdom as well.

Questions for Reflection and Discussion

1. What is your personal strategy of dealing with strangers who ask you for money?
2. How do you balance the call of Jesus to respond generously to those who ask with the teaching from the Apostle for not feeding those who won't work?
3. How could you or your church be more prepared or ready to respond in positive ways to those who beg?

CHAPTER 36

Helping the Homeless

"Lord, when did we see you hungry and feed you, or thirsty and give you something to drink? When did we see you a stranger and invite you in, or needing clothes and clothe you?"

(MATTHEW 25:37-38, NIV)

AMONG CHURCHES THAT ACTIVELY SEEK to help the poor there are some that focus especially on the homeless population. This has not been my area of expertise as we have focused on inner city families primarily, and attempted to keep many of them from becoming homeless. Homelessness and strategies to meet the need require a great deal of prayer and wisdom. It helps to know what you want to accomplish if you intend on doing ministry to and among the homeless.

The first question of course is to ask, what is your goal? What does your church seek to accomplish? One of the goals we try to articulate in ministry to the poor is to end a person's poverty, to bring them out of their situation. Many ministries have focused on sustainment, which I define as simply helping people to survive one more day. This of course is how the poor live, from day to day. They must exploit the environment they know in order to survive. Homeless people who have been on the street for a while know exactly where every free meal, every accessible bathroom, shower, or heat source might be. They know when churches arrive to give out food, and the policies of rescue missions and overnight shelters. They know all the underpasses and bridges and steam grates.

Simply surviving doesn't seem to move someone to take the steps necessary to get out of a way of living that locks them in a precarious lifestyle and keeps them living on the edge of crisis. If the goal of your ministry to the homeless is to share the Gospel, to call people to faith, then at least you have to devise some method of meeting homeless folk and getting to know them. This is much more than most churches do. One marvelous outreach to the homeless I have observed was on Skid Row in Los Angeles where one church has an open Karaoke night at the church. They give out hotdogs and coffee, allow the homeless to sing and entertain, and a few hours off of the street. People are in all sorts of conditions when they come in. One man sitting next to me kept falling out of his chair due to a drunken stupor, but he was in a safe place (at least as long as I kept his head from banging into the floor).

Many Useful Approaches

If your goal is to feed homeless people, there are many models of this kind of ministry. Many churches have weekly or monthly food distributions. These are often well-planned with cooked meals, cold sandwiches, or breakfast burritos. Most of these distributions are outside in some place where there are homeless people. Some churches invite the homeless into the church. One couple I know has a weekly meal at their own home and they have been doing it consistently every Friday night for several years. Now volunteers help them prepare and serve the food, where once it was the wife who basically did all the cooking. Having folks in their own home has given them solid relationships, and some of the new people in the group sit in the house as long as they can as it is the only house they have actually been in for a number of years. Some of the men haven't spoken to women in a long time without the women being somewhat frightened.

Church food distributions vary as to their effectiveness in actually helping anyone. Some distributions don't result in any real conversations or relationship building, and the church doesn't have any plan to help a homeless person leave the lifestyle if they wanted to do so. Some individuals and churches have run into conflict with city governments as they have created an "attractive nuisance" and create gathering places for the homeless without providing any progressive or meaningful strategies for change.

The best ministries focus on building relationships and that pretty much forces staff or volunteers to think ahead as to what resources might be available, what counseling might be available, and what immediate housing solutions might be available if a homeless person was ready to make the move. Churches and governments need to work together and not against each other in this effort.

People fall into homelessness for various reasons and get locked into in different ways. For some it is addictive, and the idea of leaving a lifestyle in which they have become adapted and skilled frightens them. Those who are mentally ill, or are alcohol or drug-addicted, can be very difficult to leverage into housing solutions. Some cities and states have taken a "housing first" approach, and then loaded up individuals with all kinds of counseling and therapy options, including employment.

Joining in a Hospitality System

Some churches have banded together to create a hospitality system where they will take in a family for a week or so at a time, housing them in the church building with volunteer supervision. A number of churches with the resources have created their own shelters, or partner with other congregations or the city to maintain one. It is important, of course, for families to be safe and wise in whom they take into their homes, but if you have a way of vetting people and checking out their stories, then it is possible to house people in our own homes. Taking people into your own home is a risk, but mercy is often a risky business.

In America we have a huge problem, and in my opinion it is a national scandal. To have children that are homeless, moving from shelter to shelter, or living in abandoned cars while still trying to go to school, is not only sad but infuriating. Stories of some of these kids who become valedictorians in their high school class are so inspiring, but why is that kind of thing allowed? What has happened to our care of children? Well, all one has to do is look at the overload of such government agencies tasked with protecting children to know the answer. Leaving a child with a loving, though homeless, parent seems so much better than institutionalizing them, or putting them in the foster care system.

We must do better at this, and can if we will use our resources wisely and cooperate with others who do have experience and wisdom in these ministries. Life on the street is precarious, violent, full of misery and sickness, and often short. I am writing this as I have just read two stories in the papers: one from Atlanta where a man went around shooting people while they slept in alleys, and another of a homeless man beaten to death by another homeless man living behind the Wal-Mart just a half-mile from my house.

Some years ago one of our young, single deacons took in a young man who said he wanted to be delivered from drugs. The drug addict had been hooked on heroin, but now was on methadone through a government clinic. He cheated with cough syrup containing codeine. He wanted Christ and desired to be saved, but felt defeated and hopeless.

Our young deacon ministered to him, sharing both his home and the Good News of Christ with him. The young addict came to Jesus, then said he wanted to come off methadone and believed God would help him. He went off the drug cold turkey, but after an interview with the clinic they elected to put him back on methadone for a slower withdrawal. The clinic folks admitted religious conversion had the best results. He came off methadone again, going cold turkey for a second time and never went back.

That's not all. A month or so later his teeth fell out, and the church got him to a dentist and paid for dentures. Then he wanted to stop smoking, so we prayed and he kicked the habit. Then he wanted to lose weight. I remember him eating carrots and mustard every time I saw him, and sure enough, he did get rid of the fat.

Then he told me, "Pastor, I want to get married." "Oh, stop it," I thought. "This is too much, a bridge too far. You have just gotten things turned around, just started working for a living. Who is going to take you?" But God gave him a wife. I still find it hard to believe, but it all began with the simple hospitality of a deacon.

Offering Somewhere to Stay

Sometimes a congregation has the resources to own or build its own apartment house and keep several apartments available for shelter. Or it can put people up in an extended stay hotel, or even rent an economically priced apartment. A support team should be built around a person or family to help them get started. Simply supplying a place to stay is seldom the solution to homelessness. It usually takes a longer-term strategy of employment, mentoring and relationships to make certain that folks can live within their means, as well as ensure bills are paid, property is maintained, and their progress is encouraged.

I was so encouraged on a visit to Hamilton, Ontario to see the work at the Perkins Center where an old neighborhood bar was transformed into a five-story apartment block for homeless people. A charitable foundation had poured resources into making that happen. We need many more of such places that have economic and occupational training available.

If people have a background of addiction or mental illness, those issues will have to be addressed and a strategy created to deal with them. If not, you will soon find the person out on the street again.

It is necessary to give attention to sound management of any ministry you pursue.

Should your congregation decide to build a non-profit by which you hope to create affordable housing, or to move people to home ownership, you must then grapple with the realities of business, real estate, government, and sound management. The struggle of combining business with ministry can becomes frustrating when material matters are confused with spiritual ones.

Bad leadership and poor management are simply that, no matter how idealistic and caring someone might be. Too many ministries have wasted resources in the attempt to house people because they can't track both business and management issues along with the spiritual and character issues. Both are extremely important. If you don't do the management well, you will lose the opportunity to do the ministry at all.

Some begin with a clear understanding of the misery of those they want to help, then add great passion and idealism, but they never develop the capacity to administer or organize a program. This is especially troubling when a ministry receives government funds to do something like housing. Inevitably the government wants a clear accounting of every dollar spent, and they should.

QUESTIONS FOR REFLECTION AND DISCUSSION

1. What does your church do – or could your church do – to help minister to those who are homeless?
2. Do you know what shelters are available for homeless people in your community?
3. Do you know of services or ministries that are available for homeless people in your community?

CHAPTER 37

Money and Justice

"For the love of money is a root of all kinds of evil. Some people, eager for money, have wandered from the faith and pierced themselves with many griefs."

(1 Timothy 6:10, NIV)

We hear a lot about economic disparity these days. Certainly there has always been disparity, and in itself that is not injustice. There will always be various levels of income because there are people who work harder, are smarter, take risks in business, and have the network of help to launch them into wealth. There are people who not only do those things but also know how to save and don't waste what they have on pleasure and consumption. The Bible addresses both kinds of people:

"He who loves pleasure will become poor; whoever loves wine and oil will never be rich" (Proverbs 21:17, NIV).

"In the house of the wise are stores of choice food and oil, but a foolish man devours all he has" (Proverbs 21: 20, NIV).

However, while it endorses the virtues of hard work, the Bible warns fairly consistently about the dangers of wealth. In America it seems we seldom hear sermons on passages that look at the wealthy in a negative light. Yet it is hard to ignore warnings of

Jesus such as, *"it is easier for a camel to go through the eye of a needle than for a rich man to enter the Kingdom of Heaven" (Matthew 19:24, Mark 10:25).*

The apostle James really goes after the rich when he says:

"Listen, my brothers, has not God chosen those who are poor in the eyes of the world to be rich in faith and to inherit the kingdom he promised those who love him? But you have insulted the poor. Is it not the rich who are exploiting you? Are they not the ones who are dragging you into court? Are they not the ones who are slandering the noble name of him to whom you belong?" (James 1:5-7, NIV).

The book of Proverbs includes a prayer that says, *"...give me neither poverty nor riches, but give me only my daily bread. Otherwise, I may have too much and disown you and say, 'Who is the Lord?' Or I may become poor and steal, and so dishonor the name of my God" (Proverbs 30:8-9, NIV).*

Now, we rejoice that what is impossible with men is possible with God (in regard to the salvation of the rich). We also rejoice in knowing wealth doesn't always lead to atheism or self-idolatry. However, we would be foolish to ignore the warnings about the dangers of materialism. Many of us struggle with attempting to gain the whole world while losing our souls.

Temptations of the Poor and Rich

We are also thankful poverty doesn't always lead to stealing. Yes, there is certainly a temptation, and when it is a choice between going hungry or stealing, that temptation gets very strong.

In God's mercy those of us in America live in a land of amazing wealth and opportunity. Yet, right here in this amazing country, the disparity of wealth is painful to witness. It is shameful to see people who work very hard, are neither lazy nor wasteful, but can barely make it on a subsistence salary when the managers, executives and owners of the company continue to get wealthier and wealthier.

All of a manager's training and experience leads them to fight for a profitable bottom line, keep labor costs low, and be competitive in a capitalist economy. Yet their wealth is sometimes – and I acknowledge, not always – a testament to how stingy they have been with their very own employees at the lowest level of their business. Shame on them, and may they feel the shame.

One of the patterns I have seen over the course of my life is the concentration of wealth in the "management class." While using the marketplace as an excuse to give higher and higher wages, benefits and stock options to managers (telling and growing the myth that only higher income will enable an organization to attract and keep the "best" people to run it), some managers have deprived their workers of a fair wage. They feel their only obligation is to the owners (and even then sometimes put owners second after themselves); hardly ever acknowledging any obligation to employees of the company.

Altruism vs. Greed

The real tragedy is to see some top executives getting "golden parachutes" even as their companies lose money. The large corporate non-profits (charities, hospitals, colleges, and even churches) have used this same rationalization of marketplace values to keep edging up compensation. These are the very folks one would expect to defend the idea of altruism, passion and missionary zeal to help create and sustain effective charitable institutions. The "worker is worthy of his hire" is a Biblical truth, but none of us are worthy of what only manipulative greed can secure for us.

The Lord enters into judgment against the elders and leaders of his people: *"'It is you who have ruined my vineyard; the plunder from the poor is in your houses. What do you mean by crushing my people and grinding the face of the poor,' declares the Lord, the Lord Almighty" (Isaiah 3:14-15, NIV).*

Isn't that scary knowing the Lord God may be saying this very thing to evangelical Christian business persons who employ many people, just as He said it to Israel? What is interesting is we have examples of owners and wealthy people who turn around and give away money in charitable contributions, but are unjust and exploitative of their workers. We want to advocate both justice and generosity. I would have to say generosity, without justice, is simply hypocrisy.

Challenges to Do the Right Thing

I want to challenge the wealthy to help the working poor by paying them a livable wage, with benefits. I want to challenge them to do this before a union makes them do it. I want to challenge them to do what is right in God's economy, not just what the market demands. I do not disparage profits, and don't believe God ever condemns wealth in and of itself. In fact, wealth is the blessing of God when He gives it and we can retain a clear conscience. *"The blessing of the Lord brings wealth, and he adds no trouble with it" (Proverbs 10:22, NIV).*

I would challenge the wealthy to use their wisdom and the gift they have of making money to think creatively and imaginatively in how to help give the poor work performing jobs they can do, ones that can still bring a profit for a company. The poor need work to make their own way in life and such work gives dignity. Yet without jobs that pay adequately, that can be maintained because the company makes a profit, we cannot help poor communities rise out of the dust.

It would be wonderful to have a world where every worker could adapt to high-skill employment, where all workers have the education and flexibility to meet a changing job market. We can curse a school system that fails the poor; we can even work to create a better one. But what about people who need to eat and feed their families this week, this month, this year? What about workers so uneducated they will never rise to those skilled jobs – how can we help them? We must do so if we are to be a just society, and we can if we will put our minds and wills to get it done.

I am convinced we must put a lot more of the resources of the church into employment strategies, and not simply on handouts to keep people surviving. This leads directly to economic development, business start-ups, and investment into the economic and job skill training of people.

Biblical Advocate of Justice

Job was a righteous man; most of us have heard that fact when we have heard of his story. But how was he righteous? Was it a personal piety in which he was clean living, didn't drink, smoke, gamble, watch dirty movies (okay, they didn't have movies then) dance, curse, or do other forms of unacceptable behavior?

Yes, Job had personal moral righteousness. But I think in our fundamentalism, we often think of righteousness as personal morality and not as social justice. Job's righteousness, the Bible tells us, extended beyond the level of personal morality. This is what Job says:

"If I have denied justice to my menservants and maidservants when they had a grievance against me, what will I do when God confronts me? What will I answer when called to account: did not he who made me in the womb make them? Did not the same one form us both within our mothers?

"If I have denied the desires of the poor or let the eyes of the widow grow weary, if I have kept my bread to myself, not sharing it with the fatherless – but from my youth I reared him as would a father, and from my birth I guided the widow – if I have seen anyone perishing for lack of clothing, or a needy man without a garment, and his heart did not bless me for warming him with the fleece from my sheep, if I have raised my hand against the fatherless, knowing that I had influence in court, then let my arm fall

from the shoulder, let it be broken off at the joint, for I dreaded destruction from God, and for fear of his splendor I could not do such things" (Job 31: 13-23, NIV).

Justice means we realize all people are made by God and in the image of God, are equal before Him, and we should treat them that way. The motivation for justice in Job's mind was the knowledge he was going to have to stand before God and answer for how he had dealt with the lowest and neediest of people. Job also says in Chapter 29:14-17:

"I put on righteousness as my clothing; justice was my robe and my turban. I was eyes to the blind and feet to the lame, I was a father to the needy; I took up the case of the stranger. I broke the fangs of the wicked and snatched the victims from their teeth" (NIV).

To me this speaks of activism in the cause of justice – standing up for the physically handicapped, the poor, and the alien. May God make His Church an army of men and women like our brother Job. It is time to do some breaking of fangs and some snatching from the teeth of the wicked.

Preventing 'Justified Anger'

Often those in situations of great need become angry with those who have resources but refuse to share them. This anger is sometimes justified, of course, when wealthier Christians don't care or have hardened their hearts. However, the apathy of the "well-off" is sometimes simply due to ignorance, along with bad leadership. True followers of Christ have a heart for God's will, and God's will is that we should love the poor and our fellow believers.

We all need each other, and it is foolish to damn people to wallow in their poverty when we could rise to the task of motivating God's people to get involved and help. This is a simple fact: Most pastors will do things that help people in their own congregation; helping another church or community is secondary. I want pastors to know that helping the poor of another congregation can be of benefit to their own church if it involves more than just sending money.

Money might be sent the first or second time, but if the people of a congregation don't get personally involved in the lives of the poor, or in personally serving a needy church, the money will dry up. Pastors of poor congregations can serve richer congregations and help other pastors bring their people into service if those saints can be given opportunities to serve where they can see results, where they can feel good about themselves, and where they feel a measure of security.

There not only are difficulties for individuals in showing mercy, but institutional obstacles as well. Some working class or middle-class churches are made up of people who still have the mindset they are poor, that help should be coming to them and not be given to others. This attitude can affect an entire congregation.

Even if the people in the congregation actually are poor, if they are following Christ and have had their values changed, they are actually better off than they used to be. They might not have realized it, and this can keep them frozen into thinking only of their own church and not about their neighbors. This is an easy trap to fall into. This is different from the attitude of the Macedonian churches as described in 2 Corinthians 8:1-2, NIV:

"And now brothers we want you to know about the grace that God has given the Macedonian churches. Out of the most severe trial, their overflowing joy and their extreme poverty welled up in rich generosity. For I testify that gave as much as they were able, and even beyond their ability...."

That statement is amazing to me. Their joy and extreme poverty welled up in rich generosity. Only God can do that. Christ calls us out of ourselves to love others.

Criticism and Misunderstanding

I cite this as one of the challenges because often in our attempts at mercy we have been criticized, even mocked, about what we were doing. Sometimes people just misunderstand how and why we are going about things. At other times folks jump to conclusions or make assumptions, and too often they come to the absolute worst conclusions about our motives and methods.

At New City Fellowship we are not perfect in how we do mercy, and have made many mistakes. We loved on people who robbed from us and then were mocked by friends for being so vulnerable and naïve. We have had our motives questioned because we wanted to have some influence on the non-profits we created, as if we were doing something underhanded.

We have attempted economic development projects that lost a lot of money (restaurants can be money pits!), and then were mocked because we seemed to have no business sense. This criticism came from business people who wouldn't come to help us and later lost millions themselves in bad business decisions.

We hold a large block party once a year in the same neighborhood, then have been criticized for only helping that community once a year – and this came from folks who evidently never asked or paid attention when we described a continuous stream of activities aimed in trying to reach out to that community. Sometimes it has felt so frustrating when Christians, our supposed brothers and sisters, seemed to give us the hardest time.

Obviously we can't please everyone, and we never know what people are thinking until it comes out of their mouths. I remember one wealthy man telling me, "You kind of people beg for a living."

I wanted to say, "Really? Seriously? You don't think we wouldn't all like to be independently wealthy and not have to depend on anyone? You don't think it humiliates us to have to assertively raise funds if we want to make any kind of impact on poor communities, and feed our own families while we do it? You don't think it is a struggle for us to live by faith and not be afraid, to trust in God to provide for us and this ministry every day?" So it is painful when someone like that comes along to mock us.

It is true those of us in this kind of ministry do ask for money, but his comment was certainly offensive and insensitive. So I am tempted to say, "May you perish with your money!" But no. God was and is patient with me in my ignorance and sin, so instead, may the Lord have mercy on him.

Unashamedly Asking

I am not ashamed to ask for money to help the poor, and fully intend to keep on asking for more of it. We need lots and lots of money to do it well. By the grace of God I have tried to share my own money, and hope I would continue to do so even if no one else joined me. I am convinced Jesus wants me to do that, to be like Him, to give my wealth and myself away so that others might know God and know His love. Thankfully, I have never had to do this ministry alone.

We have to be careful not to let our egos and pride be what mercy ministry is about. If this is God's work, He will provide. If it is God working in us, there will be success – as He wants it and when He wants it. I simply want to warn that if you seek to be given praise for this kind of work, you might be in for a surprise. Your pastor might think you are simply a nuisance for constantly bringing it up. People will tend to put you in some kind of box – the radical, strange, whiney person who is a one-trick pony. That's okay. If Jesus is in the same box, I am content.

This is not a book focused so much on the issues of justice, which deserve their own full treatment. This is a book to encourage the practice of mercy. Obviously, we believe and can agree there is much injustice in our country, and in many of the systems that affect poor people. However, we don't blame all the problems of the poor on injustice. Whatever your understanding of justice issues might be, you must not let your passion or apathy about it blind you to the reality of suffering. Not if you are a believer. Mercy calls for us to act.

Questions for Reflection and Discussion

1. What is your heart attitude toward your own money? Do you see is as something which the Lord has entrusted to you, or something that belongs to you?
2. Do you have employees? Could you live on what you pay them? Are you just in how you compensate them?
3. What resources is your church putting into employment strategies for the poor? What ideas can you come up with to help create meaningful employment?

CHAPTER 38

"You Can't Outgive God"

"Whoever heard me spoke well of me, and those who saw me commended me, because I rescued the poor who cried for help, and the fatherless who had none to assist him. The man who was dying blessed me; I made the widow's heart sing."

(JOB 29: 11-13, NIV)

"ALL THE BELIEVERS WERE ONE in heart and mind. No one claimed that any of his possessions was his own, but they shared everything they had.... There were no needy persons among them. For from time to time those who owned lands or houses sold them, brought the money from the sales and put it at the apostles feet, and it was distributed to anyone as he had need" (Acts 4:32,34-35, NIV).

Among Christians it is not uncommon to see people give generously to missions, to build church buildings, or employ pastors and staff. These are indeed often worthy of our support. But where is the pattern of the early Church among us in sharing within our own congregations to make sure there are no needy among us? Where is the pattern of the early Church to share with other churches that had needy people, as we see described in 2 Corinthians 8:1-15?

God's People Called to Share

Some Christians have decided to live in community in order to try and live out this idea, while others have attempted to live simply and set a level on their own consumption in order to share more. Some congregations have partnered with other churches, across town and around the world, to become mutually supporting congregations. All of these things can be wonderful, but they can also have temptations and problems.

We must always be careful not to become legalistic and self-righteous, especially in specific areas the Scriptures have not commanded. The godly principles of Scripture must be applied by all of us, but sometimes these matters are left to our own conscience. We need to be careful not to quickly condemn others because we judge them on how they spend their money. Yet I am afraid we often err in doing little or nothing to stop our headlong pursuit of self-centered materialism. When I say self-centered, I also speak of entire congregations that endorse selfish living.

I have been the recipient of many acts of mercy – for me personally, my family, my congregation and people. I confess at one time I had a very wary eye toward the wealthy. I had not known many of them, and it was easy for me to perceive them in stereotypes. I did not trust them.

Thankfully, over the years I have met people with lots of money who seemed bent on trying to give all of it away. I have seen them attempt to do so wisely. It is too easy to want to be friends of the wealthy, to please them, to seek to exploit a friendship for personal favors. I can't imagine how hard it is to be confronted with a new request for funding by so-called friends every day or so.

I have had to fight within myself to guard my own integrity, that I would not accept personal favors simply because I wanted or even needed something. I have tried not to take advantage but have sought rather to live under authority, with my salary published by my church, and to channel money to the truly needy. I am grateful for the many acts of love toward myself. I hope I have received this with humility and honesty.

Those of us in ministry have the opportunity to "poor mouth," so it seems we always need a new car, new suit, better home, or free meal. Since I have had the forum of the pulpit, I knew I could steer the generosity of wealthy members to help myself and my family. They often would have done so with joy, believing they were helping "God's man, God's servant."

Not Taking from Those in Need

God forbid I would steal from the widow, from the orphan, from the unemployed. It is especially important for those in ministry, in leadership, to be examples of not taking advantage of their positions, practicing material generosity and not simply becoming examples of consumption.

I don't believe God calls on us to despise the rich, but neither does He want us to suck up to them so they would fail to be held to accountability. The wealthy need to live in justice and generosity; it is a blessing for them to do so. God will give them even more in this life and the life to come. All of us need to learn to share, from the widow with her mite, to the working poor, to the middle class, to the professional, to the scary rich. As it says in Proverbs 22:9:

"A generous man will himself be blessed, for he shares his food with the poor" (NIV).

One of the great mentors in my life, Mr. David Mitchell, a ruling elder from Lookout Mountain Presbyterian Church, always used to tell me, "You can't out give God." He made it an ambition to try to do so with his kindness and generosity. But he will tell you, if you meet him in heaven, that it turned out just like he said: He couldn't out give God.

Mr. Mitchell gave me my first two automobiles to use for ministry, gave lots of men a chance to earn a few dollars working for him in his shop in the inner city, and was a fervent supporter of missions. He was an exceptionally generous man who knew how to share. I think Proverbs 11:24-25 describes him well:

"A generous man gives freely, yet gains even more; another withholds unduly, but comes to poverty. A generous man will prosper; he who refreshes others will himself be refreshed" (NIV).

There is an interesting comparison in the book of Proverbs between the sluggard, a person with a character that is lazy and that inevitably falls into poverty, and with the righteous:

"The sluggard's craving will be the death of him, because his hands refuse to work. All day long he craves for more, but the righteous give without sparing" (Proverbs 21:25-26, NIV).

Helping Some to Help Others

The righteous give without sparing, and even though there are sluggards who will not work, this does not stop the righteous from being generous – especially to those they know will benefit from it. Let me give you an example:

A call comes from the Tennessee Department of Human Services. "We hear that your church is able to help people with food and utility bills, is that correct?" "Yes," our full-time deacon answers. "We have a lady whose lights have been shut off, but we have no designated funds to cover this contingency. Can you help her?"

Our deacon suggests they send her to our office so we can meet her and find out what she needs. She is a widow who works cleaning the local library at night. She has no one in her family able to help her, had been out of work for a while and lost some income. She walks a mile home after work in the middle of the night since no buses run then.

She comes to the office and tells our deacon her story. He tells her that yes, we can pay this bill for her, but we could help her so much more if she would come and visit our church and worship with us. The deacon arranges for a ride to pick her up, and she begins to attend.

Eventually she joins the church, and not long after she has started coming the pastor making an appeal for church members to give money to provide scholarships to send some men to a conference. After the service this widow walks forward to give the pastor an envelope holding fifty dollars. She was the first to respond, the first to give, and undoubtedly she gave out of her poverty.

One of the things many of the poor that come to our church for help don't yet know is if they were to become part of our congregation, they would never again have to be hungry. Surely every church ought to be able to say that. In America this is possible – we certainly have enough to share so that we can at least feed our own people.

Radical Distribution of Assets

If we really tried, we could make sure every congregation preaching the Gospel and faithful to the Word would always have enough to care for their poorest members. However, we cannot do this without an attitude and lifestyle of sharing, and sometimes that means a radical disposing and distribution of our assets.

What an amazing example the Lord Jesus has set for us:

"For you know the grace of our Lord Jesus Christ, that though he was rich, yet for your sakes he became poor, so that you through his poverty might become rich" (2 Corinthians 8:9, NIV).

We need – and our children really need – a call to something greater than themselves. Many Christians are very sacrificial for their children, but I am afraid sometimes in reality this is just indulgence and an extension of self. We must take care of our own families, without question, but someday our children must rise up to be people of character. If they have been given a life where everything has revolved around them, how will they know how to share – and how to give their lives away for the kingdom of God?

As Proverbs 3:27-28 tells us, *"Do not withhold good from those who deserve it, when it is in your power to act. Do not say to our neighbor, 'Come back later; I'll give it tomorrow' – when you now have it with you" (NIV).*

Questions for Reflection and Discussion

1. At what level of income do we receive the responsibility to be or to become generous? (Look at 2 Corinthians 8:1-5).
2. What story about generosity can you recall concerning someone who was generous to you or your family?
3. When you sit down to eat and pray to give thanks, have you ever felt motivated then to help someone else? What did you do? If you haven't done what you felt led to do, why not?

CHAPTER 39

Considering the End Game

" 'Send the crowd away...so they...can find food.'
He replied, 'You give them something to eat.' "

(LUKE 9:12-13, NIV)

ONE ISSUE THAT HAS CONFRONTED believers desiring to help the poor comes from the warnings they have received that charity can be "toxic" and destructive to people they really would like to help. These warnings certainly need to be heeded, as many well-meaning folks have unfortunately hurt the poor by insulting their dignity, trapping them in dependency, or sustaining them in a poverty lifestyle without helping them to build an aspiration for change.

However, it is important to realize that without charity, without immediate mercy given in times of need, hunger or emergency, people can be left to go hungry, without a place to live, without heat or other necessities. It may make middle-class congregations feel better to establish a development program rather than provide relief, since that often fits into their middle-class lifestyle of doing things on a schedule and by appointment. But it can still leave people in desperate and dangerous situations.

It is also important to remember that most of the teaching we receive from Jesus about how we deal with the poor has more to do with our hearts, and our immediate response to the poor, than about what is the best organized program for them – or for us.

We should not let our confusion, or reluctance to give immediate help, freeze us from responding to the cry of the poor and their needs. We must ask God to help us develop and keep tender and responsive hearts while we grow in wisdom about how to hear a cry for help and, after responding, turn it into a change of life direction and personal development.

Front-Line Ministry, or Long-Term?

I have seen churches decide to give a ministry of charity (relief) away to other agencies as they try to build development-type ministries. At least these folks are seeking to create longer term, more in-depth solutions. However, I think they are missing the front line of mercy when they take this step, and I wish they could do both.

When I came back to Chattanooga after graduating from seminary, I visited a few local pastors and asked them, "What do you do when the poor come to church and ask for help?" The most common answer was, "We refer them to the Salvation Army, or a rescue mission." I reacted strongly against the idea that the church should be sending poor people away to someone else for help.

Today, many people are learning long-term solutions are necessary, and I believe that is true. However, it seems to me churches end up going right back to sending poor folks away because the difficulty of doing immediate mercy well is something for which they haven't prepared themselves.

While I applaud efforts to build a developmental, longer term approach, I am dismayed to know some churches still choose to send poor people away and not recognize their needs as an opportunity to bring them into the love of the church. Simply because the government, secular agencies and even church ministries have done things to harm the poor, this doesn't mean we should overreact and let children go hungry or freeze in the winter.

Immediate and Personal

The church is one institution that can act immediately and personally, especially if it has good leadership and its people have been trained in how to respond. We can do better than we have done if we will just have the will to do so and put forth the effort to prepare, train, and organize to be effective in mercy.

I am simultaneously amused and saddened by the debates I hear about being "radical" versus "ordinary" in our Christianity. I am almost reduced to bafflement when I read an apologetic for the "Emerging Church" and the desire to create a new theology because the church isn't practicing justice or mercy.

I don't think there was anything wrong with the old theology. It is certainly adequate, but many churches and churchgoers simply don't obey it. We see nothing wrong with a theology that proclaims the Bible to be true, and if you take it as written, one cannot escape God's call to justice and mercy. Obviously there is plenty wrong with our own hearts, since we haven't obeyed what has always been there. The need is not for new theology.

Some folks seem to think justice and mercy, creating churches that give a welcome to the hurting and broken, along with racial reconciliation, are their new idea. We honestly wonder where these folks have been while we have been about this work. This is neither new understanding nor has the Bible just been written.

Where have people been while the poor are dying and going to hell? We see the radical as ordinary in dying to ourselves and taking up our cross to follow Christ. We find maintaining the middle-class status quo lifestyle in a self-focused church not as "ordinary," but rather as disobedience

IF YOUR THEOLOGY IS THE THEOLOGY OF THE BIBLE, YOU SHOULD HAVE NO PROBLEM LIVING A LIFE OF MERCY AND JUSTICE. We believe that our theology (derived from our very traditional Bible) has always been adequate to meet the horrific challenges of poverty and injustice head on. It just so happens that in doing what it says, obedient and faithful believers who love "the least of these" look like radical heroes. I submit full and faithful obedience to the Word of God ought to be the pursuit and life of the ordinary Christian, made possible by the power of the Holy Spirit.

Please stop sending the poor away. Stop giving them to someone else. Make a place for them in your life, your spirituality, and your church. I fully realize this will mean a sacrifice of time and create emotional strain. It will take you beyond a Sunday-only religion or a religion that is about your self-fulfillment. It will require a restructuring of both the ministries and the budget of your church.

At the same time, it will give you friends that are very different than the ones that have come naturally to you. It will force you to depend on a mighty and awesome God. It will enlarge your soul, give credibility to your faith among those who watch you, and give pride to your children that the religion of their parents is not hypocritical.

So, I appeal to you: Join me as we *"Go and learn what this means, 'I desire mercy and not sacrifice...'" (Matthew 9:13).*

Questions for Reflection and Discussion

1. Can you identify three significant things, new insights or understanding you've learned from this book?
2. What one thing have you found yourself feeling guilty about? (As you think about this, make sure you trust in Jesus for His forgiveness and mercy, but if you need to repent, we encourage you to do it.)

3. What one thing have you read here that has encouraged you about your church, if anything?
4. What do you think Jesus wants you to do about what you've learned?

CHAPTER 40

Additional Resources

THERE ARE SOME WONDERFUL MODELS around the country of how to do mercy, how to employ the poor and the young, how to impact urban communities, and how to train the poor in values and soft skills so they can work and earn their way.

We refer you to just a few of them here.

1. **JOBS FOR LIFE** out of Raleigh, N.C. This is a curriculum to help churches train the unemployed and the under-employed in "soft" skills so they can obtain and hold jobs. Originally called Jobs Partnership, it has created a partnership between churches and businesses that provided mentors for each student, and a referral to possible jobs after the graduation. Meeting twice a week over a series of weeks, it allowed pastors to come in and teach Biblical principles, and then Human Resource folks to come in and teach how to think, prepare, and behave to obtain and retain a job. We highly recommend this program. www.jobsforlife.org
2. **CHALMERS CENTER:** The Chalmers Center on Lookout Mountain, Tenn. has some very good resources, including the Faith and Finances course. The Center is now training trainers who can help your church and community take individuals through a curriculum for helping them understand God's

view of His/their money and resources and how to manage it. Financial literacy is an important step in helping poor people come out of poverty. www.chalmers.org

3. **HOPE FOR THE INNER CITY,** providing summer week-long mission trips in the inner city of Chattanooga. We recommend them to you not simply for you to send teams, but also to learn how to use teams in creating your own host program. They combine classes on doing ministry, daily worship for the teams, service projects, and Bible club evangelism for inner city children. This ministry is connected to New City Fellowship of Chattanooga. www.hope4theinnercity.org
4. **HOPE FOR MIAMI:** Rick & Yvonne Sawyer lead and direct Hope For Miami, in Miami, Fla., A ministry to families and children through local churches. www.hopeformiami.org
5. **RESTORE ST. LOUIS**, the urban ministry and economic development program of New City St. Louis. We refer you especially to their Harambee ministry that provides summer employment to teams by teaching them how to tuck-point brick homes, thus giving them a marketable skill. Grants are provided by the city to restore homes for the elderly poor, and these youth teams do the tuck-pointing. This ministry has now spread to Chicago. www.restorestlouis.org
6. **MERCY PASTORS AND FULL-TIME MERCY STAFF:** David Apple of Tenth Presbyterian Church in Philadelphia, Pa., Chris Sicks of Alexandria Presbyterian Church in Alexandria, Va., Joe Magri of Trinity Presbyterian Church of Charlottesville, Va., Gene Johnson of New City Fellowship, Chattanooga, Tenn., and Nathan Ivey of Sojourners Church in Louisville, Ky. and Julian Russell of Park Cities Presbyterian Church in Dallas, Texas are individuals you could call on for great expertise in ministry to those in need.

7. **GLOBAL CHURCH ADVANCEMENT (GCA)**: This is a church planting training ministry conducted by Dr. Steve Childers (and a host of subject matter experts) from Reformed Theological Seminary. The concepts and techniques taught apply to all kinds of church planting settings, but it also has a mercy track in the essential part of the training. I recommend this entire training to any church planter. www.gca.cc
8. **CHRISTIAN COMMUNITY DEVELOPMENT ASSOCIATION (CCDA):**

   An association of mercy, urban, and justice ministries and practitioners, with headquarters in Chicago, IL, it has an annual conference every year in which many seminars are provided offering various levels of training. www.CCDA.org
9. **MISSION TO NORTH AMERICA STAFF EXPERTISE ON VARIOUS MINISTRIES**:
   J. Disaster Response, Arklie Hooten, ahooten@pcanet.org
   K. ESL (English as a Second Language), Nancy Booher, nbooher@pcanet.org
   L. Special Needs, Stephanie Hubach, shubach@pcanet.org
   M. Metanoia, Prison Ministry, Mark Casson, mcasson@pcanet.org
   N. Refugee and Immigrant Ministry, Pat Hatch, phatch@pcanet.org
10. **URBAN AND MERCY MINISTRIES OF MISSION TO NORTH AMERICAN, AND THE NEW CITY NETWORK:**

    Go to www.thenewcitynetwork.org for more details on the availability of Randy Nabors and team to speak or train in your area. rblevins@pcanet.org

Recommended books:

Apple, David, *Not Just Another Soup Kitchen: How Mercy Ministry in the Local Church Transforms Us All.*, Philadelphia, PA, CLC Publications, 2014.

Conn, Harvey M., and Others, *The Urban Face of Mission, Ministering the Gospel in a Diverse and Changing World,* Edited by Manuel Ortiz and Susan S. Baker, Phillipsburg, N.J., P&R Publishing, 2002. (Especially the article in Chapter 10, *Doing the Word: Biblical Holism and Urban Ministry* by Mark R. Gornik.)

Book of Church Order, Presbyterian Church in America, Atlanta, Ga., CE&P.

Fikkert, Brian and Steve Corbett, *When Helping Hurts, How to Alleviate Poverty Without Hurting the Poor and Yourself,* Chicago, Ill., Moody Press, 2009.

Fuder, John, *A Heart For The City, effective ministries to the urban community,* John Fuder General Editor, Chicago, Moody Press, 1999.

Gordon, Wayne & Perkins, John M., *Making Neighborhoods Whole, A Handbook for Christian Community Development,* Downers Grove, Ill., IVP Books, 2013.

Keller, Timothy J., *Ministries of Mercy, The Call of the Jericho Road.* Phillipsburg, N.J., P&R Publishing, Second Edition, 1997.

Keller, Timothy J., *Resources For Deacons,* Atlanta, Ga., Presbyterian Church in America, Committee for Christian Education & Publications, 1985.

Kuntz, William J., *The Collapse of American Criminal Justice,* Cambridge, MA, The Belknapp Press of Harvard University Press, 2011.

Myers, Bryant L., *Walking With the Poor, Principles and Practices of Transformational Development,* Maryknoll, N.Y., Orbis Books, 1999.

Ruby K. Payne, *A Framework for Understanding Poverty, A Cognitive Approach,* aha! Process, 2013.

Perkins, John, *Let Justice Roll Down,* Ventura, Calif., Regal Books, 1976.

Perkins, John, *With Justice For All,* Ventura, Calif., Regal Books, 1982.

Perkins, John, *A Quiet Revolution*, Pasadena, Calif., Urban Family Publications, 1976.

Scharf Graham, *The Apprenticeship of Being Human, Why Early Childhood Parenting Matters to Everyone,* Graham Scharf publisher, 2012.

Sherman, Amy L., *Restorers of Hope,* Wheaton, Ill., Crossway Books, 1997.

Sicks, Chris, *Tangible: Making God Known Through Deeds of Mercy,* Colorado Springs, Colo., NavPress, 2013.

Making Their Way

The clatter of a disturbed rock
Tumbles aside
As they make their way
Down the trail.
The careful stepping of a donkey
Bears the swollen woman.
Her betrothed holds the halter
Guides the beast
Bears his pack
Makes their way
Over Jordan
And across it again.
Travelers grousing
About government
"All this moving about;
Augustus has heartburn
And the world must move
Each to his own city,
To be taxed of course,
Paying for our own occupation;
Another building going up in Rome."
"Can we rest a moment?"
The swaying, shifting movement
Wearies, as steps turn into miles,
Making their way to some
Unreserved shelter.
"We'll find a place,
Someplace in Bethlehem."

Poor pilgrims; to all appearance
Helpless victims of larger
Political forces.
Circumstantially shifted, caught
Short, inconvenienced, put at risk;
By their poverty.
Isn't that the way of it?
By earthly appraisal
Without resource, without protection;
Flotsam on a human current.
Albeit actually sailing
Upon a Divine vessel
Of sovereign
Supernatural determination
Toward a destination
Of cosmic significance.

Guarded by legions
Without greaves or cuirass
Sword or pilum
Unseen, undetected
Immensely powerful
Intensely peering
In joyful anticipation,
Confident beyond arrogance
In the certainty of the will of God,
Toward the coronation…
-Through natal arriving
-Incarnate abiding
-Tyrants and Tempter surviving
-Loves sinners in his dying
-Salvation providing
-Rising, death defies
-Ascended, the Father glori-fying…
Angels, shepherds, wise men
Parents and redeemed say…
"Hail to the Son of God!"
– Randy Nabors
Christmas Eve, 2014

For more information and to contact
the author, Randy Nabors, go to
www.thenewcitynetwork.org.

Randy also can be reached by email,
rnabors@pcanet.org.

41905856R00196

Made in the USA
Charleston, SC
15 May 2015